HEALTHY AGEING

What does it mean to age well? This important new book redefines what 'successful' ageing means, challenging the idea that physical health is the only criteria to gauge the ageing process and that an ageing population is necessarily a burden upon society.

Using Amartya Sen's Capability Approach as a theoretical starting point, *Healthy Ageing: A Capability Approach to Inclusive Policy and Practice* outlines a nuanced perspective that transcends the purely biomedical view, recognising ideas of resilience as well as the experiences of older people themselves in determining what it means to age well. It builds to provide a comprehensive response to the overarching discourse that successful ageing is simply about eating well and exercising, acknowledging not only that older people are not always able to follow such advice, but also that well-being is mediated by factors beyond the physical.

In an era where ageing has become such an important topic for policy makers, this is a robust and timely response that examines what it means to live well as an older person. It will be hugely valuable not only for students of gerontology and social care, but also professionals working in the field.

Christine Stephens is a Professor in the School of Psychology, Massey University, New Zealand.

Mary Breheny is a Senior Lecturer in the School of Public Health, Massey University, New Zealand.

Critical Approaches to Health

Series Editors: Kerry Chamberlain and Antonia Lyons

The Routledge *Critical Approaches to Health* series aims to present critical, inter-disciplinary books around psychological, social and cultural issues related to health. Each volume in the series provides a critical approach to a particular issue or important topic, and is of interest and relevance to students and practitioners across the social sciences. The series is produced in association with the International Society of Critical Health Psychology (ISCHP).

Titles in the series

Disability and Sexual Health
Critical Psychological Perspectives
Poul Rohleder, Stine Hellum Braathen and Mark T. Carew

Healthy Ageing
A Capability Approach to Inclusive Policy and Practice
Christine Stephens and Mary Breheny

Urban Poverty and Health Inequalities
A Relational Approach
Darrin Hodgetts and Ottilie Stolte

Constructing Pain
Historical, Psychological and Critical Perspectives
Robert Kugelmann

Digital Health
Critical and Cross-Disciplinary Perspectives
Deborah Lupton

A Critical Approach to Surrogacy
Reproductive Desires and Demands
Damien W. Riggs and Clemence Due

HEALTHY AGEING

A Capability Approach to Inclusive Policy and Practice

Christine Stephens and Mary Breheny

Routledge
Taylor & Francis Group

LONDON AND NEW YORK

First published 2019
by Routledge
2 Park Square, Milton Park, Abingdon, Oxon OX14 4RN

and by Routledge
711 Third Avenue, New York, NY 10017

Routledge is an imprint of the Taylor & Francis Group, an informa business

© 2019 Christine Stephens and Mary Breheny

British Library Cataloguing-in-Publication Data
A catalogue record for this book is available from the British Library

Library of Congress Cataloging-in-Publication Data
A catalog record for this book has been requested

ISBN: 978-1-138-19392-5 (hbk)
ISBN: 978-1-138-19394-9 (pbk)
ISBN: 978-1-315-63909-3 (ebk)

Typeset in Bembo
by Apex CoVantage, LLC

CONTENTS

SERIES EDITOR PREFACE

Critical Approaches to Health

Health is a major issue for people all around the world, and is fundamental to individual well-being, personal achievements, and satisfaction, as well as to families, communities, and societies. It is also embedded in social notions of participation and citizenship. Much has been written about health, from a variety of perspectives and disciplines, but a lot of this writing takes a biomedical and causally positivist approach to health matters, neglecting the historical, social, and cultural contexts and environments within which health is experienced, understood, and practiced. It is an appropriate time to introduce a new series of books that offer critical, social science perspectives on important health topics.

The *Critical Approaches to Health* series aims to provide new critical writing on health by presenting critical, interdisciplinary, and theoretical writing about health, where matters of health are framed quite broadly. The series will include books that range across important health matters, including general health-related issues (such as gender and media), major social issues for health (such as medicalisation, obesity, and palliative care), particular health concerns (such as pain, doctor-patient interaction, health services, and health technologies), particular health problems (such as diabetes, autoimmune disease, and medically unexplained illness), or health for specific groups of people (such as the health of migrants, the homeless, and the aged), or combinations of these.

The series seeks above all to promote critical thought about health matters. By critical, we mean going beyond the critique of the topic and work in the field, to more general considerations of power and benefit, and in particular, to addressing concerns about whose understandings and interests are upheld and whose are marginalised by the approaches, findings, and practices in these various domains of health. Such critical agendas involve reflections on what constitutes knowledge, how it is created, and how it is used. Accordingly, critical approaches consider epistemological and theoretical positioning, as well as issues of methodology and practice, and seek to examine how health is enmeshed within broader social relations and structures. Books within this series take up this challenge and seek to provide new insights and understandings by applying a critical agenda to their topics.

In the current book, *Healthy Ageing: A Capability Approach to Inclusive Policy and Practice*, Christine Stephens and Mary Breheny provide a new theorised approach to health and ageing. As they note, world populations are increasingly composed of older people who are pressured to age 'successfully'. The authors discuss how notions around healthy ageing have been captured by this discourse of successful ageing, where older people are expected to sustain good health and make few demands on health and care systems. In this context, health is located predominantly within biological and medicalised perspectives. The authors argue that these notions of successful ageing are situated within oppressive neoliberal ideals of individual responsibility for health and the ongoing denial of physical ageing; successful aging is constructed as staying eternally young and as within the person's control.

Stephens and Breheny offer a critical perspective and alternative for understanding and researching healthy ageing. To do so, they take up Amartya Sen's theoretical perspective of capabilities, an approach which situates healthy ageing as involving a variety of capabilities that are valued by people as they age, capabilities that are relevant to their own material and cultural contexts. The authors provide arguments to demonstrate that this approach allows consideration of a broader conceptualisation of health, going beyond the medical to incorporate well-being and quality of life as fundamental to understandings of people as they become older.

This approach then allows the authors to raise and discuss a variety of issues not commonly considered within the scope of more restricted approaches to healthy ageing. Stephens and Breheny offer a detailed, evaluative discussion of these issues, ranging across structural concerns such as supportive housing and age-friendly communities, social concerns such as social relationships and community contributions, and personal concerns such as autonomy, independence, and enjoyment. In employing the capabilities theoretical framework the authors are able to link all of these issues directly to health and well-being.

This comprehensive coverage provides a positively-framed, yet highly critical, perspective on healthy ageing. Throughout the book the authors provide a critical account of how a capabilities approach can enhance and support the quality of life of older people in contemporary societies. The book concludes with a discerning commentary on the value of a capabilities approach, and its potential for changing the directions of policy and research around healthy ageing.

With its innovative and critical perspective on healthy ageing, this book is an important addition to the *Critical Approaches to Health* series.

Kerry Chamberlain and Antonia Lyons
March 2018

1

HEALTHY AGEING

Healthy ageing is the ideal trajectory from birth to death. As we reach older age, physical changes are inevitable, but it is not simply the effect of these changes that makes ageing healthy or unhealthy. An older person may have many years of inca- pacity as they decline slowly towards death. Or they may be well and functioning happily until a very rapid shift into loss of life (the ideal of dying suddenly in one's sleep while in the midst of life). It is the latter trajectory that many people desire and the aim of promoters of healthy ageing. However, the question raised by this recognition of the ideal trajectory is, what is health?

Concerns regarding population ageing have brought ageing and health under additional scrutiny. These concerns have coincided with new perspectives on healthy ageing, captured in descriptive phrases such as 'successful ageing', 'active ageing', 'positive ageing', or 'ageing well'. In this chapter we discuss the context of healthy ageing in the 21st century, including an ageing population and current policy dis- courses of 'successful ageing'. Critiques of these influences lead us to examine the effects of dominant discourses that view ageing as a problem to be solved and conflate ageing with poor health. Together, these discourses construct ageing as a social prob- lem which will increase the need for health care and make unreasonable demands on the public purse. This chapter describes alternative ways of understanding health for older people and introduces the Capability Approach as a socially based and ethically oriented way to understand older people's health.

Ageing population

The world's populations are ageing. Population ageing means that there is both a rise in the average age of the population as well as a growing proportion of older people within populations. According to the WHO (World Health Organization, 2012), between 2000 and 2050 the proportion of the world's population aged over 60 years will double from about 11% to 22%. Nearly a quarter of the population will be older than 60 and by 2025, for the first time, there will be more older people than children.

We might have expected that the growing numbers of older people would make a difference to their acceptance. However, recognition that the population is ageing has engendered additional fear and distaste. These shifts in the shape of the population are usually described in terms of the proportion of older versus younger people, and increased 'dependency ratios'. Dependency ratios are calculated in terms of the proportion of older and younger people in the population. As such, understandings of these changes are shaped in terms of generational shifts and intergenerational burden. Such generational changes have focused attention on the likely increased costs of health care and pensions for increasing numbers of older people (Binstock, 2010). Older people are more often portrayed as some sort of universal 'other' in the media or in policy statements where images such as a 'silver tsunami' or 'tidal wave' of ageing people about to descend upon 'us' are used (e.g., Martin, Williams, & O'Neill, 2009). Ann Robertson (1997) has critically named this the "apocalyptic demography" scenario in which the growing older population, with its ailing, retired bodies and high health care costs, drains the larger society and brings economic and social catastrophe.

Government policies today are largely driven by these concerns about the arrival of greater proportions of 'baby boomers' and subsequent generations at retirement age. From the late 20th century, policies in many countries have shifted from the focus on decline, dependence, and care of older people to those which encourage participation, independence, and good health. The overt aim of these policies is not to change ageist attitudes, but to reduce the potential burden of older people on health and welfare systems and at the same time maximise their contribution to society (Stenner, McFarquhar, & Bowling, 2011). Such policies focus on older people as a 'resource' that can be used to address the difficulties associated with population ageing (Peng & Fei, 2013).

The WHO active ageing policy framework (World Health Organization, 2002) has influenced the construction of such policy approaches. The word 'active' refers to continuing participation in social, economic, and civic affairs, as well as the ability to be physically active or to participate in the labour force (Walker, 2002). The active ageing policy framework has been influential in shaping the shift in government policies that are discussed in terms such as 'successful', 'active', 'healthy', or 'positive' ageing strategies. Such strategies lead to a focus on independence and productivity (Walker, 2002).

Government policy is one very strong influence on the ways in which people are seen as a certain sort of person in society. Peter Townsend (1981), an English sociologist, showed how policy influences citizenship and constructions of ageism in society. He revealed how UK policy in the 20th century (responding to the changing workforce needs of a capitalist society) produced a deficit model of ageing based on disengagement and dependency. This led to the stigmatisation of older people as dependent and costly. Current recognition of growing numbers of older people has made this particular construction increasingly frightening, especially as 'they' are also living longer. Townsend's (1986) influential work showed the key role of governmental social policy in constructing different versions of old age. Currently, the powerful policy notions of successful ageing, promulgated through the media (Rozanova, 2010), have contributed to a discourse of 'successful ageing' (which includes descriptors such as 'active', 'positive', 'resourceful', 'well', and 'healthy' ageing) as the dominant way to talk about old age in our societies. The general popularity of this new 'successful ageing' discourse may be understood as a response to widespread concerns regarding the ageing of world populations.

Successful ageing

An important influence on current research, intervention, and the development of recent public policy around ageing has been John Rowe and Robert Kahn's (1997) 'successful ageing' model. 'Successful ageing' stresses intervention aimed at supporting older people to avoid disease and disability, maintain high mental and physical functioning, and remain socially engaged. In their seminal 1987 paper in *Science*, Rowe (a geriatrician) and Kahn (a social psychologist) suggested a new approach to the dominant conceptualisation of ageing as a process of inevitable decline and morbidity. They noted that the effects of the ageing process had been exaggerated and pointed to the heterogeneity of older people's lives and the importance of diet, exercise, personal habits, and psychosocial factors in explaining individual differences. This model crystallised earlier work on successful ageing (Katz & Calasanti, 2015) and shaped the current focus of health researchers on the delay of illness, disease, disability, and mortality (Ryff & Singer, 2009) and the behavioural determinants of healthy ageing (e.g., Peel, McClure & Bartlett, 2005). These theoretical approaches and associated empirical focus on measuring success have contributed to a discursive construction of successful ageing which influences "retirement lifestyles, policy agendas, and anti-aging ideals" (Katz & Calasanti, 2015, p. 209). A 'successful ageing' discourse positions older people as responsible for engaging in exercise, diet, and social engagement prescriptions to produce good health.

Shifting from previously dominant discourses that featured decline and dependence to a successful ageing discourse, alongside recognition of the need to provide environments that foster participation and active contribution, has been beneficial for many older people. Thus, many gerontologists and allied social scientists have supported the development of conceptual models of successful ageing. Rowe and Kahn (2015) have recently noted that the successful ageing model suggests the 'what' and it is for psychological models to focus on the 'how'. However, the ongoing development of such models remains problematic while the meaning and location of successful ageing within broader society remain unexamined. By supporting the 'successful ageing model' uncritically, researchers and practitioners risk reinforcing a wider discourse which is potentially damaging to the well-being of older people in our society. The main critiques of the broader successful ageing discourse in this regard may be summarised within four general areas: support for biomedical constructions of health including healthism and denial of death, homogenising ageist discourses, oppressive ideals, and a dominant ideology of individual responsibility. Each of these will be described in turn.

Healthism and denial of death

Although 'successful ageing' has been seen as a positive shift in our views of older people, its ideals remain constrained by the dominant biomedical construction of health. Estes and Binney (1989) have described the ways in which healthy ageing was captured by a biomedical model which constructs ageing as a medical problem. They described the arenas of social life shaped by biomedicalisation as the scientific construction of ageing, the professions engaged in working with older people, the social policies around ageing, and the public perceptions of older people. These arenas are necessarily intertwined and together have important consequences for the ways in which we understand the roles and needs of older people and all who work with them. Although many aspects of social life and the environment may be taken into account as predictors of healthy ageing, the focus of medicalised research is on outcomes measured in terms of life expectancy, falls, multimorbidity, disability, hospitalisation, institutionalisation, and self-rated health. In *The Fountain of Age*, Betty Friedan (1994) described her personal experience of encountering this model in action during a seminar ostensibly on 'Health, Productivity, and Aging' attended by doctors and government officials:

> Day after day, when the participants broke into discussion groups after each lecture, they only wanted to talk about Alzheimer's, senility, and nursing homes. . . . Clearly they did not want to think about people over sixty-five except as helpless patients, clients of their compassionate care.
>
> *(p. xxvi)*

In the broader social context, Johnson (1995) describes how this approach to 'healthy ageing' has generally promoted ageist attitudes in Western society through which older people are seen as 'other' to be segregated, cared for, and controlled.

This powerful and pervasive construction of ageing and its effects on the treatment of older people persists today. Franco et al. (2009) described a common definition of ageing as "the progressive loss of function accompanied by increasing morbidity and decreasing fertility," and healthy ageing defined in terms of the 'Healthy Ageing Phenotype', which is "having highly preserved functioning metabolic, hormonal and neuro-endocrine control systems at the organ, tissue and molecular levels" (p. 15). Thus, a biomedical model frames 'normal ageing' in terms of biological processes with a focus on the diseases of ageing, and old age as a process of biological and psychological decline and disability to be fought against. This approach reduces people to their deficiencies and individualises their treatment by divorcing health from social and material life. Antonovsky (1993) described this process this way:

When we focus on risk factors, on a disease, and on its pathologic development, we are pressured to identify the person with the disease. Bob Scott, now at the Palo Alto Behavioral Sciences Center, many years ago wrote an unfortunately not well known book called *The Making of Blind Men*. He analyzed how we come to transform a person who is a woman, a shop owner, a mother, a devout believer, etc., etc., and who also has the very important characteristic of having extreme difficulty in seeing physical objects in her proximity – how we transform her (and how she internalizes the transformation) into a blind person, period.

(p. 6)

While focusing on achievements in conquering diseases and extending individual lives, the dominance of this model has prevented attention to the wider lifetime and social aspects of health and ageing.

The promotion of physical health is an important aspect of successful ageing models which supports the ideology of 'healthism'. First characterised by Crawford (1980), healthism describes an individualised version of the meaning of health which encourages individuals to take responsibility for that health. Crawford (2006), Rose (2001), Petersen (1996), and Lupton (1995) have drawn upon Foucauldian theory to describe the pursuit of health by the active, responsible citizen who engages, by choice, in a regime of constant self-evaluation and mastery of conduct, diet, and lifestyle. The successful ageing discourse has been identified as closely bound to the moral imperative of 'healthism' (Clarke, Griffin, & Team, 2008). In successful ageing models, good health is seen as the product of certain practices, rather than other possible definitions such as being generally well. Walker (2013) referred to these practices as "self-correction variables": diet, exercise, and social interaction. This biomedically based perspective on ageing emphasises individual lifestyle practices to prevent decline and disability. Paying attention to diet, exercise, cognitive activities, and appropriate social interaction is encouraged as part of a focus on preventing ill health and delaying death. For example, a Canadian policy workshop on healthy ageing (Health Canada, 2002) began with an introductory suggestion that healthy ageing involves three factors: low risk of disease and disease-related disability, high mental and physical function, and active engagement with life. The members of the workshop went on to focus on injury prevention behaviour, healthy eating, smoking cessation, and physical activity as key determinants of health in terms of personal health practices (pp. 5–6). Such messages have been successfully promulgated throughout many societies. Interviews with 60 people aged 55 to 70 (Pond, Stephens, & Alpass, 2010) showed that older people recognised that there were many effects on their health such as luck, genes, ageing, social and family relationships, and sometimes work stress. Nevertheless, the participants drew most strongly and consistently on particular health practice themes of diet, exercise, mental stimulation, and social engagement.

There are two main concerns about the effects of this focus on health as a product of individual behaviours. First, a moral imperative pervades: those who are healthy and diligently follow dominant health messages are seen to be living virtuously, whilst those who are unhealthy or indifferent to the prescriptions for health-related behaviour are seem as irresponsible and even blameworthy for any illnesses that develop (Crawford, 2006; Galvin, 2002; Lupton, 1995). Accordingly, older people's talk about their health can be seen to include a moral dimension in which people position themselves and others as virtuous or irresponsible depending on their body's condition and how well they engage in the recommended health-related practices (feeling guilty for not exercising or eating takeaways, or feeling proud of being active at 90; Pond et al., 2010). Health promotion discourse leads to individual responsibility and blaming, and people feel ashamed of their ill health. It is particularly difficult for older people to be subjected to this imperative because they are more likely to suffer a disability or general loss of physical abilities as they age.

Second, perhaps the even more misleading effects of healthist messages are the suggestions that focusing on maintaining physical well-being will allow us to live forever. The focus on the maintenance of health and avoidance of decline creates problems for older people because the effects of time itself on bodies are not acknowledged, and there is no space at all to consider the inevitability of death. Successful ageing discourse only includes good health outcomes and the possibility of avoiding decline; it does not include the realities of embodied ageing (Katz & Marshall, 2003; Powell & Biggs, 2004). Thus, successful ageing constructs a version of ageing in which people may never grow old. Daniel Klein (2012), writing in his 70s, provides an amusing account of his recognition of the denial of ageing among his middle-class American peers:

> All around me, I saw many of my contemporaries remaining in their prime-of-life vocations, often working harder than ever. Others were setting off on expeditions to exotic destinations, copies of *1,000 Places to See Before You Die* tucked in their backpacks. Some were enrolling in classes in conversational French, taking up jogging, and even signing up for cosmetic surgery and youth-enhancing hormone treatments. A friend of mine in her late sixties had not only undergone a face-lift but also elected to have breast implants. And one man my age told me that between his testosterone patch and seventy-two-hour Cialis, he felt like a young buck again. "Forever Young" was my generation's theme song, and unreflectively I had been singing along with them.
>
> *(Kindle Locations 132–137)*

Researchers are also affected. The ways in which the successful ageing construction presently shuts down any recognition of the effects of physical ageing within research is illustrated by the interpretation of research findings in a news media article (BBC Business News, 2013):

> Retirement has a detrimental impact on mental and physical health, a new study has found. The study, published by the Institute of Economic Affairs

(IEA), a think tank, found that retirement results in a "drastic decline in health" in the medium and long term. The IEA said the study suggests people should work for longer for health, as well as economic reasons. The government already plans to raise the state pension age.

The article further stated that "there is a small boost to health immediately after retirement, before a significant decline in the longer term." And "the effect is the same for men and women, while the chances of becoming ill appear to increase with the length of time spent in retirement." The assumption behind the article as it is quoted above is that if people stay working forever, this decline will not occur at all. Are these long-term effects the result of retirement or ageing? We found that the contradiction between these ideals and the actual experience of physical change was beginning to be noticed by our participants (Pond et al., 2010). One very active man who was working physically all day expressed concern about increasing tiredness and aching muscles; he was worried that the only solution (as suggested by health promotion advice) would be to increase his physical activity. Others expressed surprise when adherence to ideal health protective behaviour failed; they felt betrayed by the healthy ageing discourse. These were people who had followed all health promotion advice and still became unwell. They felt bewildered by the mismatch between their virtuous behaviour and their present poor health.

Death itself is largely ignored in these approaches, because of the biomedical focus on delaying death, which is seen as a poor outcome of a failed organism. Despite the growth of hospice movements and considerations of dying well (Kastenbaum, 2015), we struggle to include death within understandings of healthy ageing. Atul Gawande (2014) has written from a medical perspective about this neglect. He suggests that the medical profession and society should move from the indiscriminate focus on prolonging life towards consideration of what makes life meaningful. A reviewer of Gawande's book was moved to tell her own story thus:

> When my father-in-law was in hospital, we asked his doctor if he was dying. She blustered, looked embarrassed and, eventually, said no. He was, though, and afterwards we wished we'd known. It would have been a different, richer, kinder three months.
>
> *(Bedell, 2014)*

This account highlights Gawande's points about the damaging effects of not including death as an important aspect of ageing. He argues that this failure to confront death underlies our inability to deal sensibly with ageing. Ironically, the absence of death from the story of healthy ageing may make it more difficult for older people to age well. As people age, awareness of the proximity to death focuses attention on what they themselves value (Breheny & Stephens, 2017; Carstensen, 2006). A conceptualisation of health which does not acknowledge physical decline and death does not allow older people, or their families and caregivers, to shape the time they have remaining in terms of priorities and preparations for the inevitability of death.

Older people's sense of identity is negotiated within the context of dominant discourses of ageing and their own experiences of ageing bodies. Tulle (2008) describes how bodily ageing has been theorised as a threat to social identity in a cultural context which values youth, beauty, and physical competence. A dominant discourse of successful ageing supports these values although they do not necessarily fit with older people's assessment of their own ageing (Strawbridge, Wallhagen, & Cohen, 2002). Older people must balance the expectations of successful ageing with awareness of changes in their ageing bodies (Martin, 2007). Successful ageing discourse stigmatises the actual physical signs of ageing, undervalues some very real experiences of growing old, and denies the complexity of gains and losses in older age. The dangers of such a pervasive influence on daily practice for older people may be found in the suggestions that relentless activity and virtuous diets might allow us to live forever. This creates difficulties for those who are experiencing changes in energy and strength levels. Instead of resting a little as we age, it seems that we must engage in increasing levels of self-surveillance and discipline.

Ageism

Ageism constructs older people as members of one group (old people) once they reach 65 years of age. In Western society, different age groups are assigned particular identities and roles which also mark out relationships of power (Calasanti, 2007). Stereotypical identities that deny older people access to certain rights or full participation in society work together as ageism. Analysis of the media shows that ageing is largely represented by images of disability and dependence. These images are used to construct older people as outside of mainstream society. Irish researchers (Fealy, McNamara, Treacy, & Lyons, 2012) studied newspaper texts relating to a proposed revision of welfare for older people. They found that there were particular nouns and phrases such as 'grannies and grandads' and 'little old ladies' used to talk about older people as one group. These older people were variously constructed as 'victims'; 'frail, infirm and vulnerable'; 'radicalised citizens; 'deserving old' or 'undeserving old'. Together these ways of talking about older people placed them as 'others' who were outside mainstream Irish society. Recent research by Lindsay (2014) similarly showed that the elderly are generally represented in the media as objects of pity, as ill, or as incapable of performing everyday activities such as driving or using a computer. The result of such stereotypes is that if an elderly person is involved in a car accident, especially a 'wrong way' motorway crash, their age is usually highlighted in newspaper headlines, although a quick online search will produce many examples of headlines about a wide variety of younger people going the wrong way, and their ages are not mentioned. And what if older people do well? Even praise for a performance that was the highlight of Glastonbury in 2013 was tinged with ageist commentary. The *Daily Mail* in the UK published a story with the headline: "Glastonbury's Night of the Living Dead as Rolling Stones Rock the Festival" (Viner, 2013). While praising

Mick Jagger's performance and the Stones' longevity, the *Daily Mail* reporter could not resist making constant reference to the ages of the group members.

This sort of insidious and casual ageism displayed in the media is also part of everyday life and may be found among the most careful and thoughtful people. One of the issues raised when we requested ethical approval to invite older community dwelling people to complete survey questionnaires, was about the competence of older people to consent to participate. Simply because our participants are over 60 years old, some ethics committee members assume that they are vulnerable and should be excluded from making such decisions on their own. Such compassionate ageism views older people as uniformly frail, dependent, and in need of protection (Binstock, 2010). Thus, ageism not only stereotypes people as belonging to a certain group who all have the same characteristics, but it works (even from an apparently benign and caring perspective) to actively exclude older people from full participation in social activities.

People make sense of their own lives in terms of the cultural constructions that are available within their own social world. Thus, older people construct their own identity on the basis of the dominant discourses which shape what it means to be an older person at any particular time. We have found that these discourses contribute to people's identity in very practical ways, such as shaping their housing decisions: moving into a sheltered environment may be seen as a sensible choice in planning for one's later life if we are positioned by our own use of the discourse of inevitable decline (Matthews & Stephens, 2017). Furthermore, narratives of the irrelevancy of older people make it difficult to maintain an identity as a capable experienced citizen; one older woman volunteered to provide sexual health counselling to young women, but only on the telephone so callers would not know her age. It is an extra burden for older people to maintain the identity of a good contributing citizen in the face of these ageist assumptions. Such pervasive ageism means that older people themselves do not want to be viewed as 'old' people. Andrews (2009) describes the paradox of our wish to live as long as possible which exists alongside our fear of ageing and oft-expressed dismay at looking like an old person. Negative constructions of older people have recently led to a burgeoning anti-ageing industry which focuses on supporting our wish to appear younger looking. Calasanti (2007) has provided an excellent account of the ways in which ageism and sexism work together in this industry to further disadvantage women and exploit their fears of being cast aside by society. Meanwhile, the media celebrates those few who have managed to retain youthful looks and activities (by running marathons at 96 years old!). The effect of pervasive ageism is that we want to live a long life but do not want to be, or act like, one of those 'old' people.

At first glance, a successful ageing discourse seems to counteract ageist discourses which position all older people as subject to inevitable decline and dependence. However, in practice it supports the equally ageist view that all older people are able to age successfully. Thus, successful ageing models may reinforce the social exclusion of marginalised older people who are unable to attain these culturally specific (Liang & Luo, 2012) markers of success. For example, work with Aboriginal elders in South Australia (Bin-Sallik & Ranzijn, 2001) illustrates the practical ways in which marginalised groups are excluded from participation in successful ageing ideals which contradict their culturally based understandings of well-being. Bin-Sallik and Ranzijn note that while Australian aged care policy emphasises autonomy and independence, Aboriginal culture is collectivist and communal, with identity being located within the extended family "which is central to Aboriginal social and economic organisation" (p. 12). Thus, while successful ageing concepts of health and well-being focus on the individual, for Aboriginal older people health is part of family and spiritual well-being. Positioning all people as able and wanting to be independent as they age can be as damaging as constructing all older people as dependent (Ranzijn, 2010). Bin-Sallik and Ranzijn suggest that a more inclusive version of current ageing health policies would improve the very poor health experienced by older Aboriginal people today. Other commentators (e.g., Liang & Luo, 2012; Moody, 2005) have pointed out the cultural blindness of successful ageing policies which contributes to the oppression of marginalised groups.

Oppressive ideals

Successful ageing discourses are oppressive because they construct an ideal that not all older people can live up to. In practice, the ideal of successful ageing takes little account of lifelong inequalities and different opportunities for different groups of people to age 'successfully' (Holstein & Minkler, 2003). Several authors (e.g., Estes, Biggs, & Phillipson, 2003; Minkler & Estes, 1999; Portacolone, 2011; Walker, 1981) have pointed to the broader influence of economic, political, and social processes on the health of older people. Age intersects with other inequalities such as socioeconomic status (Victor, 2010), gender (Calasanti, 2007), and minority group status (Minkler, 1996) to shape the health chances of people throughout life, and these inequalities are exacerbated in old age. Older people who are poor are more likely to be in poor health which declines over time. For example, current data from the Aotearoa/New Zealand Health Work and Retirement (HWR) longitudinal study show the negative impact of renting a home on health over time (Szabo, Allen, Alpass, & Stephens, 2017). Specifically, home owners reported decreased levels of depression over 4 years as well as increased quality of life. In contrast, tenants indicated much higher levels of initial depression, which remained stable over the 4 years. In addition, they reported lower levels of quality of life, which decreased over time. Thus, simply owning one's own home provides for gains in mental health and perceived quality of life that are not experienced by those in more insecure housing situations. In general, successful ageing is most difficult for those older people who have experienced a lifetime of poor health and low wage insecure employment, and consequently reach later life least physically and financially able to maintain their own well-being; in other words they are failing to age successfully. Although many older people are less disabled than stereotypes suggest, many do experience disability and chronic illness, and a successful ageing discourse positions these people as failures.

People in poverty are already excluded in many ways, and successful ageing policies can reinforce this exclusion. Interviews with older people about their family life (Breheny & Stephens, 2010) showed that financially secure older people looked forward to a future located firmly within discourses of successful ageing. They saw their comfortable and active life as a reward for hard work and contributions to society. While acknowledging privilege, they also took credit for being a virtuous older person looking forward to a secure future. They often denied any suggestion that their health might decline as they aged. What was not foregrounded in their talk was the financial security and structural advantage that supports their 'successful' ageing. Poorer participants reported considerable health limitations and described how they struggled to manage financially. These participants took responsibility for their circumstances and also talked about being positive. For example, one participant living in economic hardship had chronic arthritis and many other illnesses including a twisted spine that she attributed to an abusive husband and years bent over a sewing machine for long hours. She saw her difficulties in terms of being unable to clean her cupboards properly, and her future as one of deteriorating health. Her main aim was to keep out of a wheelchair for as long as possible. She remained relentlessly positive and the interviewer praised her for this attitude. By focusing on her positive attitude, both the interviewee and interviewer provided a position of virtue for older people experiencing poor health. It could be argued that this recourse to a positive attitude is a sensible solution to come to terms with debilitating health problems in later life. However, focusing on a positive attitude supports social structures that reinforce disadvantage. Just like the wealthier participants, our poorer participants positioned themselves as good citizens through references to hard work, making good choices, and taking responsibility for outcomes.

The successful ageing discourse is drawn on, even by those who struggle, to obscure structural inequalities. Older people who age well and actively appear to do so on their own merits. Those who struggle are understood as having failed to age well. For wealthy older people, a positive ageing discourse works to support their expectation of well-being and participation in later life, and allows them to position themselves as deserving, by constructing these outcomes as due to hard work. But for those struggling with poverty and ill health, the advantage of positioning oneself as someone who works hard, and takes responsibility for oneself, is to avoid being positioned as someone who dwells on their poor health and has not made good choices. Those with low levels of living standards and poor health may be excluded from active participation in certain activities, but they are not excluded from aspirations to age well or the need to display successful ageing.

Individual responsibility

Successful ageing models, with their focus on personal activity to prevent decline, support the dominant neo-liberal economic ideology, with its focus on individual responsibility for health and economic well-being (Chapman, 2005; Lamb, 2014; Portacolone, 2011; Rubinstein & de Medeiros, 2015). Neo-liberal policies expect individuals to be responsible for managing their own later life and achieving the ideals of successful ageing through financial planning and adherence to health promotion advice (Kemp & Denton, 2003; Murray, Pullman, & Rodgers, 2003; Pond et al., 2010). Such policies position people as making decisions based upon material or economic considerations in the pursuit of self-interest (Coburn, 2000) which has important implications for the ways in which a society cares for people in later life (see Chan & Liang, 2013). This focus shifts responsibility for health from the public sector and social care agencies to families and individuals, while constructing later life circumstances as the culmination of good individual decision making. Along these lines, successful ageing models encourage a position of self-reliance (Kemp & Denton, 2003; Murray et al., 2003), surveillance, and personal blame for any failure to age successfully (Pond et al., 2010). In the context of individual responsibility, longevity shifts from a demographic concern for governments to manage to an individual responsibility for older people to manage. These critiques point to the ways in which individualism has been co-opted to organise community contribution, while alternative understandings of interdependence and community responsibility for vulnerable older people are neglected.

Constructing successful ageing as an individual achievement means that those who age successfully may take personal credit, and those who end up in poor circumstances are blamed, while the structural basis of inequalities in older people's life circumstances are masked (Breheny & Stephens, 2010; Rozanova, 2010; Rubinstein & de Medeiros, 2015). The impact that previous life circumstances and present social and physical conditions have on access to a healthy and participatory older age is ignored. The material effects of these discourses are that when poor health is blameworthy and independence is prized, older people may deny their need for help and support (Portacolone, 2011).

Older people construct their identity on the basis of dominant discourses (Gilbert & Powell, 2005) which shape what it means to be an older person at any particular time (Townsend, 1986). Successful ageing discourse restricts the criteria for success to two dimensions: (ill) health and (in)dependence (Powell & Biggs, 2000). Thus, older people living in restricted material circumstances and with poor health may be excluded from participating in society, but they are not excluded from the imperative to age independently. These neo-liberal constructions of dependence/independence ignore the interdependence of individual and community in social life (Robertson, 1997). Accordingly, a successful ageing discourse works hand in hand with neo-liberal policies to develop a divisive "two class system of older adults" (Rubinstein & de Medeiros, 2015, p. 35), to blame those in poverty and poor health, and to encourage independence in those who could well seek help in a more supportive society.

Can 'successful ageing' be saved?

As the volume of these sorts of critiques has grown over the years, others have responded with attempts to mend the cracks in the framework through attention to methodological issues in research, or to the conceptual framework itself as a basis for research and policy.

Methodological issues

There have been many critiques of the methodological application of the successful ageing ideal in research and practice (Katz & Calasanti, 2015; Martin et al., 2015; Martinson & Berridge, 2015; Rubinstein & de Medeiros, 2015; Stowe & Cooney, 2015). An early critic within psychology, Ryff (1989) criticised the failure of quantitative researchers to recognise the cultural construction of the notion of successful ageing and the lack of theorising applied to the measurement of the construct. Ryff described the broad array of psychological indicators such as quality of life and subjective well-being that have been used to assess successful ageing. More recently, Depp and Jeste (2006) identified 29 definitions of successful ageing in the 28 studies they examined. Bowling (2007) has reviewed successful ageing research and pointed to inconsistencies in the conceptualisation and framing of research questions in which particular aspects of well-being are seen variously as predictors or indicators of successful outcomes, or as part of the successful ageing model.

One approach to investigation has been to include older adults' own perspectives. The general neglect of what successful ageing means to older people themselves has been addressed in some qualitative work (Katz & Calasanti, 2015). Bowling's (2007) review of qualitative investigations of older people's perceptions and values of successful ageing reported that, although somewhat in accord with different research models, lay models of successful ageing are more multidimensional. Similarly, Andrews (2009) suggests a focus on gathering multiple narratives of ageing to resist the dualism of the inevitable decline and individual achievement stories that are available to us today. However, qualitative studies of older people's accounts of ageing successfully (e.g., Stenner et al., 2011) are also limited because they are generally constructed within the dominant discourses that reproduce current moral and political values. To ask people about their own 'successful' ageing is asking people to reproduce the dominant constructions of how we should age today (Stephens, 2016). Ironically, although Andrews addresses the possibility of alternative narratives which include positive identities for people who are positioned negatively by the decline and independence narratives (using the example of Alzheimer's disease), her own examples of successful ageing only include stories of outstanding achievements at very old age; stories which inevitably position those of us who are not seeing patients and swimming laps, or running our own farm, or studying and writing in our 80s and 90s, as not ageing successfully. Research on lay conceptions generally neglects to be critical of the successful ageing discourse itself. Such research has not examined the ways in which questions about successful ageing position the respondent. To be asked to evaluate the success of one's own ageing, or to comment on the attributes of successful ageing, is to be positioned as a subject of the successful ageing discourse. Why should older people be asked to evaluate the 'success' of their ageing at all? This very question positions the older person as one who may or may not be 'successful' and presupposes the possibility of individual failure to achieve ideals of health and participation.

The problem with attempts to respond to critique by simply including older people's views lies in the dominance of the successful ageing discourse. Although representing ageing in terms of success is relatively recent, elements of the successful ageing discourse are not new to our social world. On the contrary, people draw upon related discourses with a longer tradition which include a puritan work ethic, notions of independence and being beholden to none (which is a powerful working class discourse), and resistant discourses including withdrawal and preparation for death. It is the dominance of successful ageing discourse in current research, policy, and the media that leads to the current strong focus on talk about independence, contribution, and health as virtues, and pushes alternative equally historical discourses, such as care, respect for elders, or rest, contemplation, and disengagement as appropriate activities for older people, into the background (Breheny & Stephens, 2010, 2017; Martinson & Halpern, 2011). Active, healthy, and successful ageing discourses only include venerated subject positions for healthy, coping, and independent individuals.

Conceptual framework

Other critics have suggested that we must address the conceptual framework within which we conduct research and frame policy. Alan Walker has prominently supported the concept of active ageing (Walker, 2002, 2008), but criticises current policy applications, such as a narrow focus on working longer, as "blunt instruments" which produce problematic effects (Walker, 2013). Foster and Walker (2015) build on Walker's earlier work to propose eight key aspects of an improved strategy for active ageing: it should include all meaningful pursuits, it should involve all age groups preventatively across the life course, include the frail and dependent, embrace intergenerational solidarity, include both rights and obligations, be empowering with opportunities and support for citizens to take action, respect national and cultural diversity, and include individual differences in ageing throughout the life course. Others have suggested similar adaptations including understandings of cultural and gendered differences (e.g., Baker, Buchanan, Mingo, Roker, & Brown, 2015; Fabbre, 2015; Iwamasa & Iwasaki, 2011) or the importance of life course approaches (Stowe & Cooney, 2015). These critiques have highlighted the weaknesses in the conceptual frameworks of successful ageing and attempt to address aspects of health and quality of life that are neglected by the successful ageing model. However, including additional variables does not shift the focus of the successful ageing ideal itself. The ideals of successful ageing match the currently powerful neo-liberal economic and political ideology and the ideology of healthism. Together, these dominant ideals are part of a construction of ageing that cannot include a virtuous subject position for one who is physically dependent and does not allow for withdrawal, or preparation for death.

Alternative constructions of health

Although the successful ageing discourse remains dominant, there are alternative understandings of healthy ageing available. Critics of the pervasiveness of bio-medicalisation aim to broaden the possibilities for enjoying good health in older age, while recognising the benefits of medical science. Studies of older people show that well-being is not just affected by illness but by many other factors such as material conditions, social and family relationships, and social roles and activities, and these factors also change with age (Sprangers et al., 2000). Alternative views of healthy ageing go beyond illness and disability as the basis of well-being in older age to include the role of supportive environments in improving positive psychosocial states that contribute to well-being (Marengoni et al., 2011). The extent to which a person can live the life they want, a life they find satisfying, purposeful, and enjoyable, has been shown to mediate the effects of physical health on overall well-being (Berg, Hassing, Thorvaldsson, & Johansson, 2011; Devins, 2010). When older people with poor physical health are able to engage in activities and participate in society, they experience increased well-being (Tannenbaum, Ahmed, & Mayo, 2007; Van Campen & Iedema, 2007)

A well-known, if less influential, broader definition of health that takes into account these aspects of wellness was provided by the World Health Organization (WHO) as long ago as 1948: "Health is a state of complete physical, mental and social well-being and not merely the absence of disease or infirmity." This famous definition is included in the preamble to the constitution of the WHO and has not been altered since (World Health Organization, 1948). This more holistic approach to health has influenced many in the field of health promotion, particularly from the time of the Ottawa Charter, which states that all people should be able to reach their fullest health potential, realise their aspirations, and be able to satisfy their needs (World Health Organization, 1986). Dixey (2013), in her book on global health promotion, reflects many of the arguments for this more holistic model of health, suggesting that quality of life, happiness, and social relations should be the fundamental elements of health promotion in the 21st century.

Internationally, different cultural understandings of health are being brought to bear on Western understandings of healthy ageing. For example, Liang and Luo (2012) explain the importance of the Chinese philosophy of balance and harmony to understanding healthy ageing. Harmony, as a conceptual framework, emphasises a holistic approach which includes balancing complementary forces (yin and yang) in all spheres of life, including mind, body, and social relationships in time and space. Tse (2014) found that this same theoretical background was essential to understanding the experiences of older Chinese immigrants in Aotearoa/New Zealand. Her participants' narratives showed that well-being was dependent upon each person achieving a balance between their mind, body, and environment; Tse's participants told stories about their ongoing need to achieve a balanced dynamic interplay between their individual agency and the changing contexts and situations in which they found themselves.

Indigenous models of health have also contributed to a broader view within countries with a history of colonisation. In Aotearoa/New Zealand, Mason Durie (1985) provided an account of traditional Māori constructions of health. In Durie's model, 'Te Whare Tapa Wha' (the four-sided house) provides an image of the four cornerstones of health that are essential to ensure the strength of the house and support for the roof: bodily health, psychological health, spiritual health, and family health. This metaphor emphasises the importance of all aspects of health and includes collective well-being as an essential aspect; older Māori see their health status as strongly connected to the health status of their wider family (Edwards, 2010). In a similar way, Australian indigenous people's broader understandings of health encompass spiritual well-being and social health which includes the morale and well-being of the whole community (Bin-Sallik & Ranzijn, 2001; Maher, 1999).

A key element of a broader conceptualisation of health is recognition of spiritual values. Spirituality is a vital component of many indigenous frameworks of health, including connections with the environment (Ranzijn, 2010) and a sense of belonging to the past and future (Butcher & Breheny, 2016), which opens spaces for the importance of family and care. Although older people of many cultures may express interest in spiritual aspects of well-being, the dominant emphasis on maintaining physical health neglects these spiritual dimensions of ageing (Liang & Luo, 2012). Crowther, Parker, Achenbaum, Larimore, and Koenig (2002) have reviewed literature that supports the role of spirituality as a positive aspect of health. For example, there is evidence that spiritual beliefs provide a framework to reduce stress, increase a sense of coping, and increase a sense of purpose and meaning in life.

What people value in terms of their own goals and desired outcomes as markers of health often differ from the medical approach to deficits and challenges (Bryant, Corbett, & Kutner, 2001). Strawbridge et al. (2002) showed that medical approaches do not accord with older people's assessment of their own well-being. Using a model of absence of disease and disability, maintenance of physical and mental functioning, and active engagement in life (as defined by Rowe & Kahn, 1987) less than one-fifth of 867 people aged 65 to 99 were classified as ageing successfully. However, over half of these people rated themselves as successfully ageing. Bowling and Dieppe (2005) concluded that

> there is ample evidence that many elderly people regard themselves as happy and well, even in the presence of disease or disability. Doctors should be aware that many elderly people consider themselves to have aged successfully, whereas classifications based on traditional medical models do not.
>
> (p. 1550)

Alternative views of health are also reflected in qualitative studies of ageing and well-being. Bowling and Dieppe (2005) reviewed a range of qualitative studies which showed that many older people describe successful ageing in terms of having good physical health and functioning. However, people also contributed other ideas about what constitutes ageing successfully, including valued accomplishments, enjoyment of diet, financial security, neighbourhood, physical appearance, sense of humour, sense of purpose, and spirituality. Bryant et al. (2001) found that older people in general described health as doing something meaningful which included having something worthwhile to do, achieving a balance between their abilities and challenges, having access to appropriate external resources, and expressing positive personal attitudes. Participants in our research (e.g., Pond, Stephens & Alpass, 2010; Stephens, Breheny, & Mansvelt, 2015a) made it very clear that health meant an absence of disease, and functioning joints and limbs. In addition, these participants also took a broader view of the meaning of health, or wished to focus on other ways to be well. One 67-year-old woman eloquently expressed resistance to the health promotion ideals that she saw around her:

> You know, culturally, there's a sort of a thing I keep coming across that we shouldn't be ill, you know? If we're sick we've done something wrong and that somehow our expectation is that we will be well and happy all the time if we've got our acts together, you know and there's this thing about having our act together too, which is a sort of moral duty you know and I suppose that I think, actually life's not like that. Actually, all of us are going to die and most of us will probably have some ill health at some time and so that's part of being a human being. And you know, these difficult experiences we have are part of our, you know, they're part of our life in the world and to meet them with some sort of patience and graciousness and to sort of learn from them.

To encompass these broader understandings of health, we use the notion of quality of life.

Quality of life

Quality of life is a concept that shifts our perspective from a medical definition of health to one which encompasses the broader aspects of well-being recognised by older people themselves. Netuveli and Blane (2008) note that our ideas about quality of life have shifted over time from a focus on norms (often medically based), which were determined objectively, to more recent concepts of quality of life as a socially constructed version of individual experience. Although sometimes criticised as a nebulous concept which has been measured in many different ways (Cummins, 1997), quality of life provides an opportunity to consider individual perceptions of the positive and negative features of life, and the many aspects of life that contribute to well-being.

Research employing qualitative and quantitative surveys to study the quality of life of older people has grown in recent decades. Those studies which focus on people's own perceptions of their quality of life provide an opportunity to assess the things that people value in this regard. In general, findings such as those of Farquhar (1995) show that different kinds of physical losses experienced with ageing, such as poorer physical health and functional limitations (e.g., loss of mobility or sight), are seen by older people as making their quality of life worse. At the same time, there are many other aspects of life that people take into account, and often give greater weight to, when assessing how well their life is going. A wide range of studies has shown that older people generally identify a similar range of factors related to their quality of life: family, friendships, emotional well-being, religion/spirituality, independence, social activities, finances, standard of living, their own health, and the health of others (Walker, 2005). Netuveli and Blane (2008) reviewed a range of qualitative studies in which older people were asked what they thought contributed to their quality of life. The general findings of their review were that assessment of quality of life should include factors other than physical health. Older people's perceptions of the important factors contributing to the quality of their life included having good social relations with family, friends, and neighbours and being able to participate in socially and personally meaningful activities, as well as having no functional limitations. In addition to psychological factors such as having an optimistic outlook, older people often mentioned environmental factors such as being in a nice neighbourhood, having access to good public transport, and living in comfortable houses. Gabriel and Bowling (2004) conducted interviews with 80 people over 65 years old in various regions of the UK. Of the factors contributing to good quality of life, it was social relationships, home and neighbourhood, and psychological well-being which were mentioned by almost all of the participants. These were also often endorsed as aspects that contributed to poor quality of life (e.g., as loss of friends, poor family relationships, or bad neighbourhoods). Health and financial circumstances were also mentioned as aspects of poor quality of life. The other commonly mentioned aspects of good quality of life were activities done alone, social roles and activities, and independence. Gabriel and Bowling used their findings to emphasise that the influences on quality of life go beyond physical health and functional capacity to include the interplay of people's circumstances with the social structures of their society.

The importance of the social context is emphasised by examining studies with people in different environments. A Brazilian study of a group of rural people over 80 years old used qualitative methods to enquire about their satisfaction with their quality of life (Xavier, Ferraz, Marc, Escosteguy, & Moriguchi, 2003). Just over half (53% of 67 people) were satisfied, and these people mentioned good health, good relationships with the family, financial security, work, friends, and other people as important aspects of their good quality of life. When asked what was 'well with your life', most mentioned work as their main source of satisfaction (whether they had reported good or poor quality of life). Given that these were retired people, the investigators were initially surprised by this emphasis on 'work', but further analysis showed that in this context, work referred to the domestic and rural activities that the participants had performed for their whole lives (not just paid employment). Sometimes referred to as 'lending a hand', they meant contributions to the community rather than individual activities. The work included shared activities such as baking a cake or gardening, or contributions to family activities such as "dealing with the vineyard, tying a tomato plant, sewing, or collecting firewood" (p. 38).

These contributions to shared domestic life bound the participants to their community and provided a sense of reciprocity. The authors noted that these activities were lifelong ones and not special retirement activities, and suggested that this continuity of roles contributed to the satisfaction with their quality of life. This finding supports Atchley's (1989) continuity theory which stresses that the values of older people are developed over a lifetime, and the adjustment and adaptation to the challenges of ageing occur gradually for most people. One important source of good quality of life is continuing to engage in the valued activities developed across a lifetime and a sense of being important within one's social group (Xavier et al., 2003). The experience of very poor health, in a context of poverty and loneliness, is most likely to impact perceptions of one's quality of life (Smith et al., 2004).

New definitions of healthy ageing

Given awareness of the critiques of medical perspectives, and alternative understandings of health, new ways of understanding healthy ageing are being proposed. The recently published WHO report titled *World Report on Ageing and Health* (World Health Organization, 2015) includes many of these perspectives and draws on aspects of the Capability Approach. This document summarises the key issues to be addressed in healthy ageing policies (p. 27) as the need to:

- Consider the heterogeneity of experiences in older age and be relevant to all older people, regardless of their health status;
- Address the inequities that underlie this diversity;
- Avoid ageist stereotypes and preconceptions;
- Empower older people to adapt to and shape the challenges they face and the social change that accompanies population ageing;
- Consider the environments an older person inhabits;
- Consider health from the perspective of an older person's trajectory of functioning rather than the disease or comorbidity they are experiencing at a single point in time.

The background to this new framework makes it clear that the architects are addressing many of the critiques of current approaches to healthy ageing, such as ageism, lack of attention to diversity, and inequalities. The focus on functioning is seen as a shift away from characterising health in terms of disease states towards recognising the importance of a person's ability to live well within their society. Finally, a strong focus on the environment and the support it provides to retain quality of life in older age clearly signals a shift away from the focus on personal responsibility of previous health promotion thinking. However, the definition of healthy ageing provided in this report, namely "the process of developing and maintaining the functional ability that enables well-being in older age" (p. 28), can be read from many perspectives. The strong focus on functional ability in the new policy framework could map on to a dominant biomedical discourse, and is in danger of being captured by individually

oriented ideologies. Without a theoretically cohesive framework behind such a definition, the holistic and inclusive intent of this new framework could be rapidly lost.
In the rest of this book, we will outline a theoretical framework which can support
the development of more inclusive ageing policies.

Conclusion

There are diverse definitions of health used for different purposes; however, the term
'healthy ageing' has presently been largely captured by a 'successful ageing' discourse.
Within successful ageing discourse, health itself is narrowly defined from a biomedical perspective and further narrowed to a focus on the behavioural version of health
promotion constructed by 'healthism'. In critiquing concepts such as healthy ageing,
Johnson (1995) has suggested that we need multiple images of ageing well, rather than
the single version of ageing described by Rowe and Kahn (1987) as "usual ageing."

We suggest that Amartya Sen's (1993) Capability Approach provides the basis
for distancing the construction of the well-being of older people from oppressive
ideals of individual responsibility and the denial of physical ageing. The Capability
Approach is an alternative construction of well-being which focuses on the social
and environmental supports to enable people to live a life they value, rather than
promoting individual responsibility for achieving physical health. Quality of life is a
useful concept that encompasses the broader aspects of well-being described by the
WHO definition of health. We will draw on Sen's (1987) Capability Approach to
provide a theoretical framework to describe quality of life for older people. Sen has
proposed that capabilities are fair and useful indices of well-being which may be used
to measure quality of life.

Chapter 2 will introduce Sen's (1987) Capability Approach to suggest that healthy
ageing may be more usefully understood in terms of capabilities valued by older people themselves in different cultural and material contexts. The Capability Approach
leads us to see healthy ageing as a constellation of valued capabilities rather than
a narrow biomedically oriented definition. From a capabilities perspective, there
is little concern with finding the correct definition of healthy ageing. Rather, the
focus is on people's own valued capabilities within their own context. Using this
approach, our intention is to broaden the view from the dominant lens by considering the valued aspects of healthy ageing. Sen (1993) uses the broader notion of
'quality of life' (often interchangeably with 'well-being'). We will generally use the
terms 'quality of life' and 'well-being' as used by Sen to denote a broader construction of health, while acknowledging that aspects of physical, mental, and spiritual
life currently defined as 'health' are very important to older people. Having good
physical health and access to good health care is valued, although this may mean
many different things in different contexts. In this book we aim to acknowledge
the importance of health to older people, to point to the diverse understandings of
the constituents of health, and highlight the ways in which a capabilities approach
can support the quality of life of older people in our societies.

2

CAPABILITIES

This chapter introduces Sen's (1993) Capability Approach as a conceptual framework for research, practice and public policy in regard to the well-being of older people. The Capability Approach is a socially based and ethically oriented way to understand the quality of life of older people, and we suggest that thinking about older people's well-being in terms of capabilities solves many of the issues raised by the dominant frameworks critiqued in Chapter 1. The Capability Approach frames people's well-being in terms of their capability to function in the ways that they value. In doing so, this framework focuses on social rather than individual responsibility for health, on a more nuanced view of well-being instead of healthism, and allows for freedom rather than oppression. We include a discussion of how other theories of ageing may be included as explanatory aspects of a capabilities approach to well-being, provide examples of the use of the Capability Approach in relevant empirical research to date, and discuss the findings of our own research into the capabilities valued by older people.

A capabilities approach to healthy ageing

Sen's (1987) Capability Approach provides us with a basis on which to theorise healthy ageing by taking into account and examining the influence of the social and material environment, and asking what older people themselves value. The Capability Approach is a theoretical perspective rather than a set of guidelines, and as such it remains an open and often contested framework that can be used for a variety of aims (Robeyns, 2005a). Sen's (1987) description of the Capability Approach began as an economic analysis that shifted the focus of well-being (or quality of life, or living standards) from concerns with access to material goods to a concern with the values of people's actual lives. Rather than focusing on the consumption of goods, Sen's (1985) economic analysis distinguished between a material good, the utility or benefit of the good, and the functioning, or the individual's use of the good. The functioning itself and the capability to achieve that functioning is an important focus, and so the central principle of the Capability Approach is that a person's well-being or quality of life is not located in their ownership of material resources but in the opportunities that they have to lead the life they value.

From this perspective, understanding the nature of well-being shifts to understanding the level of freedom that people have to pursue the life they value. A capabilities approach includes recognition of differences in health, education, resourcefulness, and social connections that may influence the process of transforming resources into quality of life. It also accounts for social and cultural diversity in preferences. People may prefer different ways of living, but those with higher levels of capability have more freedom to choose what they prefer. Quality of life conceptualised in terms of capabilities takes account of these preferences by focusing on the extent to which people are able to pursue their preferred way of life, whatever it may be (Robeyns, 2005a).

Functionings

A core concept of the Capability Approach is the 'functioning' or the individual's use of a good to 'be and do'. To explain how functioning differs from other focuses of analysis, Sen (1985) used the example of a bicycle. It is not the possession of a good such as a bicycle that is important, but the functioning that it enables; that is, the ability to ride around on it. A disabled person may own a bicycle but not be able to cycle around; an older person may own a bicycle but the danger of the streets forbids its use. For Sen (1983), these 'functionings' include basic needs, such as being well fed or physically healthy, which are strongly valued by all. Other functionings are more complex although still widely valued, such as being literate or socially respected. The ability to be involved with one's community and friends may vary a great deal, even within wealthy countries (Sen, 1985). Writing specifically about capability and well-being, Sen (1983) noted that people may differ in the importance they attach to these different functionings and that these differences are context dependent. Important functionings such as 'not being ashamed to appear in public' were recognised as such by Adam Smith (Sen, 1987), who demonstrated how the goods required to achieve this functioning "varied with social customs and cultural norms" (p. 17). Functionings (being and doing) are seen as central to the nature of well-being.

Capabilities

Sen's theoretical focus is on a second core concept, a person's 'capability' or the extent to which they are able to function in a particular way (Sen, 1993). Capabilities reflect the various combinations (the "whole set," in Sen's words) of valued functionings a person can achieve, given their circumstances (Sen, 1985).

Focusing on capabilities allows us to include many possible ways of living, for example, across cultural and historical differences in values. 'Capability' describes what individuals are able to do and be, and their freedom to "achieve outcomes that they value and have reason to value" (Sen, 1999, p. 291). Thus, Sen (2002b) distinguishes between the achievement of certain levels of functioning, and the capability to achieve desired functionings. From a capability perspective, well-being is about command over physical, social, psychological, and environmental resources and the possibilities that they make available to an individual.

Values

An important part of the capability concept is the notion of values. Sen (1985) notes that while some easily defined functionings may be important, others may be seen as trivial. Thus the Capability Approach is concerned with the identification of valued functionings and capabilities to achieve these functionings. This is an aspect of the Capability Approach that has attracted some concern given the subjective and shifting nature of different values. How do we decide whose values are important or whose values to focus any analysis on? In response, Sen (1985) points to the advantages of this approach in terms of inclusion. Including values as a focus is important because it allows us to include "a variety of human acts and states as important in themselves" (p. 33). From Sen's perspective, it is the freedom to live well that capabilities provide (whether or not a person chooses to achieve their capabilities) that is the important factor.

Justice and inequality

Sen (2010a) argues strongly for taking the Capability Approach to the idea of justice. Raising the importance of the wide variety of abilities to use primary goods that might be available, he cites the additional needs of a disabled person, the additional requirements for nutrition and support of a pregnant woman, and the impacts on capabilities of inherited diseases or environmental surroundings. Thus, Sen argues for a focus on freedoms and capabilities as integral to our understandings of justice, noting that the Capability Approach points to "the central relevance of the inequality of capabilities in the assessment of social disparities" (2010a, p. 232). Sen has further argued across several works (especially 1992, 2010a) that a theory of justice must value equality. In discussing health equity in particular, he suggests that achieving good health and inequalities in access to good health care are pointers to underlying capabilities. It is these capabilities that would form a practical focus for an investigation of social justice and inequities.

An important contributor to these ideas of justice and capability is Martha Nussbaum (2011), another highly cited author on the Capability Approach. She has collaborated with Sen but their approaches are significantly different. In contrast to Sen's focus on individual freedom, Nussbaum's theory is based on Aristotelian notions of flourishing. While Sen (2004) describes developing context-related lists of valued capabilities using democratic deliberation, Nussbaum (2007) has developed a philosophically and empirically based list of 10 capabilities that she claims are essential to human flourishing. While Sen has developed a general framework that is applicable to evaluating the quality of lives people can lead, Nussbaum's aim is to provide a normative theory of justice. Although Nussbaum's work is philosophically coherent and has contributed to the development of a social justice focus to capabilities, the scope of Sen's practical framework, a focus on justice in terms of actual lives rather than philosophical or institutional ideals, is more helpful towards our interest in understanding the well-being of older people.

Capability and well-being

The concept of a capability may be applied generally, but understanding the capabilities of particular groups of people depends on specific local circumstances and needs. For example, the capability to participate in society is recognised as an important basic functioning; however, for older people such participation is culturally prescribed and constrained in particular ways. In Aotearoa/New Zealand, older Māori are respected and expected to take on cultural responsibilities which increase with age, and this respect is viewed positively. However, their everyday life is likely to be increasingly circumscribed by these social demands and increasing public involvement may lead to a sense of burden (Durie, 1999; Dyall et al., 2014). Older European New Zealanders are not generally accorded this higher status and are also more likely to report loneliness and isolation with its associated well-being decrements (Stephens, Alpass, Towers, & Stevenson, 2011). Thus, the value of participation as well as the capability to participate can have different meanings for different groups of people even within the same country. The value of, and the capability to achieve, any basic functionings, such as eating well, enjoying life, or feeling secure will have different meanings in different cultural and physical situations.

These differing situations in turn require considerations in terms of justice. If a shortage of financial support prevents older people from achieving their valued capability of physical functioning, or social participation, then this becomes a focus for change. If social circumstances, such as negative social norms, exclude older people from their need to participate, then these should become the focus for support. If older people are financially supported and well fed, but not able to be respected as full members of society, the Capability Approach holds that the capability of social participation must also be addressed by focusing on social change. By addressing all valued capabilities equally, neglected aspects of well-being and the possibility of social injustice may be highlighted and addressed.

Thus, the Capability Approach provides a theoretical framework that is able to take into account the material and social situation of people's lives, and account for different culturally based values. We now turn to a systematic consideration of how the Capability Approach can help us to overcome some of the problems of the 'successful ageing' approach (individual responsibility, healthism, and oppression) highlighted in Chapter 1.

Capability rather than successful ageing

Social rather than individual responsibility

Sen (2002a) distinguishes between the achievement of specified aspects of well-being such as good health or physical functioning, and the capability to achieve valued aspects of well-being which may also include access to friends and family or personal enjoyment of life. Thus, from a capability perspective, well-being is about command over physical, social, and environmental goods and the possibilities made available by these goods for an older person to achieve their desired functionings. The Capability Approach may be used to understand differences in well-being by considering people's freedom to make certain choices. In this way, it takes into account differences in health, education, resourcefulness, and social connections that may influence the process of transforming resources into well-being, and additionally accounts for social and cultural diversity in preferences. In his 1979 lectures, Sen focused on the example of physical disability (an example he has often drawn on since) to demonstrate the importance of a person's circumstances in converting goods into well-being (the disabled person who owns a bicycle but is unable to use it for transport). This example fits well with the experiences of embodied ageing which may be disabling, and focuses on the social and cultural location of older people's lives because 'capability' describes the level of peoples' freedom to pursue the lives that they themselves value (Sen, 1987). This focus on the 'level of freedom' brings to our attention the environmental aspects that support or prevent all valued functionings (Sen, 1992, 1993).

Thus, the Capability Approach shifts our constructions of ageing from a focus on individual responsibility for well-being with its moral implications, to one which includes the social and environmental context of ageing and well-being. For example, Allmark and Machaczek (2015) have described how the Capability Approach may be used to consider the financial capabilities of people with disabilities. Such an approach directs attention away from the current focus on individual shortcomings. Their use of a capability perspective points to the environmental and social changes that would be required for individuals to improve their financial capability, and accordingly their health, without requiring them to develop "extraordinary abilities" (p. 4) in financial knowledge that fit with the current economic ideology.

Health and ageing bodies rather than healthism and denial of death

Paying attention to capability is particularly important for understanding the well-being of older people who have different levels of physical capacity as they age. Rather than drawing upon dominant discourses in which physical health, independence, and productivity are normative demands to be produced by individual effort, the Capability Approach focuses on the needs of older people and the ways these needs may be met. For example, Venkatapuram (2011) argues that health itself may be understood as the capability to achieve a cluster of connected capabilities. The core of Venkatapuram's detailed argument for health justice from a capabilities perspective is that "a person's health is most coherently conceptualized as her abilities to be and do things that make up a minimally good, flourishing and non-humiliating life for a human being in the contemporary world" (p. 20). This conceptualisation of health as a meta-capability brings us closer to understanding differences in well-being for those from different social backgrounds and at different levels of physical capacity. Stephens, Breheny, and Mansvelt (2015a) demonstrated the use of the Capability Approach to identify a cluster of such connected capabilities valued by older people. Analysis of interviews with older people revealed six commonly valued functionings: physical comfort, social integration, contribution, security, autonomy, and enjoyment. The capability to achieve these valued functionings was of high importance regardless of physical health status although often limited by social and material circumstances. Grewal et al. (2006) similarly analysed data from interviews with older people in the UK to identify five related functionings that were seen as important attributes of quality of life: attachment, role, enjoyment, security, and control. Their findings suggested that the quality of informants' lives was limited by their ability to pursue these functionings, and they drew on Sen's theorising to suggest that it is the capability to achieve such functionings that contributes to quality of life.

Freedom rather than oppression

Sen's Capability Approach is a theoretical approach to social justice. In practice, this means that, rather than inquiring about levels of particular predefined attributes of success, which in turn may be oppressive, people assess their freedom to achieve their own valued functionings. Anand and Van Hees (2006) assessed well-being using the Capability Approach to purposefully shift the perspective from individual achievement. Rather than inquiring about levels of actual social participation or quality of the environment, participants assessed their levels of choice in these areas. In another example, Alkire (2002) used a participatory approach to evaluate development work in Pakistan. She used a capability perspective to show that for those experiencing poverty, values often neglected by institutional approaches to evaluation, such as religion and social status, were important development needs. Similarly, Horrell, Stephens, and Breheny (2015) studied the needs of carers for older people from a capability perspective. Their findings highlighted caring as an emotional relationship with the caree, and showed that carers need support for caregiving itself as a valued capability. This is in contrast to much of the literature which treats the caree as an anonymous burden from whom the carer deserves respite and relief. Using the Capability Approach enabled the researchers to highlight the values and needs of caregivers from their own perspective and contributed new understandings of the interdependent and relational nature of care. Such enquiry can provide new understandings of valued needs and people's ability to meet those needs.

Critiques of the Capability Approach

There have been many critiques of the Capability Approach from developmental, philosophical, and methodological perspectives. Here we briefly describe three main critiques relevant to our focus on well-being, where highlighting values and freedom has drawn criticism, and discuss the responses to those critiques.

Several critiques of Sen's focus on individual freedom suggest that Sen generally ignores social arrangements, social values, and interpersonal relationships. For example, Dean (2009) argued that a capabilities approach neglects understandings of human interdependency, power relations, and the powerful impact of socially structured arrangements on the possibilities for freedom. Crocker (2007) resists such arguments by claiming that power imbalances silence the voices of the poor or ill-educated. Crocker argues for ongoing commitment to democratic agency for all, which must involve a concerted critique of failed democratic processes at every level. Researchers with an interest in social perspectives on health and social justice have followed this line with reference to Sen's framework. For example, Marmot, Allen, and Goldblatt (2010) suggested that capability may be assessed individually, but differences in the capacity to choose the life that is valued may be understood as reflecting and revealing the structurally produced access to lifelong advantage or disadvantage. In general, many of those who draw on Sen's approach use it to point to its value in working towards socially supportive societies. Venkatapuram (2011) has developed a capabilities approach to health on the basis of the understanding that "for human beings to be able to live a full lifespan and experience as few avoidable physical and mental impairments as possible they need to be surrounded by a supportive environment" (p. 1). Sen (2002b) himself noted the importance of distinguishing between the capability on the one side, and the facilities socially offered to achieve that capability on the other (p. 660). Achieving individual capability requires social action to remove the structural barriers to participation and to developing capability. Thus, the Capability Approach may be used to evaluate the impact of social arrangements on the freedom of people to live the life they value (Alkire, 2005b). For older people, this understanding is particularly pertinent. People's values are constructed by the society in which they live; however, if that society is ageist and rejects those whose movements or appearance are affected by their ageing body, then the individual is excluded from achieving other valued capabilities. In terms of living conditions and health disparities, Sen (2010b) added that capabilities are to be understood as the basis for assessing advantages and making interpersonal comparisons, while Robeyns (2006) agrees that assessments of justice and equality may also be made on this basis. In regards to inequalities, it may be used to understand the nature of differences in living standards by considering people's freedom to make economic and social choices. The extent of choice and freedom available will reflect a person's relative position in an unequal society and their access to the resources that support well-being. In this way the Capability Approach draws attention to the social and material conditions that support capabilities.

Sen's rather abstract construction of persons and agency has contributed to critiques of his theoretical neglect of social structure and interpersonal relationships. Wells (2016) summarises suggestions that this is the result of his background in economics and philosophy and lack of grounding in anthropology, sociology, or psychology. There is space within a capability framework for development from these perspectives. More nuanced theorising of social relations, the importance of the social construction of personal values, and the workings of power and agency which are better understood from sociological and psychological perspectives may be incorporated into a capability framework as its use is developed.

Another critique of the Capability Approach is Sen's focus on opportunity and freedom to achieve valued functionings, rather than on the achievement of the functionings themselves (e.g., Arneson, 2007). This practical criticism suggests that possibilities for functioning are less useful than understanding what things people are actually able to do and be. Such achievements are also more readily assessed than capabilities. Sen (2010) responded to these critiques by noting that the idea of capability can provide a more inclusive account of disadvantage by distinguishing between those who choose not to function in a particular way and those who cannot function. This distinction between achievement and capability can be particularly important in situations such as immigration, in which people are able to choose between functionings according to different cultural values. For understanding the capabilities of older people, this distinction may be particularly important. For example, a moral imperative to volunteer one's 'leisure time' following retirement and thereby contribute to society can conflict with the value of rest as a reward for a lifetime of contribution, or values of care for older citizens (Breheny & Stephens, 2017). Sociological and psychological analysis can provide more understandings of the clash of such values and their implications within a capabilities framework. The strength of the Capability Approach's focus on the social and material environment and justice makes its precepts valuable, and its status as a general framework makes it open for ongoing theoretical development.

Capability and theories of ageing

Robeyns (2005a) specifically notes that applying the Capability Approach to issues such as policy or social change will "often require the addition of explanatory theories" (p. 94). To explain ageing itself within a capabilities approach to research and practice, we will require theories which enhance our understanding of values, agency, and contexts of ageing. For example, other theorists of ageing interested in enhancing the well-being of older people have developed guidelines for optimum ageing that could be understood as capabilities from Sen's perspective. These sets of theoretically or empirically derived capabilities could be incorporated into a capabilities approach in specific areas of enquiry or intervention as an important part of the procedures outlined by Alkire (2005b). Here we outline theories that could complement a capabilities approach in empirical and evaluative work on ageing. These are generally from developmental theories of ageing, social psychological theories, and critical social theories.

Andrew Scharlach's (2012) socially situated developmental model of 'optimum ageing' fits well with a capability perspective in that it accounts for environmental influences and cultural values. Scharlach's model includes five core concepts: continuity (the ability to maintain established preferences), compensation (support from the physical environment), connection (meaningful social interactions), contribution (a lifelong need to have a positive impact), and challenge (opportunities for stimulation). Each of these developmental achievements is supported by the physical and social infrastructure surrounding the older person, and so these key concepts are used by Scharlach to structure the basic requirements of an 'age-friendly' community. As such they are used to provide a guide for town planning and public policy. For example, empirical work which shows the types of housing and living arrangements which generally support the capability of connection is used to formulate solid practical guidance for the development of urban environments to support this aspect of healthy ageing. The core concepts in Scharlach's model map on to valued capabilities that have been identified using qualitative enquiry with older people (Grewal et al., 2006; Stephens et al., 2015a) and together provide a set for practical application or for further development to suit specific contexts. Further research questions could be: How are these capabilities valued by older people in a particular context? Or, what are the environmental and social conditions which support these particular capabilities?

Another influential theory is Paul Baltes and Margaret Baltes's (1990) theory of Selection and Optimisation with Compensation (SOC). From a life span perspective, this theory is based on the premise that development at any age is a process involving three components related to important goals: selection, optimisation, and compensation. When faced with changes and new limitations this suggests that, to achieve valued goals, people select favoured or meaningful activities, optimise the use of strengths and abilities that they do have, and compensate for losses by changing the ways in which they meet their goals. Paul Baltes (1997, p. 371) used the example of 80-year-old Arthur Rubinstein. When asked how he maintained his expert piano playing, Rubinstein said that he played fewer pieces (selection), practiced more often (optimisation), and to compensate for his loss of mechanical speed he played at slower rates overall (compensation).

Importantly, Baltes and Baltes (1990) suggested that the realisation of these components depend on the personal and societal circumstances of people as they age. Baltes (1997) held that to maintain human development further into the life span, culture-based resources (psychological, social, material, and symbolic) are increasingly required as the ratio between gains and losses in functioning becomes more negative. Thus selection, optimisation, and compensation become increasingly important in older age. From a capabilities perspective, SOC would lead us to ask questions about the valued goals of older people and their capability to select, optimise, and compensate to achieve those goals. These goals will be determined by the social context, personal resources, and values. In different contexts, different cultural resources will be required to support ongoing development as we age.

Laura Carstensen's (Carstensen, Isaacowitz, & Charles, 1999) socio-emotional selectivity theory could be seen as focusing on a particular set of valued goals which change over time; it predicts that older people (across cultures) value emotional connections rather than knowledge, and that this is because of awareness of time. Carstensen (1995) argues that the perception of time is linked to the selection and pursuit of social goals which are oriented to both emotional and knowledge needs. In particular, the recognition of shortened remaining time profoundly effects our motivation, cognition, and emotion. As we age, we usually become increasingly aware of the brevity of time left. A perception of limited time left, rather than limitless time as in youth, has important implications for people's choices in older age. The use of time for learning and pursuing novel experiences becomes less important than a focus on important emotional connections. This influences people's decisions, actions, and social contacts. As people age, they generally choose to interact with fewer social connections, focusing on intimate and important relationships. Older people are also more likely to emphasise the experience of positive emotions and avoid circumstances that instigate negative feelings. Carstensen et al. (1999) have employed a range of empirical studies to demonstrate these effects of awareness of limited time on human choices and emotional connections at any time of life. When time in life is apparently limited, both younger and older people pay more attention to the emotional aspects of life and prefer emotionally based social contacts. These preferences are used to explain the 'paradox of ageing' in which, although physical health declines, psychological health (including happiness and satisfaction with social networks) generally increases among older people (Löckenhoff & Carstensen, 2004). The important thing about this theory from a capabilities perspective is the important differences that awareness of limited time makes to our values and choices at the end of life, and the possible impact on well-being. As we have seen, dominant discourses of successful ageing ignore the limitations of time, and suggest that we can expand time by altering decisions about its use. Carstensen's work, suggesting an adaptive process from a developmental perspective, has been very influential in gerontology and yet does not sit well within a successful ageing framework. The clash of ideals between the values suggested by socio-emotional selectivity theory, and the development of new social connections and participation suggested by successful ageing models, could be fruitfully explored in terms of their implications for older people's well-being.

Toni Antonucci's convoy model (Antonucci, Ajrouch, & Birditt, 2014) addresses the importance of social relationships for health among older people. The convoy metaphor essentially describes the small group of significant others who accompany individuals through life with a special emphasis on emotional closeness. In old age, it is these social convoys that provide important support for well-being. The convoy model has enabled recognition of the complexity of human relations and their changing nature, both in depth or quality of relationships, and their changes across time, while highlighting the contextual nature of social relationships. This focus on context has been more recently developed by Berkman, Glass, Brissette, and Seeman (2000), who describe a model which includes the impact of the broader social and physical environment on the development of social networks and the social support they provide. Berkman and colleagues drew on social theory to raise questions about the constructive nature of the broader social and physical environment of social networks. Their model suggests that many social and structuring forces such as differences in culture or socio-economic status shape social networks, which in turn affect people's perceptions of social support and their social integration. Such theorising around the importance of the social and physical environment to social relationships can inform a capabilities approach to this important aspect of health. Both the idea of convoys and Berkman et al.'s focus on the environmental basis of social networks raise questions about the types of social support and social engagement valued by older people and the ways in which the environment supports the maintenance of these relationships.

Capability and social and critical theories

The move to social theory exemplified by Berkman et al. (2000) is needed as we shift the focus more towards recognising the importance of the social context of capabilities. Robeyns (2005a) has noted that the Capability Approach does not pay enough attention to social structures, although we must develop our understanding of the social determinants of relevant capabilities. Robeyns suggests that drawing on hitherto unexplored disciplinary areas would develop the potential for using the Capability Approach in the analysis of society and institutions. Here, critical and social theories would usefully inform a capabilities approach.

A political economy approach to understanding ageing was introduced in the 1980s when social scientists from the UK and the US (Estes, Swan, & Gerard, 1982; Phillipson, 1982; Townsend, 1981; Walker, 1981) critiqued the ways in which older people had been treated as a homogeneous group, separate from wider society, facing common problems of biological decline and inevitable dependence. Social policy interventions were seen to reflect this perspective resulting in age-segregated services for older people who were constructed as isolated from, and dependent on, the rest of the population. In contrast, the political economy approach examined the relative social and economic status of different groups within older age as well as between older and younger generations. A political economy of ageing takes the whole life course into account and highlights the problematic effects of social history, current social structures, and the political environment, including the role of social policies in constraining the social position of older people, their opportunities, and outcomes in old age. Walker (2005) has extended the approach to a global political economy of ageing, one which would take account of global inequalities, development and ageing, and the reach of international government and non-governmental organisations, supra-national structures, and trans-national organisations in regard to human rights, development, and ageing. The political economy approach has clear affinities with a capabilities perspective through its focus on different contexts and trajectories, and on the structuring effects of the social and political environment.

Gilleard and Higgs (2000) suggested that the political economy approach does not allow for individual agency (although this has been contested), and they outline a cultural studies approach to understanding ageing, one which takes into account the fragmented social meanings of ageing as well as the structural contexts in which older adults address their identity. A cultural studies perspective suggests that in post-modern society, issues of agency and identity are more important than the structural determinacy focused on by early critical gerontologists. The focus on culture reveals the variety of cultures of ageing available in the 21st century and the broadening of meanings and resulting identities of ageing that are possible. From a capabilities perspective, the attention to discursive constructions and shared narratives that cultural studies brings to the field provides an important perspective on the values of older people in particular contexts. A cultural approach also draws on critical theories to show that these values are inevitably socially constructed and shared; critical work by social scientists (e.g., Biggs, 2001; Stephens, Breheny, & Mansvelt, 2015b) can reveal and challenge the influence of powerful commercial and political institutions on the construction of ageing identities and values such as youthful appearance or productive contribution.

Feminist theorists also provide useful critical approaches to the construction of ageing by foregrounding diversity and power relations. Calasanti (1999) describes the importance of feminist perspectives in locating the experiences of ageing which are shaped by intersecting forces of power relations between classes, ethnicities, and genders. By focusing on the voices and experiences of different groups in society, feminist approaches can reveal the ways in which activities, such as 'retirement', are shaped by dominant values and have quite different meanings for many women, meanings which have been generally ignored in mainstream analyses. Gasper and van Staveren (2003) claim that Sen's view of freedom has important commonalities with feminist economics. After describing the ways in which Sen's Capability Approach has been drawn upon to support and develop feminist economics, these authors also point to some deficiencies in Sen's (1999) proposals. They draw on feminist theorists, including Nussbaum, to point to the importance of actions, meanings, and neglected values such as those associated with friendship, respect, and care. Gasper and van Staveren's work provides one example of how feminist approaches can help to provide recognition of the commonality and diversity of ageing experiences, and a broader understanding of the valued beings and doings of all older people.

Health as capabilities

Sen's Capability Approach is a theoretical approach to social justice as well as a field of praxis and a framework for social change (Venkatapuram, 2011). From a capabilities perspective, health research, policy, and intervention would focus on the capability of all older people to achieve valued functionings, rather than being responsible for ageing 'successfully' or achieving 'health' as a commodity. Sen's Capability Approach provides a theoretical approach to research as well as a framework for social change. The adoption of a capabilities approach to frame research, practice, and social policy will influence the way in which ageing is constructed by all, including older people themselves.

In this book, we use the Capability Approach as a framework for conceptualising the health of older people. This approach to health in older age points us towards a more nuanced version of health which includes the role of social structure, unequal incomes, spatial contexts, and social provisions. Venkatapuram (2011) argues that health may be seen as the capability to achieve a cluster of connected 'functionings' so that health in older age may be seen as the capability to continue to do valued things in later life.

A focus on support for individuals' abilities to meet their practical, social, and participatory needs begins with an assessment of valued capabilities. Various authors have used theoretical and methodological approaches to identifying valued functionings and capabilities in different contexts (e.g., Alkire, 2007; Burchardt & Vizard, 2011; Horrell et al., 2015; Robeyns, 2005b; Schokkaert, 2009; Walker, McLean, Dison, & Peppin-Vaughan, 2009). The World Health Organization (WHO, 2015) report on ageing and health has drawn on the Capability Approach to summarise the literature in this area. They conclude that some of the beings and doings that people value include a role or identity, relationships, the possibility of enjoyment, autonomy, security, and the potential for personal growth. Van Ootegem and Spillemaeckers (2010) found that people draw on their experiences of daily life when making decisions about what is important to them, and this was also found in a qualitative study of older people in the UK (Grewal et al., 2006), who talked about their quality of life in terms of five functionings: attachment, role, enjoyment, security, and control.

These domains are very similar to the findings from a large-scale qualitative study of older people in Aotearoa/New Zealand (Stephens et al., 2015a). Analysis of interviews with 153 older people (63–93 years of age) identified six broad domains of functioning which were noted as important in all respondents' accounts. These were labelled social connectedness, contribution, security, autonomy, enjoyment, and physical functioning. Of course these domains overlap, or may be combined, as when participants describe food, not in terms of physical needs, but in terms of being able to share with friends and family. Although the functionings were universally valued, there were different levels of capability to achieve all six; some people were not able to contribute or did not have the physical comfort or security that they desired, and many participants described their lack of capability to meet desired levels of social integration, autonomy, or enjoyment. Older people were not simply excluded from achieving valued functionings because of physical limitations. Many were excluded by having to make choices, such as between social integration and healthy diets, or were excluded simply by lack of money or appropriate transport. In general, this talk showed that, although they value physical functioning and its effects on their quality of life, many downplayed their infirmities and were determined to enjoy their life or present themselves as capable citizens despite ageing bodies. According to our analysis, well-being was understood in terms of physical functioning but also in terms of other capabilities. Well-being was seen as having choices around food and enjoying treat foods like chocolate, or wine when desired. It was understood in terms of being surrounded by family and friends who could provide enjoyment and security. And well-being was seen as participating in social life and making contributions to others despite physical disabilities. In addition, well-being could be seen in the gracious acceptance of change by those whose physical decline denied them access to past pleasures. Thus, the Capability Approach provides a basis for considering what constitutes well-being despite physical decline, and include all older people as having the potential to achieve healthy ageing.

We will use this initial list from our own empirical work, not as a definitive list of capabilities valued by older people but as examples of how a focus on the freedom to realise valued capabilities draws attention to the wider context and the influence of social, cultural, and material factors on well-being in older age. Each of the following chapters will address the realisation of each of the following capabilities in turn: physical functioning, security, contribution, social connection, enjoyment, and autonomy. Each chapter will include examples of the voices of those older people who contributed to our understandings of these capabilities. After detailing each valued capability, we will return to a discussion of research using the Capability Approach that can include the interconnection of these capabilities.

3

PHYSICAL FUNCTIONING

DECLINING INTO INVISIBILITY (FREIDA, 81 YEARS)

I'm getting unsteady, terribly unsteady. Someone was talking on the radio, an old person, about how he feels. He was saying you know in the house or in the garden, you go from one handhold to the other, sort of stagger along, grab hold, steady yourself a bit, stagger along to the next one. And that's where I'm at.

I walk to the supermarket and taxi home. Here you can, it's within my walking distance. They're very nice taxi drivers. The older ones help you inside with the groceries. The younger ones tend not to, but by and large they're very good. You see I'm on a walking frame so they have to load that in as well and it's quite a business for them. It's extra.

I've managed to get someone that comes in to help, only an hour and a half a week and a very awkward time. She's a very nice lady, but they're stopping it. And I really need her. The hospital board has run out of money.

Oh dear this is a sad tale. I went for a hearing test, and I found it very unsatisfactory because all it is, is a hearing aid salesman. So he's going to sell you a hearing aid whatever. It's completely wasted. It's sitting in its case in my bedroom and I just can't use it. The battery thing, a little tiny thing you put in your ear, it falls out. And I thought, you know, he doesn't really care a damn now he's gone and sold me the thing. I felt, "I don't like you, I'm not coming back." He was very, very polite and professional but I thought well I don't think you like old women. You know, people don't. There's a feeling, you see it is still superstition of the witch, the old woman is a bit, is either invisible or rather repulsive. Some people are very kind and very polite and

> treat you like a person which is marvellous. But for most people you are, they prefer that they didn't see you. You walk down the street and you're invisible. You pass lots of people but they don't look.

All living beings decline towards death, although the timing and trajectories of functional decline are highly variable (Lunney, Lynn, Foley, Lipson, & Guralnik, 2003). As we now live longer and are less likely to die suddenly, chronic conditions and multiple illnesses which affect physical functioning can be part of the ageing experience and may restrict participation and negatively influence well-being (Marengoni et al., 2011). Because of awareness and experiences of bodily changes, older people value the maintenance of physical functioning highly (Walker, 2005); however, illness or physical disability does not preclude healthy ageing (Farquhar, 1995; Netuveli & Blane, 2008). This chapter focuses on understanding the interactions of the social and physical environment with physical limitations, illness, chronic conditions, and disability in influencing the capability of older people to achieve valued physical functioning.

A capabilities approach highlights the ways in which physical changes, disability, and chronic illness will affect an older person's quality of life in relation to the support or lack of support available in that person's immediate social and material environment (e.g., friends and housing) or in their wider environment (e.g., health care and social stigma). To develop a capabilities approach to physical functioning, this chapter will draw on the wealth of work in ageing research which addresses the social and material aspects of the environment which support the physical functioning of older people and the ways in which the environment physically disables older people. By including aspects of the social environment, such as stigma, assumptions about the health conditions of ageing, and aspects of the physical environment such as provision of transport or the design of neighbourhood or urban facilities, the chapter will point to the ways in which the broader environment can support physical functioning. A capabilities approach shifts the focus from the shortcomings of the individual and individual responsibility to improve personal situations, to a consideration of the provisions of the social and physical environment to support the values of healthy ageing.

Physical functioning is valued

A capabilities approach leads us to consider physical functioning as one aspect of the quality of life of older people. Studies of older people's own perceptions of their quality of life show that people over 65 (Gabriel & Bowling, 2004; Stephens et al., 2015a) and people over 80 (Xavier et al., 2003) value physical functioning and good physical health. Older people are more likely to include physical functioning as an aspect of quality of life than younger people (Walker, 2005). For those who are living in the most difficult material circumstances, these aspects of life assume greater importance in constraining the experience of a good life. However, those in more favourable circumstances are able to reveal that other aspects of life can be seen as of greater importance, and that physical functioning is important largely to the degree that it may limit the achievement of other valued capabilities like social participation and contribution. By considering physical functioning in terms of the broader valued functionings of life, the assessment of well-being does not necessarily focus only on the individual's capability to achieve certain levels of physical functioning. Rather, functional capability is limited as much by the material and social environment, and the expectations for what is a good life in the person's society, as by changes to the body.

From this perspective, support for improved physical functioning by the individual is not seen as an end in itself, but rather understood as support to achieve all the important aspects of well-being that contribute to quality of life. For example, an older person able to walk successfully in their own home may not experience well-being if they are not able to participate socially. Loss of physical functions (such as mobility, sight, or hearing) and the experience of chronic illness are certainly limitations, and ones that older people are more prone to experience. However, a person's quality of life need not be limited by these changes.

The disability paradox

Being physically fit or able to walk well is not necessarily the central focus of an individual's perception of well-being, although medical perspectives have assumed this would be the case. This assumption has given rise to the notion of the 'disability paradox':

> [If the] common understanding of a good quality of life implies being in good health and experiencing subjective well-being and life satisfaction . . . one can argue that if people have disabilities, they cannot be considered to be in good health nor possess a high level of life satisfaction.
>
> *(Albrecht & Devlieger, 1999, p. 978)*

Such assumptions conflated life satisfaction and physical functioning and led to surprise when it turned out that there was not a general agreement between people's own perceptions of their health, well-being, and life satisfaction and the objective assessments of their health status (p. 978). When Albrecht and Devlieger studied the experience of disability in the general population, they concluded that those who reported higher quality of life had achieved a balance between their body, mind, and spirit which was supported by their social and physical environment. Bowling, Seetai, Morris, and Ebrahim (2007) studied the disability paradox among a sample of 999 people aged over 65 in Britain. Although around 20% of respondents reported functional difficulty between 'fairly' to 'very severe' levels, 62% of these rated their quality of life as 'good'. Those who reported poor physical functioning but good quality of life were more likely to feel in control of their lives, and used psychological coping strategies such as acceptance and compensation to find that balance. Thus, physical functioning may be understood as only one part of a satisfying life, and undesirable changes in physical functioning may be compensated for, to achieve good ongoing quality of life in older age.

Within gerontology, there is an increasing focus on the role of the environment in supporting healthy ageing. Baltes and Baltes's (1990) theory of selection, optimisation, and compensation describes how older people with psychological, material, and social resources are able to compensate for changes in physical functioning to maintain valued activities, social connections, and identities as valued contributing members of their communities. The following sections consider the modifiable social and material aspects of the environment which may support good quality of life for all.

Disabling social environments

Ageist stereotypes, which remain strong in many societies, view older people as a homogenous group, and adversely affect the social standing and identity of older people (Angus & Reeve, 2006). Popular constructions of the older person as either 'declining and dependent' or 'youthfully capable and productive' (Hodgetts, Chamberlain, & Bassett, 2003) serve to exclude many older people because of changing physical functioning. Discourses of ageing in which the self-regulating older person who maintains good physical health is the epitome of a functioning participating citizen can be disabling and demoralising for older people who experience physical change. The focus on physical health as the hallmark of a contributing citizen includes a moral dimension in which people position themselves and others as virtuous or irresponsible depending on their body's condition. Those who maintain good physical functioning are proud of this achievement. For example, after describing his physical health and flexibility, a 77-year-old participant in a recent study summed up his good health by saying: "I boast about it a lot and I'm entitled to." The interviewer agreed: "I know" (from Breheny & Stephens, 2017). This entitlement (reinforced by the interviewer) means that those whose bodies display age-related changes are often ashamed. People who do not participate in healthy practices may be positioned as failing and hesitate to venture out of doors. A dominant medical perspective on health which sees ageing as a preventable ailment and physical changes as the result of individual choices contributes to the continuing stigmatisation of older people who display signs of disability.

Such ageism has material effects on people's physical functioning. Angus and Reeve (2006) describe the marginalising effects of ageism on those who would benefit from physical assistance in very old age. They described older people who were isolating themselves from any social or physical support owing to fear of the total loss of independence and self-hood signified by hospitalisation. Angus and Reeve note that an ageist society has produced a problem for older people who fail to age successfully and must "access punitive and fragmented service systems" (2006, p. 143). These ageist stereotypes function to disempower older people and deprive them of basic rights in social and institutional settings such as health care. Safiliou-Rothschild (2009) reviewed health care for elders in several European countries to show that older patients are less likely to be provided with appropriate treatment. Older patients are discriminated against because they are not represented in clinical trials, physicians are less prepared to risk treatment, and insurers are unwilling to risk expenses. Illnesses that affect any age group such as deafness, poor sight, depression, anxiety, insomnia, and various chronic illnesses may not be taken seriously by health professionals when they occur to the frail old, or the treatment offered older people may be considered from a different perspective (Stephens & Flick, 2010). Many common problems such as alcohol abuse are overlooked by physicians because of assumptions about the basis of illness in old age (Berks & McCormick, 2008). Reed and Clarke (1999) provide a particularly pertinent analysis of the ways in which the construction of older people as a problem, because of physical impairment and costs to the public health care system, shapes the provision of nursing care through social policy and professional practice. These authors describe a system that provides home support according to system requirements, rather than older people's everyday needs, such as to stay in their lifelong home or for a couple to spend the evening together. They show how these attitudes create a pathway to the unnecessary and disabling institutionalisation of frail older people. Latimer (1997) further demonstrated how treating older people as a category or group with particular characteristics impacts directly on the treatment of their physical or mental health problems by health professionals in hospital settings.

The practices of ageism are used to perform particular identities by older people themselves and these have very practical consequences for physical functioning. Latimer (1999) later described how health professionals in an acute hospital ward worked to assign identities and categorise older people in terms of their problems as medical or otherwise to determine their access to treatment. This identity assignment in turn affected the conduct of patients:

> Through their encounters with practitioners, some patients come to realize that their conduct, rather than their views, concerns, and experiences, is significant to how clinical practitioners categorize them. Specifically, the ways in which practitioners manage their encounters with patients provoke patients' awareness of the ordering of the medical domain.
>
> *(p. 199)*

Latimer described the ways in which this realisation leads to people "lying low" or effacing their own social identity in order to assume a valued clinical identity and access to medical care.

Older people themselves assume the identities assigned to them in their social world. Wearing (1995) used a discursive approach to describe the dominant discourse of ageing in the 1990s as one which constructed the old as inferior on biological grounds. Wearing argued that such discursive construction worked to isolate and disempower older people. The subject position of one in biological decline was taken up by older people themselves to "incorporate and perpetuate powerlessness" (1995, p. 265). Latimer (1999) noted: "It is as though, by being categorized as old, older people are put in a cultural space that inhibits both their participation in social spaces and their performance of self-identity" (p. 188). Just like younger people, older people negotiate their identities in the context of the expectations of the present situational, cultural, and historical moment (Biggs, 2001). Recent social changes, including population ageing and a neo-liberal focus on individual responsibility for health, influence the social identities available to older people to negotiate their place in the world (Biggs, 2005). These changes make available a new set of identities based around imperatives to live a long and healthy life, actively manage contribution and participation, and resist decline and dependency.

Accordingly, ageism affects how individual old people are viewed by society and how they are treated in social spaces including in health care and support service settings. Even within the system designed to provide care, "negative and nihilistic attitudes" (Reed & Clarke, 1999, p. 208) towards older people shape health professionals' understandings of their needs and the appropriate ways of delivering care to meet those needs. Ageist assumptions work to exclude older people from participation as active and respected citizens and are the reason that older people may be discriminated against, excluded, and subordinated, to the detriment of their physical functioning.

The 'social model' of disability (Humpage, 2007) has provided a conceptual framework for a shift from a focus on the impaired individual who needs to be changed to function well in society to a focus on the whole environment as the producer of disabling circumstances. " 'Social Model' approaches generally argue that the disabled are excluded by unnecessary societal barriers . . . In this view, the 'problem' is not the disabled person, but the lack of appropriate goods and services" (Dewsbury, Clarke, Randall, Rouncefield, & Sommerville, 2004, p. 148). In focusing on the ways in which disability is socially produced, the social model has succeeded in shifting debates about disability from biomedically dominated agendas to discussions of politics and citizenship (Hughes & Paterson, 1997). Such discussions have the power to continue to change society's perceptions of the role of the older person and provide political and practical gains. Among these practical gains are the increasingly recognised understandings of the importance of a physical environment which supports the physical functioning, full participation, and well-being of older people.

Supportive housing

Since the 1970s, gerontologists such as Lawton and Nahemow (1973) saw the person–environment interaction as fundamental to defining quality of life, especially for older people, because any change in functioning makes people more dependent on their environmental circumstances (Peace, Holland, & Kellaher, 2011). The ecologically based theory of person–environment fit has been influential in research with older people, particularly in regard to assisted housing and institutional situations.

More recently this work has included housing in the community. In general, research has demonstrated that problems in the environment do cause difficulties in relation to physical functioning ability; older people are more vulnerable to the consequences of poor housing conditions due to reduced mobility, spending greater proportions of time at home, and having higher rates of disability and health-related conditions (e.g., Costa-Font, Mascarilla-Miró, & Elvira, 2009; Houben, 2001, 2000; Sommers & Rowell, 1992). Researchers in southern Africa have found that provision of basic household amenities such as indoor water and toilets, electricity, and appliances improve older adults' daily functioning and independence by reducing their workload and increasing their capacity to cope with daily demands (van der Pas, Ramklass, O'Leary, Anderson, Keating, & Cassim, 2015). The concept of person–environment fit suggests that, rather than considering the separate effects of individual changes or environmental aspects on health, well-being must be considered as a balance between individual competence and the demands of the environment.

Oswald et al. (2007) use the term "accessibility" to capture this aspect of individual well-being in relation to housing needs. Their study of housing needs and well-being across five European countries found that rather than simply the number of barriers in the home environment, it is the magnitude of accessibility problems (understood as a balance between a person's functional ability and the barriers in their home) that is substantially related to healthy ageing in very old age. Peace et al. (2011) extended the person–environment fit theory to encompass the lives of older people living in the community or in supported accommodation to consider both their personal housing situation and the wider community environment. An intensive ethnographic study involving 54 people across three different areas of the UK showed that changes in a person's physical functioning or their environment will result in compensation. When everyday compensation cannot achieve the balance needed between the person's needs and the wider environment, then people reach a critical point of change. At this point people generally modify their daily activities or their environment, access support from formal or informal services, or relocate if they have this option. Keating, Eales, and Phillips (2013) observed that some people, such as those in impoverished rural communities, have few such options when the environment no longer supports them.

Designing for care

An increasingly common approach to providing living spaces for older people with disabilities is specialised housing, which includes care services known as 'extra care housing' in the UK (Evans, Fear, Means, & Vallelly, 2007) or 'assisted living' in the US (Spitzer, Neuman, & Holden, 2004). These specialised housing models are designed to support good, ongoing quality of life despite any physical health problems or disabilities in older age, rather than moving older people with disabilities to institutionalised nursing homes. The principles of extra care housing include a 'home for life' philosophy (Evans et al., 2007), and this philosophy is best exemplified by the organisation of Humanitas which aims to provide 'apartments for life'; a home from first entry until death. Humanitas, a Dutch company, now organises its housing for older people on this innovative model developed by Hans Becker, with an emphasis on happiness rather than nursing care (Birkbeck, 2014). The basic principles of Humanitas buildings are self-determination; maintaining whatever one always did in one's life or wants to go on doing; all residents, staff, management, suppliers, family, and members of the neighbourhood are part of the Humanitas family; and a 'yes-culture', in which any wish is met by 'yes' as the first answer. Becker's model concentrates on supporting desired values and a quality of life which enables the resident to live happily even with a chronic condition. Whatever assistance is required by a resident, including nursing level care, is brought to them in their own apartment (Glass, 2014). The spirit of Becker's approach, which may be found in other housing models in the Netherlands or US (e.g., the 'Eden Alternative'; Bergman-Evans, 2004), has the potential to reform the provision of housing for older people in a practical and achievable way by allowing for the needs and values of the residents themselves.

Despite the popularity of Humanitas apartments among older people in the Netherlands (Glass, 2014), there is a lack of systematic evaluation of models which focus on housing designs to allow older people to maintain their own lifestyle as physical functioning changes. Orrell et al. (2013) reported on a study of building design and quality of life in 23 extra care housing schemes in the UK which showed significant associations between several aspects of building design and quality of life. In general, the findings suggested that good quality building design can support the quality of life of ageing residents, although the needs of highly dependent users are not so well supported by such arrangements. These findings are not unusual and reflect some of the tensions around moves to provide more normal living situations for those who need care to support frailty or illness. These have been critiqued for failures to provide sufficient care (see Wilson, 2007) or evaluated and shown no differences in medical outcomes between those in traditional nursing homes and those based on maintaining other valued functionings (e.g., Coleman et al., 2002). Such evaluations point to the ongoing dominance of a medical model which values physical health above other values such as pleasure, company, lifelong customs, and autonomy. Provision of such facilities in many parts of the world may be hampered by legal regulations, or the requirements of families, or investors and shareholders in traditional nursing homes. We can see the dominance of medical approaches to end-of-life care, and ageist expectations about the rights of older frail people, expressed in the attitudes of well-meaning lawmakers, nursing home managers, and family members. These attitudes reveal the importance of the wider community in supporting the capability of ageing members of society to live well despite physical changes.

Housing design

Well-designed housing is recognised as an important aspect of the quality of life of older people (Orrell et al., 2013). Surprisingly, although many older people do either choose, or are compelled by circumstances, to relocate to more supportive housing, much of the housing purpose-built for older people is constructed without consideration for the users. People moving into new retirement village units complain about cupboards placed too high to reach and dishwashers or ovens unused because they are too low for easy access (Herd, Street, & Wells, 2016). Simple objects like faucet handles are often difficult to operate. Modern units break important design safety principles by including features such as apartment access only through the kitchen area. One way to increase the understandings of the needs of users is simply to include their views in the design process. To work towards including older people's voices in housing design, Fang et al. (2016) describe the use of participatory community mapping workshops to identify facilitators and barriers for older people's use of a new community housing development. These techniques were used to enable senior housing and social care professionals and decision-makers to work with older tenants to understand their needs. More work along these lines beginning at the very inception of the design and building processes would be fruitful.

Kitchens are an important part of daily living and an important aspect of remaining independent and being able to host others in one's home. Recent work has begun to focus on the ways in which modern kitchens do not suit the needs of older people. Sims et al. (2012) suggest changes to the contemporary 'rules' for kitchen design which have become taken-for-granted ways to construct kitchens that do not suit all users. For example, windows placed over the sink may be inaccessible and are not needed when dishwashers are available. The modern fitted kitchen does not include flexible units such as some at lower levels that enable seating for chores, just as the old kitchen table used to do. Maguire et al. (2014) analysed data from the same study to reveal that the common impairments related to difficulties in the kitchen (especially among older people in their 80s and 90s) were sight (e.g., lack of appropriate lighting), hearing (confusion of sounds), mobility (access through doorways), reaching and bending (storage and implements at inappropriate heights), and dexterity (trouble using kitchen utensils). These authors, who included psychologists and ergonomists, provided a comprehensive list of design recommendations including adequate lighting, easier access, useable devices (such as lever faucets), and more flexible options.

Good design may also be applied from a broader social perspective. Oosterlaken (2009) advocates a capabilities approach to designing for society and the world's poor. She describes how capability-sensitive design would allow for diversity and encourage participation. Oosterlaken herself notes the similarity of these ideas to the concept of universal design.

Universal design

Ecological theories and the person–environment fit hypothesis in particular have been influential in drawing our attention to the importance of the environment and its effects on the quality of life of individuals from a psychological perspective.

Consultation with users is a first step towards taking account of particular group's needs; however, it may be seen that many of the practical recommendations for supportive housing reflect good design principles for all. The concept of universal design (Carr, Weir, Azar, & Azar, 2013) focuses on the environment alone and deliberately does not focus on individual needs at all. The first principle of universal design is "equitable use" (Whitney & Keith, 2006). This means providing a built environment that is the same for all users, can be used by anybody, whatever their stage of life or disability, and avoids stigmatising any particular users with special provisions.

The Declaration of the Rights and Responsibilities of Older Persons (International Federation on Ageing, 1999) was first published in 1990 and thereafter adopted by the United Nations General Assembly in 1991 as the United Nations Principles for Older People. "Incorporate Universal Design principles to assure older persons access to all environments" was one of eight recommendations to the United Nations for National Plans on Ageing. Whitney and Keith (2006) note that the incorporation of universal design principles in all buildings would support the participation of older people both materially and socially. Providing an environment that is automatically supportive means that "taking account of age is not simply taking account of disabilities and functional limitations" (p. 126). Carr et al. (2013) elaborate on the ways in which universal design is based on the understanding that there is only one population with varying characteristics, rather than groups with special needs. Thus a universally designed environment allows anybody, including older adults, to participate in social life and live in places without stigmatisation. Universal design options (e.g., lever handle faucets or wider doorways, or no-step doorways, that benefit people of all ages) support continuing engagement in everyday life for all. Although this principle would benefit everybody in the built environment, universal design remains to be embraced by planners and society in general.

Age-friendly communities

The features of housing for older people are inter-related with the broader local and national environment. Local norms and expectations around housing, local resources, planning regulations, and national laws and policies are critical influences on housing design and provisions. In their research in South Africa, van der Pas et al. (2015) observed that features of the home and neighbourhood (safety, access to amenities, participation) that were associated with quality of life were similar across both home and neighbourhood environments. In the US, Cho, Cook, and Bruin (2012) found that neighbourhood features had a stronger effect on housing satisfaction than individual housing amenities among over 1,000 participants in the US Housing Survey. Recognition of the need for local environmental support for older people's physical requirements has been growing worldwide, and Scharlach (2012) has provided a conceptual framework for developing the 'age-friendliness' of community environments. The key concepts in Scharlach's framework are derived from developmental theories and are also supported by research on the values of older people in regard to their quality of life. Each of the five key concepts of his model (continuity, compensation, connection, contribution, and challenge) is able to be supported by the physical and social infrastructure surrounding the older person and so provide a guide for town planning and public policy.

The model of 'age-friendly cities' developed by the World Health Organization (WHO) provides a policy framework for urban communities around the world to optimise these aspects of quality of life. The WHO age-friendly cities guide (World Health Organization, 2007) highlights eight domains within which cities and communities may adapt their structures and services to fit the needs of older people: outdoor spaces and buildings, transport, housing, social participation, respect and social inclusion, civic participation and employment, communication, and community support and health services. The checklist of age-friendly community action points was based on focus groups in 33 cities worldwide. Older persons, caregivers of older persons, and representatives of service organisations were asked to identify those factors that make urban environments "age-friendly." The identified focus group themes were similar between cities in developed and developing countries, although the age-friendly features were more likely to be endorsed in developed countries (Plouffe & Kalache, 2010). A major focus of this framework is on the needs of older people in urban environments because the majority of the world's population now lives in cities (World Health Organization, 2016). Universal design is applicable in this wider environment. For example, self-opening doors enable older people, young parents with pushchairs, or wheelchair users to enter public spaces easily. The WHO framework suggests that the action points should make cities 'friendly for all ages' and not just 'elder-friendly': "it should be normal in an age-friendly city for the natural and built environment to anticipate users with different capacities instead of designing for the mythical 'average' (i.e. young) person" (WHO, 2007, p. 72). Cities which meet the minimum set of standards set by the framework are encouraged to participate in the WHO Global Age-Friendly Cities Network, which is supported by the WHO to promote the concept of age-friendly cities, and share the results of projects in many cities worldwide.

To determine which aspects of the environment have been found to support the participation of older people in their community, Vaughan, LaValley, AlHeresh, and Keysor (2016) conducted a meta-analytic review. They used the WHO International Classification of Functioning, Disability, and Health environmental taxonomy to structure the environmental domains of products and technology; the natural environment; support and relationships; norms and attitudes; and services, systems, and policies. They found that within these domains, land-use diversity and planning, perceived social support, and neighbourliness were the most commonly measured environmental categories. In addition, street connectivity and walkability, living near family and friends, transport services, and policing or security services were examined. Twelve studies included both urban and rural participants, generally older than 65 years. As examples of the sorts of findings in these studies, street-level characteristics such as sidewalk conditions, resting places, and pleasant walking spaces were usually positively associated with walkability and community participation. Studies measuring transport services found positive associations for people over 80 years old or people with physical limitations. Vaughan and colleagues concluded that features of the environment are significantly associated with community participation of older adults and that these and similar reviews support the implementation of age-friendly initiatives.

The 'age-friendly' community perspective has been influential in raising awareness about the needs of older people, particularly in large city environments. However, further changes are required. Phillipson (2011) has drawn attention to the complexities of cities and the larger-scale forces affecting urban communities in Europe. Buffel, Phillipson, and Scharf (2012) additionally proposed that the question of 'how age-friendly are cities?' raises issues about the conflicting demands of commercial, social, and political interests. Although there are advantages for older people in urban environments including access to amenities, public transport, and supportive communities, Buffel et al. also describe various pressures: hazards and risks, such as negotiating traffic; exclusion from influential organisations; poverty and poor housing; and high rates of crime. Phillipson and Buffel (2016) have more recently elaborated on these issues. Even in cities which espouse overt 'age-friendly' policies, many of the broader challenges are not addressed, including reduction of social spending, gentrification of housing, and ownership models that exclude many citizens from good quality housing. They cite evidence for the resulting decline of affordable housing, the increase and greying of homeless populations, and lifetime renting for those on low and middle incomes staying in cities. They point to the role of international developers and global economic elites in distorting housing markets and the increase in slum properties. In general, the major issues raised for older people revolve around a housing crisis in many cities across the world today. Lawler (2015), while acknowledging the impact that the age-friendly community movement has had on the awareness of planners and social service providers, has argued for the need to focus on 'big' policies if there are going to be any changes in the supportive structures in cities in the coming decades. Lawler notes three big policy areas that will need to respond now to the needs of older people if communities are to be able to be age-friendly: transport, housing, and economic development policies will need to adjust.

Like Phillipson and his colleagues, Keating et al. (2013) acknowledge the contributions to awareness made by the WHO age-friendly model, but question the applicability and utility of predefined lists of attributes for an age-friendly community. In particular, they question the applicability of the attributes of urban environments to rural contexts, as population ageing also has relevance for rural areas. In many developed countries, the proportion of older people in rural areas remains higher than in urban areas. Although research based on the WHO model has shown that the concerns about the physical and social context for rural residents are similar to those in urban settings (with context-related differences such as snow ploughs instead of public transport featuring), Keating et al. maintain that the great diversity of rural settings is not accounted for in this approach. To develop our understandings of age-friendly communities, these authors draw on the theory of person–environment fit. The important interaction of the individual and their environment at the heart of this model is seen in terms of the different needs of the older person living rurally and the resources available in the type of community in which they dwell. Different communities have different levels of fiscal and social resources to bring to 'age-friendly' programmes, and these must be taken into account as part of the conceptualisation of person–environment fit. To illustrate these interactions, Keating et al. provide examples from a study of two different types of rural community, named 'bucolic' (rural retreats for retirees) or 'bypassed' (poorer rural communities whose members are losing support and services). Within these different communities, the researchers focused on the experiences of two groups of inhabitants (classified as marginalised and community-active older adults) to show the different effects for both according to place. Community-active older adults in the 'bucolic' community experienced good support for their wish to have an active, engaged retirement, whereas community-active older adults in the 'bypassed' community reported having a more difficult time creating and sustaining a fit within their community. In contrast, marginalised older adults in the 'bucolic' community did not experience support, while those in the 'bypassed' community felt a good fit between the community and their needs. The foregrounding of community needs and resources in a conceptualisation of person–environment fit highlights the diversity of communities as well as that of older people.

In addition, Keating et al. (2013) argue that the rapid changes facing people in rural communities must be taken into account. Again, they support Phillipson (2011) in his recognition of the broader social forces impacting on communities that must be recognised by social policy makers. They note the patterns of decline and change in economic circumstances and population structures in rural communities worldwide which have changed the nature of rural living. For example, in Aotearoa/New Zealand, older people in small rural and provincial communities face isolation and increasing difficulties in accessing transport and key health and social services, as these services have become increasingly centralised (Ministry of Social Development, 2014). Because of these considerable changes, Keating et al. suggest a temporal dimension to the age-friendly model: "There is a need to move from a static concept of what constitutes age-friendly to an approach that incorporates place, people, and time" (p. 328). They argue that the World Health Organization (2007) definition must be developed to be inclusive, interactive, and dynamic. Accordingly, they propose a revised definition: "An age-friendly community strives to find the best fit between the various needs and resources of older residents and those of the community. Age-friendly is dynamic, addressing changes over time in people and place" (Keating et al., 2013, p. 330). To acknowledge these understandings, higher-level policies aimed at age-friendly communities must attend to both community and individual needs. To begin to address these needs, van der Pas et al. (2015) draw on the concept of 'liveability', a term used by environmental researchers for over 50 years to describe the aspects of the environment most relevant to the lives of the people living there. Van der Pas et al. describe this concept, which takes into account diversity and local needs, as appropriate for use in developing countries.

As we focus on the importance of the environment as the source of support for older people's well-being in the face of physical changes, it becomes apparent that the social environment is as important as the built environment. The WHO age-friendly cities guide (World Health Organization, 2007) highlights social participation, respect, and social inclusion among their eight guidelines. Lui, Everingham, Warburton, Cuthill, and Bartlett (2009) note that the built and social environments are interdependent. Scharf, Phillipson, and Smith (2002) interviewed 600 older people living in inner-city communities in Liverpool, London, and Manchester and reported that older people experienced a strong sense of exclusion from many of the organisations and institutions that were influential on the quality of life in their neighbourhoods. Many respondents were excluded from involvement in both formal social relationships and civic activities. Such studies reveal how many older people today are disabled through the social and physical environment.

Conclusion

From a capabilities perspective, good physical functioning means supporting an individual's ongoing quality of life, including their family and community relationships. Person-centred care, which has become good practice in caring for people with dementia (Downs, 2015), is also being utilised in other areas of support for those with chronic illnesses, such as diabetes (Grohmann, Gucciardi, & Espin, 2015). This approach focuses on the valued functionings in the lives of older people and challenges practitioners to explore alternative and pluralistic definitions of age and ageing. Other expressions of this person-centred focus, which allows for the expression of all valued aspects of life while supporting physical functioning, may be seen in new models of social housing such as Humanitas. Such demonstrations of critical approaches in actual practice are a good start towards influencing wider policy and practice approaches (Reed & Clarke, 1999). A social ethos which recognises the human needs of older people and respects their role as functioning members of society will support the development of 'age-friendly' buildings, communities, and cities, as well as appropriate social services and health care. More general recognition of the values of all people in society will foster the adoption of principles such as those of universal design which will go further towards developing an environment which allows all to function well without discrimination.

A NEW BEGINNING (BRIAN, 76 YEARS)

We had a large property, it was a lovely house. We enjoyed it, we had a lovely garden, but as you get older you haven't got quite to sort of energy that you've had. And it always needs something doing to it. The garden, we worked every day at the garden. Well the house always needed something doing to it, plus the fact is you looked around and you saw security was a great concern. Plus the fact as you get older and you realise that unless you're in a car accident or something you're not going to die together, and so if you come into a place like this there's always somebody there to take up the reins give you a helping hand, and they're absolutely brilliant in a place like this. And now we're surrounded by people that we know, and that's it.

I've done things in here that I've never ever done before, I sing in the choir, I sing solo, I would never, I never did it before I came in here. I play bowls, I never played bowls before, I play croquet, I've never played croquet before. I used to play table tennis, I still do, or when my knee's alright. There is so much going on I mean I can play snooker if I wanted to, but I am hopeless at it so I don't. But there is something going all the time. If I was outside of a place like this, I'd have to look for something to do. Here it's around you all the time and you don't have to make a special journey or a special effort to do it.

I didn't know what to expect really when we came in, and we had no, sort of false hopes, it was going to be absolutely marvellous. But it turned out to be absolutely brilliant.

4

SECURITY

FALLING APART (MARIA, 87 YEARS)

I thought I was going to have my husband all my life. I never, never, expected his heart attack. It came suddenly. It was heart-breaking. And then everything went down, slowly, slowly, slowly, you know? I moved to be with my family, and be nearer them. Things have not worked out as I thought they would. No, I feel very, very lonely.

I've lived in this house almost six years now. It was a real shambles. With the help of my two sons, we were able to do it up a little. It's very cold, extremely cold. I really do feel the cold. It's a very old house. The wood has rotten, and it's falling apart. There's holes in the carpet. I have a habit in the night to visit the bathroom. Sometimes I worry, what if I go through, shouting and nobody to hear me? Even a visitor, she wouldn't enter the house because she was so frightened. And here I have to live. It's very dangerous but what am I to do? My son doesn't have money, I don't have money.

I do get an allowance but it's hardly anything a week. Every month we have to pay water tax, electricity tax. It's so much. Nobody helps me with the finances. When the bills come, they come in my son's name because it's his house. And then I have to pay it. He says, "Come on Mum, it's due. Pay up, pay up." I have to pay.

If my money was reduced? Oh God. I don't know what I'd do. I'm frightened to know about it also because I don't think I can, you know, how can I live then? I mean I'd have to live in one room, doing every blessed thing in one room. I'd much rather die. Come and live with me, whoever is responsible for looking after old people. Then you will know.

The experience of ageing can often be one of declining health and social networks and increased support needs. These changes can undermine the experience of security in older age, making later life a time of "stress, worry and illness" (Roberts, Schuh, Sherzai, Belliard, & Montgomery, 2015, p. 3). Because of this, the capability to feel secure is highly valued by older people. The experience of security reflects not only personal circumstances but also depends upon the social and political context. Uncertainty regarding eligibility for publicly funded pensions, health care, and social services compounds insecurity. In this chapter we will examine the social context that shapes older people's experiences of security, what experiencing security means for older people, and the ways that environmental structures and social policy can support older people to experience security.

Understanding security

All aspects of security, whether physical safety, access to economic resources and health care, or availability of social networks, may be understood in terms of ontological security (Giddens, 1991). Ontological security refers to a sense that the roles, relationships, and contexts of life are predictable. Ontological security provides people with a sense of control over the future, a sense of feeling secure in place and time, and a means of managing unpredictability. This is particularly important in later life, as older people are often faced with changes in physical functioning, social relationships, and material environments. Older people may struggle to maintain a sense of security when they feel such changes are beyond their control (Skey, 2010). The ways that older people realise a sense of security may vary, as people have different mechanisms for promoting secure relationships and safe environments (James, Ardeman-Merten, & Kihlgren, 2014). Ontological security is not an isolated individual process, it includes ones' place within a set of collective expectations (Bamberg, 2011; Kinnvall, 2017). To maintain ontological security, older people need to be able to situate themselves in relation to expectations of what later life will hold in terms of esteem, care, and support. Through this process, older people are able to understand their identity and develop expectations for practical assistance. Not knowing what the future holds is an inevitable part of the experience of life, but ability to expect a certain sort of future and respond in ways developed in the past is a means of ensuring security.

The counterpoint to security is precariousness. Precariousness is defined by Portacolone (2013) as "the intrinsic insecurity and unpredictability of the human existence" (p. 167). Although unpredictability is part of human existence, insecurity arises not from this unpredictability alone, but from the interaction between unpredictability and social provisions available to respond to it. The rise in precariousness over the last few decades is not caused by an increase in intrinsic unpredictability, but a reduction in social provisions to mitigate risk. This is illustrated by the loss of provisions that protect against precariousness, acknowledged in terms of a "political economy no longer equipped to guarantee essential resources – a secure job, retirement income, affordable health coverage – to its citizens" (Portacolone, 2013, p. 167). Although precariousness has become a key topic in social scientific research, it has tended to be examined in relation to youth and the working age population rather than older people (Alstott, 2017; Craciun & Flick, 2015; Portacolone, 2013). When precariousness is discussed alongside demographic change, population ageing is viewed as the cause of insecurity among younger people rather than as producing insecurity among older people (Breheny, 2017; Phillipson, 2012). Yet, population ageing and economic shifts have profoundly influenced the security of older people.

Demographic ageing and the pension crisis

In the context of population ageing and predictions of escalating health care and financial costs, the relative financial position of older people has become a prominent topic in the media, in research, and in social policy. The comparison between the needs of older and younger people is discussed in terms of affordability of public pensions and the sustainability of health and social services. Solutions typically focus on ways to limit the expansion of government spending on older people. As part of this debate, spending on pensions, health, and social care services are compared with spending to address social issues such as child poverty or youth unemployment earlier in the life course (Alstott, 2017). Such comparisons tend to imply that expenditure on older people is a comparatively wasteful use of scarce community resources (Breheny, 2017). Older people are viewed as causing financial insecurity among younger people rather than experiencing insecurity themselves (Hagemann & Scherger, 2016).

Part of this shift is due to changing expectations for the role of the individual in funding his or her old age. Financial provision in later life, previously a risk assumed by the state, is increasingly viewed as the responsibility of the individual to plan and save (Ekerdt, 2004; Laliberte Rudman, 2015). Although population ageing is acknowledged as a global issue, the economic uncertainty of a long life is increasingly viewed as an individual problem (Phillipson, 2012). Older people are advised to calculate how long they will live and what retirement savings they will need for a future of unknown length and with uncertain health. When individuals are responsible for managing such risk and uncertainty, it leads to fear regarding "having a long life that ends after your money has run out" (Koh, 2016). Recent shifts from collective responsibility for older people to individual responsibility for managing one's own later life contribute to insecurity (Biggs, McGann, Bowman, & Kimberley, 2017).

This shift from government and employer responsibility to individual responsibility is illustrated by recent changes in pension systems. In the US, there has been a shift from defined benefit pensions, which provide an agreed value throughout the lifetime of the recipient, to defined contribution pensions, which provide a lump sum payment and require the holder to manage the fund. Defined contribution funds shift the responsibility for a long life to the pension recipient, rather than the state (in terms of state funded pensions) or the employer (in terms of defined benefit pensions) (Quinn & Cahill, 2016). Similar reforms have occurred in the UK (Department of Work & Pensions, 2012), Australia (Gerrans, Clark-Murphy, & Speelman, 2010), and Israel (Litwin & Meir, 2013). In Aotearoa/New Zealand, there has been a similar shift to encourage contributory pension savings, which provide a lump sum on retirement. Although Aotearoa/New Zealand still retains a comparatively generous universal superannuation system, the future security of this increasingly uncertain (Breheny, 2017; St John, 2016). Pension reform shapes the resources available and profoundly influences the capability to experience security.

Security of economic resources

Security is largely absent from the economic literature on ageing; income and wealth tend to be the focus rather than the security that economic resources enable. Research has particularly focused on calculating the amount of economic resources required to maintain financial security in later life (Duay & Bryan, 2006). This discussion has tended to focus on ensuring one of two things: that older people have sufficient resources to maintain health as they age (O'Sullivan & Ashton, 2012), or that older people have the ability to maintain a level of consumption that approximates that experienced during their working life (James, Matz-Costa, & Smyer, 2016). As a result of focusing on consumption, suggestions for maintaining the security of older people tend to narrowly focus on income and wealth, in particular encouraging savings and promoting remaining in paid employment for longer (Quinn & Cahill, 2016).

Economic resources are a critical part of security in later years, and certainly, economic resources have an important effect on older people's ability to age healthily and to participate in their communities (Stephens, Alpass, & Stevenson, 2014). Lower economic living standards are related to poorer mental and physical health outcomes and to diminished opportunities for social support (Stephens, Alpass, & Towers, 2010; Stephens et al., 2011). Economic resources are reliably linked to mortality and morbidity, and such relationships persist in older age (Huisman et al., 2004; Jatrana & Blakely, 2008; Seeman et al., 2004). Ability to make economic preparations for later life depend on earlier life circumstances, and inequalities in earlier life tend to compound in older age (Alstott, 2017; Chandola, Ferrie, Sacker, & Marmot, 2007). Although there is evidence that early life disadvantage is sustained over the life course (Vineis, Kelly-Irving, Rappaport, & Stringhini, 2016), poverty in later life also matters. Montgomery, Netuveli, Hildon, and Blane (2007) examined the intersection of earlier life advantages and late life financial disadvantage. They found that early advantage is not sustained in the context of later life poverty, and conclude that inadequate pension provision in later life may have significant consequences for health and health care provision. As employment and pension insecurity has risen, and financial markets have provided unreliable returns on investment, many older people have found themselves in the position of having inadequate economic resources. This has occurred unevenly, and there are now significant inequalities among older people in terms of income, wealth, and living standards in developed countries (Alstott, 2017; Perry, 2016). Financial anxieties in later life are linked both with individual socio-economic position and rates of income inequality in the country of residence (Hershey, Henkens, & van Dalen, 2010). In countries with lower income inequality, older people worry less about their financial position in later life than those living in countries with high income inequalities. Equality of position promotes a sense of solidarity and security. Income inadequacy and rising income inequality have increased insecurity and undermined the conditions for healthy ageing (Craciun & Flick, 2016).

Seeking security in later life

Although much of the rhetoric around pensions is around maintenance of pre-retirement lifestyle, security for older people encompasses much more than pensions and economic resources. For example, Grewal et al. (2006) analysed data from interviews with older people in the UK and identified six important attributes of quality of life, which included security. Their analysis indicated that for older people "security incorporated ideas of feeling safe and secure, not having to worry and not feeling vulnerable" (Grewal et al., p. 1897). Although financial provision was part of this broader experience of security, other aspects included enjoying sufficient practical and emotional support and experiencing good health. Our research on older people's living standards also identified security as a key capability (Mansvelt, Breheny, & Stephens, 2014; Stephens et al., 2015a). This included security of economic provision, but also a sense that wider social supports such as health services, home support services, and family relationships provide a web of reliable relationships that could be anticipated to last into the future. Concerns were encompassed by having enough resources to ensure sufficient nutritious food, adequate housing, access to transport, timely health care, and opportunities for social participation (Stephens et al., 2015a). Reichstadt, Depp, Palinkas, and Jeste (2007) also noted that security and stability were vital to the experience of ageing in their study of older Americans. In this context, security was discussed in terms of living environments, financial resources, and social support. Their accounts focused on the security of knowing that they would be taken care of if their health declined or other changes in circumstances occurred (Reichstadt et al., 2007). Even when financial resources were discussed, it was in terms of the options that resources enabled for better health care or more options for living arrangements. All these studies note the importance of finances, supportive relationships, physical functioning, and availability of health and support services to enable security. Understanding security in terms of these intersecting domains points to the need for supportive provisions in a wider environment that values well-being for all irrespective of individual economic resources.

Older people understand security in terms of stability. Older people seek security in the domains in which later life change might make accumulated economic resources insufficient: health, housing, and social support. Older people experience uncertainty regarding how long they will live and what needs they may have (Litwin & Meir, 2013; Mansvelt et al., 2014). These experiences depend upon the social and political context, which includes fears regarding eligibility for publicly funded health and social services. In our research on the economic living standards of older people, their concerns were encompassed by having enough resources to address anticipated future needs: having enough to last, having enough to guard against unforeseen circumstances, and having enough to guard against tragic trade-offs between current needs and future requirements (Mansvelt et al., 2014; Stephens et al., 2015a). When one older woman was asked whether she had enough money, she expressed her uncertainty by saying: "But you don't know how long you're going to live and you don't know what your needs are going to be." This uncertainty pervaded any discussion of sufficiency. Similarly, Litwin and Meir (2013) found that the most common worry amongst older Israelis was in terms of the insufficiency of their pension funds to last for the remainder of their lives. Schultz (1997) noted that economists puzzle over the high level of savings among non-frail elders, but explained that this reflects the savings required to guard against an unknown future. Precautionary savings are one way to manage anxieties regarding the future. Research on the living standards, quality of life, and well-being of older people suggests it is not wealth or significant income that older people seek, but income adequacy and stability – enough to last and to weather physical and social uncertainty (Bowling & Gabriel, 2007; Grewal et al., 2006; Mansvelt et al., 2014; Stephens et al., 2015a).

Concerns about financial insecurity were often expressed in terms of the ways that financial worry would overwhelm the capability to enjoy the time one had remaining (see Iwamasa & Iwasaki, 2011; Reichstadt et al., 2007). Participants in Reichstadt et al.'s (2007) study suggested that the security and stability derived from financial and social resources provide a foundation for engagement and enjoyment of later life. Without this foundation, some of the older participants in Nagalingam's (2007) research avoided friendships and social relationships, as social relationships were unable to address their primary financial concerns.

Concerns regarding economic resources are important to older people, but older people understand security differently from the focus in the economic literature on pensions and wealth. For older people, concerns regarding financial resources are in terms of a sufficient annuity to address changing needs as long as they live. Finances are only one part of the web of relationships that enable older people to feel secure. Beyond a sufficient annuity, older people discussed security in terms of access to secure housing, their ability to live in secure communities, and their access to reliable health care and social services.

Secure housing

The home has been identified as a key site and source of security, with the 'home as haven' providing autonomy and social status (Foye, Clapham, & Gabrieli, 2017; Gilbertson, Stevens, Stiell, & Thorogood, 2006). Most of the older people

Colic-Peisker, Ong, and Wood (2015, p. 178) interviewed stated, "their home was at the top of a list of 'things' they needed in order to feel secure." Housing provides sanctuary, physical safety, and the location from which people navigate social relationships and social networks (Severinsen, Breheny, & Stephens, 2016; Sixsmith et al., 2014). Improvements in housing quality and facilities can increase a sense of security and autonomy (Hiscock, Kearns, MacIntyre, & Ellaway, 2001). Evans, Kantrowitz, and Eshelman (2002) found that living in a home in good repair and with amenities such as handrails and accessible cupboards improved place attachment and increased well-being. The relationship between security, housing quality, and socio-economic status is also significant. Low income and minority group older people are more likely to live in substandard housing, which presents issues of safety or poor access (Clarke & Nieuwenhuijsen, 2009). Housing quality matters for a sense of well-being, security, and attachment.

Housing tenure is also critical to security in later life and inextricably linked to wider household financial circumstances and life transitions. Owner-occupied housing is often viewed as providing additional security through stability of tenure, freedom to make alterations in response to changing needs, freedom from surveillance, and through the capability to use housing as a source of economic security to mitigate instability in other life domains (Fox O'Mahony, 2012). Home ownership enables older people to feel in control of their lives (Howden-Chapman, Signal, & Crane, 1999; Rohe & Basolo, 1997; Sixsmith & Sixsmith, 2008; Wiles, Leibing, Guberman, Reeve, & Allen, 2012). Research in Aotearoa/New Zealand has found that older home owners have better quality of life and better mental health than older renters (Szabo et al., 2017). This finding can be partly explained by the insecurity of rental tenure in the Aotearoa/New Zealand context, which tends to provide short-term tenancies and poor protection for tenants. This insecurity of rental tenure is similar in Australia. Older people renting in Australia face instability when rental houses are sold, or rent increases make the rental situation unaffordable (Colic-Peisker et al., 2015; Sharam, Ralston, & Parkinson, 2016). When this happens, renters tend to manage by moving to lower cost areas, which tend to have poorer access to services, particularly poor access to medical facilities required by older people (Sharam et al., 2016).

Although there are insecurities associated with rental tenure, it is important not to ignore the insecurities that are associated with home ownership in later life. These can include a lack of resources to adapt owned housing to changing needs and anxiety regarding repair and maintenance needs (Colic-Peisker et al., 2015; Davey, 2006; Hillcoat-Nallétamby & Ogg, 2014). Owned housing can also bring financial insecurities, as transferring housing equity into economic resources can be complex (Sharam et al., 2016), and having a mortgage in later life can create anxiety (Colic-Peisker et al., 2015; Zumbro, 2014). In support of this, Zumbro (2014) found that home ownership in Germany was associated with increased life satisfaction only if the dwelling was in good condition and ownership was not financially burdensome. Similarly, Smith, Cigdem, Ong, and Wood (2017) note that the path to outright home ownership is now too precarious to ensure the long-term security of home owners. Zumbro (2014) concludes that policies should support not home ownership in isolation, but should include support for maintenance costs and sustainable financing options. In the context of these possibilities, rented accommodation may provide security, bringing with it the possibility of more easily moving to more suitable accommodation, the ability to rely on others to maintain the property, and capacity to use economic resources to meet other needs. International evidence suggests that the effect of housing tenure on the experience of security depends upon context. In countries with strong protections for tenants, home ownership may not be required to experience housing security (Zumbro, 2014). This points to the role of policy and legal contexts in shaping the experience of security in later life.

Social housing has traditionally provided housing security for older people. Social housing acknowledges the many impediments (financial, mobility, social networks) that might require interventions in the housing market to enable older people to feel securely housed. Morris (2012) compared the capabilities of older social housing tenants to those renting in the private market. The results indicated that the fixed cost and security of tenure of social housing enabled housing security, which in turn supported strong social ties and community integration. By contrast, renting in the private market left tenants with insufficient income to engage in the wider world. In addition, older private renters seldom knew their neighbours, and this increased their sense of vulnerability and isolation. Similarly, Colic-Peisker et al. (2015) found that moving from private rental to social housing increased security of tenure and reduced housing costs. Although social housing historically provided housing security for older people, particularly those in poverty, social housing has generally become less available to older people in Europe and Australasia (Sharam et al., 2016). Scanlon, Fernández Arrigoitia, and Whitehead (2015) note that the pressure on social housing in Europe has increased. As limited housing stock is stretched, municipalities have tended to prioritise social housing to families with young children and residents with high and complex needs. This shift in housing priorities has also altered the composition of social housing areas, making them less secure for older renters (Colic-Peisker et al., 2015; Morris, 2012).

Residential housing options also present opportunities for increased security in later life. Retirement villages particularly can offer freedom from household maintenance and a sense of safety (Graham & Tuffin, 2004). However, the development of retirement villages as profit-making ventures often restricts these options to very wealthy older people. In addition, not all retirement village complexes are able to support ongoing care and security as needs change.

A capabilities approach to security shifts attention from income and wealth to the ways that environments can support physical and social needs as people age. Using housing security as an example, the capability to experience security is achieved variously through support and adaptations to enable older people to age in their own homes, through the provision of social housing suitable to meet the needs of older people, or through residential care that maintains security of identity and enables dignity when living independently would undermine security. For some, long-term rental tenure may better enable security than providing support to maintain or enable home ownership in later life. All meet the capability to be securely housed without prescribing the ways by which this capability should be achieved.

Secure communities

Beyond housing, wider environmental, community, and neighbourhood settings have an important role to play in supporting or undermining the capability to experience security among older people. Security is located at the intersection of networks of services and relationships. Security is enabled by attachment to place of residence, which supports a strong sense of belonging and trust (Dale, Söderhamn, & Söderhamn, 2012; Fang et al., 2016; Theurer & Wister, 2009; Wiles et al., 2009). This includes the security of being known and knowing others in the community and confidence in one's ability to manage the physical environment (Walker & Hennessey, 2004). Walker and Hennessey (2004) found that feelings of safety were key to the experience of security, with older people reporting reluctance to venture out in more deprived neighbourhoods. Characteristics of the physical environment also support security, with accessible outdoor space and warm climates supporting access outside the home (Todorova, Guzzardo, Adams, & Falcon, 2015). This is particularly important for older people as changes in mobility and reductions in access to transport often mean that older people are restricted to their local area (Bowling & Stafford, 2007). Older people report difficulties in forming new neighbourhood connections, which means that moving communities can be particularly damaging in later life (Colic-Peisker et al., 2015). An ability to access the community outside of the home enhances a sense of security and belonging.

Financial resources and community characteristics are not separate, but intersect to enable security in later life. Older people who reside in deprived neighbourhoods are more likely to be socially isolated, in poor health, and have poor quality of life (Bowling & Stafford, 2007; Scharf, Phillipson, & Smith, 2004). Portacolone (2015) found differences in security by both economic resources and age segregation profiles of the housing of older people. This suggests that wider contexts of housing and neighbourhood relationships are key to maintaining security. Portacolone found that living alone in age-segregated communities provided advantages both for wealthy people in gated communities and for those in more deprived senior housing developments. In wealthy gated communities, older people benefit from access to onsite services that promote a feeling of security. In age-segregated senior housing developments, deprived older people gain access to subsided rent and home care supports that may be unavailable to those ageing in the wider community. By contrast, living in intergenerational communities exacerbated the insecurity of older people living alone. Older people living alone in conventional housing situations maintained a low profile to avoid surveillance that might lead to nursing home residence (Portacolone, 2015). Similarly, Morris (2012) noted that older renters in straitened circumstances avoided letting people in their community know they lived alone, as this heightened their sense of vulnerability. Such strategies compounded their social isolation, however. These studies demonstrate how living circumstances and individual characteristics intersect with housing environments and neighbourhood environments, which mean that none of these can be considered in isolation.

Different cultures and societies understand security for older people in different ways. Among older Māori in Aotearoa/New Zealand, security is understood in terms of a comforting and comfortable dependence upon land and people (Butcher & Breheny, 2016). Among Māori, security is best achieved by ageing in places of spiritual significance in which intergenerational family relationships are fostered. In this way, security is located in a set of relationships with others, with physical surroundings, and with dependable and reliable structures. In rural China, older people tend to live with their adult children, and children provide economic and social security for their parents (Calvo & Williamson, 2008). Similarly, in Latin America, family support networks are key to security in later life (Calvo & Williamson, 2008). For older Puerto Ricans, family support and intergenerational reciprocity are bound up with experiences of ageing (Hilton, Gonzalez, Saleh, Maitoza, & Anngela-Cole, 2012). Insecurity in later life centred on being forgotten by family members and left to age alone and unsupported (Todorova et al., 2015). This cultural disconnect is particularly stark for older Puerto Ricans ageing in the US, as they fear the abandonment of older people they view as part of American culture. They contrast this abandonment with the adoration of older people in Puerto Rico (Todorova et al., 2015). Thus, ageing outside of their cultural context engenders insecurity and sadness for older Puerto Ricans in the US. Similarly, older Inuit peoples experience insecurity as their expectations of care and support are undermined by observations that such expectations are no longer held by younger community members who would provide such support (Collings, 2001). Such changes were viewed as 'the way things are now' which contributed to a lack of control and sense of insecurity. These understandings point to the ways that secure communities in later life reflect shared or dissimilar value systems.

Health and health care

Physical health and functional change influence the capability to experience security. The experience of insecurity is particularly profound for older people living with poor health in precarious situations (Portacolone, 2015; Morris, 2012). For such people, poor health both undermined their well-being and their ability to make economic provision for themselves (Craciun & Flick, 2016). Financial insecurity compounds functional health difficulties. Financial concerns exacerbate poor health status (Krause, Newsom, & Rook, 2008; Rios & Zautra, 2011) and poor functional health might also increase financial anxieties (Litwin & Meir, 2013).

Reliable health care and social support services are key to mitigating the insecurity of changes in physical functioning. As people age, they become more concerned about access to good quality health care (Hogan, Leyden, Conway, Goldberg, Walsh, & McKenna-Plumley, 2016). Access to health care is also dependent on socio-economic status, with health care facilities typically clustered in areas of relative advantage (Clarke & Nieuwenhuijsen, 2009). This, combined with poorer availability of public transport and less private transport among disadvantaged older people, can compound issues of access to health care. For example, Portacolone (2013) investigated the difficulties that older people had navigating a range of services designed to meet the needs of older people with different health conditions. Access to services was complicated by the presence of a variety of non-profit and private provider systems. Many older people in her study exhausted their limited resources fighting for the services that they needed in the communities they lived in. To address issues of access such as transport and mobility restrictions, Portacolone (2013) suggests a single point of contact for services for older people. Rather than requiring older people to travel, services could be provided to places that older people are already ageing in or already going to.

As older people's health declines, support services in the home and long-term care options also become increasingly important to maintain security. In our research, the provision of home help services and in-home nursing care were regularly mentioned as providing security. Recognition that these services are subject to changes in eligibility increased anxiety. Although the number of older people ageing in their own homes has increased due to population ageing and reduction of institutional aged care, there has been a reduction in spending on home care support (D'Souza, James, Szafara, & Fries, 2009; Draper & Sorell, 2016). Older people recognise these services are uncertain and this lack of predictability of support into the future undermines security. Changes in eligibility and availability of services mean that older people often have no recourse but to rely on family when formal services are discontinued. One participant in our research noted that since funded aged care services had been reduced, he now had to depend upon his son to provide care and support, support the son struggled to manage given his employment and family commitments:

> there was a lady who used to come and make my bed and do my washing for two hours a day. It was good assistance for me, but that good service was cut, by whatever organisation which ran that programme. It wasn't long hours or that much work to do in the house, but to me it was great help. Those people came and said that the service is cut because I'm living with my son and he should be doing those things . . . I don't think it's fair, but I can't do much as they run and control their own things. If they want to cut, they will just cut it.
> —*Manaia*

This leaves older people in a position of relying on others or facing increasing physical limitations (Breheny & Stephens, 2009; Breheny & Stephens, 2012). As Schultz (1997,

p. 130) noted 20 years ago, "The economic costs of growing old in a post-industrial society will not go away just because we reduce or abolish government programs." Service eligibility might change, but needs do not correspondingly diminish.

Social relationships

Security is nested within social relationships. As people age, they become more reliant on social support as the foundation for security. Security of family and community relationships is often conceptualised as separate from economic provision, as if it occurs in different spheres and is maintained through different mechanisms. However, the security of intergenerational and interpersonal relationships is not separate from social identities and economic resources. As the example from Manaia illustrates, the provision of funded services enables older people to rely less on family, friends, and neighbours. Reliance on family for long-term care is worrying for many older people (Breheny & Stephens, 2009; Litwin & Meir, 2013). Research with older care recipients demonstrates that they view such services in terms of mutuality, care for those who need it, and care as a return on lifetime contributions to society (Hanratty et al., 2012). Receiving home support services does not require older people to accept a positon as burdensome. Such services do not replace informal support, but supplement the caring of family, friends, and neighbours. Rather than leaving people isolated, funded care supports older people to manage their social relationships to meet their own valued capabilities.

For some older people, family were viewed as a security blanket, providing secure social relationships, welcome monitoring, and evidence of positive regard (Stephens et al., 2015a). But this is not the case for all older people. For many, family relationships may be absent, strained, or exploitative (Portacolone, 2013). Even when loving family relationships are present, lack of resources can compound the difficulties family members face, and such difficulties can strain otherwise supportive relationships. In these situations, rather than providing a security blanket, such situations compound the insecurity of older people. The reduction in funded support services for older people (D'Souza et al., 2009; Draper & Sorell, 2016) means that older people in poverty must rely on family and friends to meet any social service shortfall. Those without supportive social relationships suffer from a lack of services as the expectation increases that they will manage by themselves, rely on others, or purchase support if required. Although reliance on family and community is normative and welcome for many, particularly elders from non-Western cultures (Butcher & Breheny, 2016; Iwamasa & Iwaraki, 2011; Todorova et al., 2015), such expectations can be troubled when people age in communities that do not share these expectations for support.

Future security

People live in current circumstances and at the same time live in an imagined future of unknown length. A person's well-being depends upon both their current capabilities and their ability to sustain capabilities into the future (Morris, 2012; Wolff & de-Shalit, 2007). Even those currently coping with their situations have concerns about the future (Colic-Peisker et al., 2015; Mansvelt et al., 2014). Older people with limited economic resources must trade off the current conditions of their lives against future security in the context of unpredictability regarding how long they might live and what resources might be adequate to address changing health and social care needs in the future (Mansvelt et al., 2014). Older people with lower levels of economic resources have less room to negotiate as the conditions of their lives are already less comfortable, and consequently reducing living standards has more profound effects on their current circumstances than those with greater resources. What older people are seeking is not so much the purchasing power of economic resources, but the management of later life unpredictability (Mansvelt, Breheny, & Stephens, 2017).

Capability to experience security

The Capability Approach asserts that a person's well-being or quality of life is not located in their ownership of resources but in the opportunities that they have to lead the kind of life they value. A capabilities approach shifts security from the responsibility of the individual to make provision for an uncertain later life (as in the current emphasis on individual economic management) to a consideration of the provisions of the social and physical environment to enable older people to securely access those things that they value in later life. These are summarised by Schultz (1997, p. 130) as "nondemeaning economic security, affordable health care, supportive services to compensate for frailty, and companionship." Using a capabilities approach we can acknowledge that ageing brings challenges to security, but from this perspective, the ordinary challenges of ageing are able to be mitigated if supports are in place. To address these ordinary challenges requires a focus on the ways that supportive social and environmental provisions can enable security for all. A capabilities approach takes into account differences in health, education, resourcefulness, and social connections that may influence the process of transforming resources into security and accounts for social and cultural diversity in how people achieve security.

To understand security, we also need to pay attention to the intersecting domains that influence security. Insecurity of housing and lack of economic resources undermine the ability to develop and nurture secure social relationships and supportive social networks. To promote security, older people need people to rely on reliable health care and economic resources received as a right. To enhance the capability of older people to experience security, we need to understand how security may be practically supported in the community. A broader understanding of supports to engender security can be found in Portacolone's (2013) approach to the role of resources. Resources are understood as the stable sets of circumstances and supplies that are available to assist in meeting life changes or challenges. Resources can include

> financial support with paying rent or maintenance expenses, wider access
> to public home care aides and case managers, connection with neighbours,

easier transportation, subsidies to pay for private services, promotion of interdependent (instead of independent) living, all exemplify initiatives that would quell the precariousness of older adults.

(Portacolone, 2015, p. 301)

These suggestions recognise the concerns that older people have expressed in terms of fears regarding housing quality and maintenance, uncertainty regarding what health and social care needs they may have in the future, and desire to live in supportive communities where they are known and valued. Security can be maintained, not only through an increase in income in later life with the attendant requirement to plan and manage this independently, but also an increased eligibility for funded services and supports. These services offset the need for economic resources to maintain security in later life. But to achieve security, these supports and services need to come with certainty of provision into the future.

Conclusion

A capabilities approach shifts security from expectations that older people will make provision for themselves to focusing on the resources available in communities to support changing needs. Older people may face numerous challenges to maintaining security as they age, including changes in economic circumstances, declining health, changing family circumstances, and altered social networks. If these changes are nested in an environment that is supportive of security, they can be accommodated. Framing security in older age as a capabilities issue means examining the securities that older people have or are restricted from having, such as secure housing, access to timely and appropriate health care, and reliable access to resources needed for full participation in life. Although ageing brings changes, the inherently uncertain nature of later life should not be used to undermine the social and environmental arrangements that can mitigate insecurity. The wider environments, including social provision, equality of provision with others, and predictability in social arrangements enables security. Security is best achieved by the expectation that we all, as members of a community and society, can rely on one another.

THE COMFORT OF SUPPORT (PRIYA AND VIKESH, 69 AND 74 YEARS)

The children forced us to come over here. And we are very happy since we came here. Once we bought a house, then, of course, the place appears to grow on you. Everything is very near and it's a lovely quiet neighbourhood too. A very warm house and lovely neighbours. So you don't feel you are out of place.

We get a pension at the moment, very adequate. We bought the house and we get help for the rates and everything. The government did the insulation for us. Medically, just the normal problem, age. Our GP is very happy except for my weight. I had my two knee operations done and then the hospital came and put in whatever I needed. We just take each day as it comes. How much time do we have left? We don't know what time we will kick the bucket.

We're happy with the way things are, very happy. The biggest consolation is that we have our kids and all of them are very, very affectionate and loving and caring. That's a big sort of security blanket around here. They ring up in the morning, they ring up in the night. The girls will call up, all three of them so they're constantly in touch with me and if anyone of us is sick we don't have to ring up everyone. We have to rely on one another, that's really what it all boils down to, isn't it? Not living in a shell.

5

CONTRIBUTION

MANAGING CONTRIBUTION (ANDREA, 77 YEARS)

I play games and do a bit of research and do a lot of work for the church you know so, minutes and things on the computer. That sort of stuff. Yeah so I'm usually on the computer at least two to three hours a day. I chair the maintenance committee of the church. I'm also involved as a reader, and a lay minister. I'm also in the community choir so I sing in the choir. That's the one that we do all the gigs at Christmas. You know the entertainment, the Events Centre, all those sorts of things.

Also for the last twelve years I do a bit of singing and acting on stage. Though I think I'm going to have to let that go this year because I can't move as easily as I could and I, I get very tired so I can't take late nights anymore and that really upsets me but I'm going to have to give it up.

Older people do wish to and do contribute to society. Being positioned as a contributing citizen is an aspect of social identity that is essential for well-being, and research with older people (particularly around volunteering) shows that contribution is an important aspect of quality of life. A capabilities approach draws attention to contribution as a valued capability among older people. Exploring the context of contribution reveals the practical barriers older people face to contributing in ways that they value. Society can recognise and support the contributions of older people in practical ways such as opportunities to engage in paid work and volunteer labour. Although older people are encouraged to contribute, the social environment provides a complex set of barriers through contradictory social expectations of ageing which may disrupt the positioning of older people as contributing citizens. Active ageing policies to promote volunteering and civic engagement among older people may support social mores of contribution and reciprocity which are at the heart of the need to contribute; however, this support is contradicted by economic discourses of productivity and those which construct older people as dependent and a drain on economic resources. These contradictory discourses create difficulties for those who wish to participate in economic activity and problematic positions for those who cannot contribute economically. To counteract these effects, some authors have suggested new constructions of interdependence and social productivity to resist the economically based productivity discourses and support all older people as valued contributors to society.

Valued contributions

The contributions of older people are many, valuable, and important (Siegrist, von dem Knesebeck, & Pollack, 2004). Practices of contributing, giving, and passing on have an important role in the self-identification of older people as contributing citizens; as individuals with self-worth, significance, and meaning (Mansvelt, 2012; van Dijk, Cramm, & Nieboer, 2013). The socio-emotional benefits derived from contributing include basic psychological needs of self-esteem, socialisation, life satisfaction, and contribution to others (Morrow-Howell, Tang, Kim, Lee, & Sherraden, 2005).

One of the most socially respected ways in which a person is currently seen as contributing to society is through paid work. The attitudes to and need for older workers has changed considerably according to economic circumstances across recent decades, and across countries (e.g., Taylor and Walker, 1994). Changing compulsory retirement legislation in many countries and policies to encourage workplace participation in recent decades, and to support work and caregiving responsibilities, have meant a renewed interest in working for longer – an interest supported by government policy in Australia, Aotearoa/New Zealand, the UK, and other European countries. There is also increasing evidence to support the importance of older workers in the workplace. However, age discrimination (largely by employers) is now understood as a determinant of early workforce exit and exclusion, and is also associated with lower recruitment, training, and retention, and poorer mental health (Noone & Bohle, 2017; O'Loughlin & Kendig, 2017; Walker & Maltby, 2012). Once people have left the workforce, whether willingly or unwillingly, the legitimacy of their contribution to society is questioned from an economic perspective. To discuss these issues around contribution by older people, this chapter will focus on the issues around contribution beyond paid work.

Rather than deliberately withdrawing into dependence upon retirement, many people continue to want and need to contribute to society. One of the main expectations of an actively participating member of society is that they should support others (Martinez, Crooks, Kim, & Tanner, 2011). A qualitative study of 153 people aged from 63 to 93 years in Aotearoa/New Zealand (Stephens et al., 2015b) showed some of the ways in which older people wanted to contribute to their communities; participants described their contributions in terms of child care and family contributions, gifts of time and goods to others, formal voluntary work, informal helping, making monetary donations, and civic engagement. These descriptions demonstrated the importance of activity that is "not so much for myself" and an engaged life that is focused on the needs and concerns of others. Such contribution not only provided a sense of value and self-fulfilment, but was part of the exchange that was seen as a 'natural' part of community relationships.

Other research has shown that older people are often keen to contribute to their communities (e.g., Heenan, 2011) and value opportunities to use their time productively (Townsend et al., 2014). Social contribution provides a positive identity for those in later life as active members of their society. All this has very positive implications for older people who are able to contribute in these ways, and such contribution has been often studied in terms of volunteering.

Volunteering

Both formal and informal volunteering are a major resource for any community, large or small, because volunteers provide services that are outside the remit of social institutions or could not be otherwise afforded (Seaman, 2012). In Australia, it has been found that older people are most likely to volunteer for community and welfare organisations (Warburton & Cordingly, 2004). Although older age groups generally volunteer less than those in the mid-age groups, older people are more likely to be highly committed volunteers; they give more time to their volunteering and stay with organisations longer (Lyons & Hocking, 2000; Zappalà & Burrell, 2002).

Volunteering has also been shown to have many positive health effects for volunteers. A recent comprehensive review concluded that "volunteering among older adults is related to better psychosocial, physical, and cognitive health, as well as better functional performance" (Anderson et al., 2014, p. 19). In regards to physical health, older volunteers are more likely to have better specific outcomes such as reduced hypertension (Burr, Tavares, & Mutchler, 2011) and better self-reported health (Piliavin & Siegl, 2007; Thoits & Hewitt, 2001). Several recent reviews (e.g., Grimm, Spring, & Dietz, 2007; Harris & Thoresen, 2005; Oman, 2007) and a meta-analysis (Okun, Yeung, & Brown, 2013) have supported the relationship of volunteering to decreased mortality. Research has also shown better psychological health for volunteers compared to non-volunteers (Greenfield & Marks, 2004; Piliavin & Siegl, 2007; Thoits & Hewitt, 2001), and longitudinal studies have found that volunteering over time resulted in lower rates of depression among older adults (Morrow-Howell, Hinterlong, Rozario, & Tang, 2003).

Closer examination of the evidence shows a strong emphasis on contribution as a valued aspect of well-being itself, rather than solely a predictor of health as an outcome. Seen in this way, volunteering has been shown to foster aspects of well-being such as increased self-worth and enjoyment (Narushima, 2005; Townsend et al., 2014). Particular psychological benefits noted are maintenance of self-identity, a sense of social connectedness, and feelings of belonging (Battaglia & Metzer, 2000; Musick, Herzog, & House, 1999). In a range of studies, engaging in helping behaviours has been related to increased energy and to greater feelings of joy and happiness among older adults (Dulin, Gavala, Stephens, Kostick, & McDonald, 2012; Midlarsky & Kahana, 2007; Wheeler, Gorey, & Greenblatt, 1998). Descriptions of formal volunteering services by older people show what the volunteers themselves gained from the experience (Stephens et al., 2015b); they described meeting new and interesting people, having something to look forward to, and having a structure to their daily and weekly activities. These participants recognised that volunteering provides benefits to the volunteers, as well as those who receive the services. In general, contribution through formal volunteering provides a way to remain engaged with the community, to enjoy the company of others, and to use the skills developed during one's working life to benefit society.

Social participation

How do we conceptualise the important positive effects of giving time to others? One important aspect of volunteering is participating in social life. Social engagement among older people has been well recognised as a predictor of health status, cognitive functioning, and mortality (Thomas, 2012), and evidence supports a view that the benefits to well-being observed among volunteers might be explained by opportunities for social engagement. Volunteers are less likely to report feeling lonely or socially isolated (Warburton & Cordingly, 2004), and volunteering can help people withstand losses such as widowhood or retirement (Utz, Carr, Nesse, & Wortman, 2002). Volunteering also offers opportunities for contributions to younger generations (Narushima, 2005; Warburton & Gooch, 2007). Qualitative studies also show that volunteering may be described in terms of social engagement as an important aspect of well-being itself. The Aotearoa/New Zealand study (Stephens et al., 2015b) showed that volunteering was an important means of maintaining an identity as a contributing citizen and an engaged community member. For example, one woman detailed her weekly round of formal volunteering for organisations such as meals on wheels, a Bible study group, and the round of visiting and telephoning elderly friends and neighbours and explained the importance of her weekly commitments in this way: "I think it must be awful to have no purpose to your life. Whereas every day I've got something to get up and look forward to doing, being involved."

Although social participation is clearly an important benefit of giving time to others, Anderson et al. (2014) have reviewed many studies which point to the well-being benefits of volunteering over and above those of social engagement. Altruistic motives or helping others and providing support rather than receiving support have been shown to be directly related to better physical and mental health. Although people have various motives for volunteering (Narushima, 2005), it appears that the altruistic aspect of volunteering is particularly beneficial. A key way in which the social function and benefits of helping others has been theorised is in terms of reciprocity.

Reciprocity

Reciprocity is often understood simply as a social exchange of benefits, with each party expecting some return. For example, Zaninotto, Breeze, McMunn, and Nazroo (2013) summarised recent research with older people that supports such notions of reciprocity. Cross-sectional studies showed that those engaged in volunteering were more likely to report greater well-being if they also felt adequately rewarded for their activities. However, social theorists have developed more complex accounts of the functioning of these exchanges.

Gouldner (1960) made the seminal distinction between reciprocity as a pattern of exchange and reciprocity as a moral norm. Thompson (2013) has drawn upon this work to understand reciprocity in terms of socially constructed identities. For older people this is seen in terms of 'giving back' to society or community in general, rather than as a simple rational sense of exchange and accounting (Quandt, Arcury, Bell, McDonald, & Vitolins, 2001). From this perspective, reciprocity (mutual exchanges of help or gifts) may be understood as a general moral belief that is an important social force (Offer, 2012; Uehara, 1995). Uehara (1995) demonstrated that the normative nature of reciprocity means that, not only giving without return, but receiving more than one gives, is an uncomfortable moral position for a person. While there are differences in specific expectations between cultural groups, the force of the reciprocity norm may generally be considered in terms of the whole life course, which is particularly pertinent to older people (Antonucci, Fuhrer, & Jackson, 1991). Several studies (Akiyama, Antonucci, & Campbell, 1997; Breheny & Stephens, 2009; Heenan, 2011) have illustrated how older persons draw on concepts of both direct and long-term reciprocity between friends and family to actively construct their own independence and connectedness. Furthermore, Moody (2008) demonstrated that reciprocity is not necessarily immediate, but may be 'serial' in that, to meet the expectations of the moral norm, the return does not necessarily need to be to the same person but can be to others. Thus, exchanges of help within the community, rather than between specific people, meet the demands of the reciprocity norm.

Although there are different motives for volunteering, moral values such as social obligation and returning benefits to society, are often reported in studies of older volunteers (Narushima, 2005). Cattan, Hogg, and Hardill's (2011) review found that being able to 'give something back' is often mentioned as a motivation for volunteering. Okun's (1994) study of American seniors reported that the three most frequent reasons for volunteering were to 'help others', 'to feel useful or productive', and 'to fulfil a moral responsibility'. Their study showed that the specific motives for volunteering – to feel useful or productive and to fulfil a moral obligation – were significant predictors of the frequency of volunteering. Buys and Miller (2006) interviewed older Australians who saw 'giving back' through volunteer activities, either presently or in the future, as an essential component of engagement in their community. In Narushima's (2005) qualitative study with 15 older Canadian volunteers, all participants referred to concerns for others and society at large, although nobody used words like 'social obligation' or 'altruism'. "Instead they used expressions like 'feel responsible', 'want to work for social causes', or 'want to give something back to the community': four participants called this 'pay-back time' in retirement" (p. 575).

Many of the studies in this area (e.g., Narushima, 2005; Okun, 1994) enquire into the ways in which altruistic and personal motives are inter-related. Cattan et al. (2011) noted in their review that personal motives such as gaining a sense of control, feeling appreciated, and having a sense of purpose are also mentioned alongside notions of being able to 'give something back'. Rather than see these motives as separate and conflicting, understandings of reciprocity show how older people can draw on personal and normative motives to create a positive identity as a participating citizen. Thompson (2013) described how social entity is important to older people in making sense of their place in the world. Isolation from participation in their communities threatens the identity of older people and denies them the opportunity to be 'useful' members of those communities. Thompson notes that older people who are not able to contribute may feel a burden on others (an uncomfortable moral position given the moral norm of reciprocity) and that they lack purpose in life. These feelings compromise well-being. Thus, social contribution provides a positive identity for those in later life through a sense of fulfilling reciprocal obligations of return for both past and future benefits (see findings of Narushima, 2005). The moral imperative of reciprocity has important implications for older people and their capability to contribute.

Exclusion from contribution

Although the notion of contribution is positive, and volunteering is beneficial for both society and older people, opportunities to volunteer are not equally available to all older people. Holding up work or volunteering as an ideal for all is an example of an apparently positive ideal which may serve to oppress those who are already disadvantaged. Research findings provide us with a high degree of confidence in the association of volunteering with greater well-being, even for those whose economic circumstances are usually associated with lower well-being. Volunteers with lower income and less education perceived more benefits from their volunteer experience than older adults with higher socio-economic status (Morrow-Howell et al., 2009). Dulin et al. (2012) reported that the average increase in levels of happiness for volunteers with low living standards was significantly greater than, and almost reached, the reported happiness of volunteers with high living standards. Such findings suggest that those at the low end of the economic spectrum are even more likely to benefit by volunteering than those at the high end. However, not all people are able to volunteer, and this is particularly true for people of low socio-economic status. Research shows that disadvantaged people do not have the same opportunities to contribute as wealthier people do.

In the Aotearoa/New Zealand study described above, it was found that people in more challenging circumstances used various strategies to manage their obligations to contribute to others. In terms of financial challenges, many had explicitly negotiated limits on the extent of their gift-giving and donations to church and charity. These agreed limits on expectations allowed older people to continue to contribute without shame. Managing others' expectations was a recurrent concern with regard to a variety of contributions, including donations, gift-giving, and time given to volunteer services. Difficulty making such contributions meant re-negotiating these exchanges by explaining limitations or by withdrawing completely.

In addition to financial and health challenges, older people were constrained from contribution by ageing identities which positioned them as no longer having anything relevant to offer others. One 80-year-old woman felt that she was able to contribute to the community only because of the anonymous nature of her voluntary counselling work: "Nobody knows how old I am, I'm talking to them over the phone, it's just a matter of common sense I think a lot of that sort of thing. So that's something I do." In contrast to those who focused their volunteer energies on supporting older people or addressing social issues among the elderly, this woman's work was outside the expectations of expertise for those in later life, even though she may have much to offer.

Certain groups of people are more likely to be able to contribute to formal volunteering. Warburton, Oppenheimer, and Zappalà (2004) reported that older volunteers are more likely to be found among higher status occupational groups and among those who report good health. In general, socio-economic status, measured by education or income, is one of the most significant predictors of volunteer engagement (e.g., Tang, Morrow-Howell, & Choi, 2010; Burr, Caro, & Moorhead, 2002). The reasons for lack of participation by members of lower socio-economic groups may be found in a common set of barriers. Several authors have described the barriers to community contribution for older people which include poor health, disability, lack of transportation, and finances (Balandin, Llewellyn, Dew, Ballin, & Schneider, 2006; Fischer, Mueller, & Cooper, 1991; Martinez et al., 2011; Warburton et al., 2004). Given the benefits of volunteering, it is important to support the capability of all older people to contribute in meaningful ways that they value.

Structural and material exclusion from contribution has been shown to lead to wider social exclusion. One of the expectations of an actively participating community member is to contribute to society in some way. Gouldner (1960) showed how norms of reciprocity also provide a basis for exclusion, by pointing to the inherent imbalances in expectations of reciprocity and the respective resources of the giver and receiver. The moral norm of reciprocity means that the ability to reciprocate is seen as an important aspect of a person's identity as a participating citizen (Funk, 2012). Offer (2012), while noting the importance of reciprocity to the maintenance of social integration and social ties, has described the way in which inability to reciprocate among low-income families leads to lack of social integration and withdrawal from community involvement. Thus, the lack of ability to contribute in various ways leads to further withdrawal from community activities (Offer, 2012) and having few resources to contribute means that older people are often excluded from social exchanges (Komter, 1996). Studies of reciprocity show the social and psychological imperative to give, and also the difficulties for those who cannot reciprocate in a social world in which reciprocity is so important (Moody, 2008).

Expectations of active contribution may place older people who are unable to meet norms of reciprocal exchange in the position of either being excluded from or choosing to withdraw from engagement in social life. Such difficulties are likely to increase as centralised government provision of health and social care services based on notions of need and entitlement are being replaced with family and community care provision based on norms of individualised reciprocity (Robertson, 1997; van Dijk et al., 2013; Wiles & Jayasinha, 2013). These arrangements favour those most able to give and disadvantage those most in need of support (Offer, 2012).

Supporting the capability to contribute

The capability to contribute to community is valued and these contributions are beneficial to well-being. From a capabilities perspective, Nussbaum (2006) insists that all people should be included in regard to supporting valued capabilities, and each should be supported according to their needs. One policy priority must be to support the many ways older people wish to be involved in their communities and to provide structures necessary to support these preferences. In particular, organisational policies could include a more considered approach to the needs of older people. Institutional ageism in the workplace and in volunteering organisations means that older people are often excluded or given less meaningful work (Siegrist et al., 2004). Some volunteering organisations are beginning to recognise the wealth of potential volunteering power that will be increasingly available as the 'baby boom' generation reaches retirement. In addition to recruiting appropriately, volunteering organisations can develop policies that care for older people's particular needs (for examples of such considerations, see Hong, Morrow-Howell, Tang, & Hinterlong, 2009; Tang, Morrow-Howell, & Choi, 2010). They must recognise the different practical and social supports required to allow all older people to participate when they want to, and enable them to retire gracefully when they need to.

To allow these developments in practical, organisational, and community arrangements, a broader social shift is required. An examination of the ways in which contribution by older people is presently constructed by economic and social discourses reveals more complex problems for older people who wish to be included as contributing members of society.

Discourses of contribution

Although contribution is generally valued in society, public discussions of the contribution of older people are a relatively recent phenomenon arising from concerns about population ageing, generational conflict over resources, and the development of active ageing discourses. Siegrist et al. (2004) describe theories which suggest that withdrawal from social interaction is an inevitable part of ageing and construct older people as a drain on economic resources. These constructions of older people as dependent and costly persist today (Walker, 2009). Alongside these discourses, more recent constructions of the active, contributing 'successful ager' draw attention to the important contributions to society by older people. Both Siegrist et al. and Walker support the value of recognising and supporting the contributions of older people; however, these authors also critique the ways in which an economic discourse of productivity has dominated active ageing policies so that their effects are damaging rather than supportive.

Critics in general have pointed to various effects of these policies on understandings of contribution and participation by older people. First, current productivity discourse which constructs contribution as an economic imperative has colonised active ageing policies, and these economically driven notions of productivity create a very narrow view of contribution (Walker, 2009). Martinson and Halpern (2011) note the recent focus of active ageing discourse on volunteering and civic engagement, framing older people's contributions in terms of economic productivity. Alan Walker (2009) has been particularly vocal about the narrow focus of European policy on paid employment only, advocating for a broadening of policies to include all meaningful contribution by older people to maximise participation and well-being. Kimberley, Gruhn, and Huggins (2012) describe how Australian government policies around inclusion of older people are also grounded in a 'social integration' discourse which constructs

> paid work as the primary or the sole legitimate means of integrating people of working age into society and thus excludes those who are 'workless' such as most adults in later life. Not surprisingly then, there is no specific reference to older adults and only the broadest statements of the agenda can be interpreted to include them.
>
> *(p. 2)*

Second, discourses of productivity are divisive. The dominant economic view of contribution in terms of productivity has led to the construction of older generations as not contributing and blameworthy for the rising costs of health care and income security programmes, the poverty of children, and increases in real estate prices, thus creating a battleground between generations seen in Aotearoa/New Zealand, the UK, and the US (Hurley, Breheny, & Tuffin, 2015; Phillipson, Leach, Money, & Biggs, 2008; Robertson, 1997). Robertson (1997) has critiqued the 'marketplace' version of reciprocity in which older people are caught between expectations of dependence and the requirement for independence. To resist being positioned as economically dependent, the alternative constructions of active ageing require 'productive' contribution. The twin constructions of older people as either economically dependent or productively contributing creates tensions for older people who need to be seen as valuable contributing members of society. In this way, economic discourses work to link productivity and agency with citizenship (Lamb, 2014) in ways that work to exclude many older people. Kimberley et al. (2012) note that the exclusion of older people "is confirmed by the three Intergenerational Reports (Australian Government, 2002, 2007, 2010a) where Australia's ageing population is regarded primarily as an economic burden" (p. 2). These authors call for a focus on areas of social inclusion not related to employment which support the rights of older adults to full citizenship.

Once volunteering and other contribution is understood in terms of productivity while being related, through norms of reciprocity, to the worth of all older people in society, then we must raise concerns about those who cannot contribute in this way. The extent of opportunity for, and capability of, economic contribution varies across the life course. Older people must work harder to maintain an identity as a contributing citizen, and those with fewer resources are even less able to meet the ideal of the contributing active older person (Martinson & Halpern, 2011). When contribution is understood only in terms of paid work, caregiving, formal volunteering, or other community contribution, obligations to contribute (reinforced by norms of reciprocity) create difficulties for some older people in the face of poor health, low income, or ageist attitudes. Without consideration of the barriers to contribution, a focus on individual responsibility for active engagement in society, which does not take account of individual circumstances, can be harmful.

If social policies continue to focus on developing the sense of individual obligation to contribute, we also need to fully understand the experiences of participation and the difficulties that some older people face meeting expectations of contribution. The moral norm of reciprocity is foregrounded by current active ageing policies which include a focus on contribution and volunteering, but this becomes a psychological burden when people are unable to reciprocate. Highlighting obligations to contribute, and in particular to volunteer time to others, may further oppress those who are already unable to live up to the ideals of active ageing. Older people vary greatly in their health, financial resources, social networks, and their preferences for contribution, and should not be seen as a homogenous group who must contribute in the same way (McMunn, Nazroo, Wahrendorf, Breeze, & Zaninotto, 2009; Wiles & Jayasinha, 2013). Tensions arise for older people who are attempting to maintain an identity as an active independent community member (and not a dependent 'other') while coping with the burdens of older age which may include lower social status, possible loss of employment or diminished income, loss of personal relationships, declining health and mobility, and diminished opportunities for community engagement. Although research to date has shown that contribution is beneficial for older people, we must be alert to the ways in which such advantages are situated within wider social and structural contexts which reinforce existing inequalities. At present an individually focused ideology centres on the economic importance of community contribution, while alternative understandings of community responsibility for vulnerable older people are neglected. Such messages about contribution which are developed in social policy and promulgated through the media (Hodgetts et al., 2003; Lamb, 2014) suggest that people must contribute in certain ways whatever their circumstances and need.

Contribution is the hallmark of a participating citizen. To be seen as non-contributory is to be seen as unworthy, one who is not reciprocating. Current social policies support and exploit this social norm with the aim of encouraging independence and minimising dependency on the public purse. In doing so, they have adopted marketplace notions of reciprocity which are based on an exchange of benefits between equally functioning citizens. However, such conceptualisations of reciprocity cannot include people with impairments and disabilities. An example of this is provided by Lilburn, Breheny, and Pond (2016) in their discourse analysis of promotional materials for a befriending service for lonely older people. The volunteers were positioned as developing new skills and contributing to the lives of others. By contrast, those they visited were constructed as the passive recipients of another's kindness. Although both visitors and those they visit are older people, the position available to the service recipient is as a dependent 'other' to the actively ageing citizen volunteer. Although the receipt by older citizens of social support and care has often been explained in terms of their past contributions, current discourses expect older people to maintain active contribution and increasingly devalue those who are unable to maintain physical activity or need care.

Alternative discourses of contribution

Several critics have raised these issues to suggest alternative constructions of contribution. Siegrist et al. (2004) question the current economically driven notions of productivity to suggest a broader view of 'social productivity' based on understandings of reciprocity. Extending psychological theories of effort and reward imbalance in the workplace, these authors suggest that if people's contributions are not socially valued (rewarded) then important aspects of well-being such as self-agency and self-esteem suffer, leading to withdrawal and ill health. Social structures presently act as barriers to social productivity and need to be explored to improve the potential for contribution and health for older people. These arguments bring a psychological perspective on reciprocity to support Walker's (2009) call for broadening the policy recognition and support for older people's contributions to society.

Robertson (1997) brings a moral economy perspective to these issues. Her arguments shift the discussion along from a focus on the practical barriers that organisational and social policy can address, to a focus on the constructive basis of policy. Robertson offers a "moral language" that will return social policy to the moral basis of reciprocity in which

> our very individuality exists only as a result of our embeddedness in a network of relationships both private and public. None of us is totally independent of our context; social, political and economic; rather, we are located and live within complex webs of mutual dependence or interdependence.
>
> *(Robertson, 1997, p. 436)*

Robertson's focus is on the notion of interdependence and the ways in which such a broader understanding of community relations would enable us to recognise the real contributions of all citizens to social life. She argues that a moral economy perspective brings a language of needs and our obligations to one another into the discussion and accordingly acknowledges all contributions. Rather than focusing on the rights and entitlements of individuals, and seeing reciprocity in terms of individual exchange, members of society identify with their community as a whole and this broadens the notion of reciprocity. The needs of all the members of that community are their needs, and community members understand that all life prospects are part of a common endeavour. Thus older people, as integral members of the community, may be valued as part of the whole and their needs accepted as communal needs.

Nussbaum (2006) draws on the Capability Approach to develop theories of justice in a similar way. From a philosophical perspective, social contracts form the basis of modern societies. Theories of justice describe social contracts, but Nussbaum notes that modern theories do not include people who need care or cannot participate in society without support. She points to two problematic assumptions of these theories about the bases of social cooperation that apply to older people in modern contexts: power differentials and the nature of personhood. If members of society are assumed to be equally able to contribute economically then anybody who is impaired in any way cannot achieve the status and rights of membership of the group. Nussbaum calls for recognition of the equal citizenship of anybody who requires support. A capabilities approach "begins from the conception of the person as a social animal" (Nussbaum, 2006, p. 98) and the benefits of social co-operation are moral issues. Therefore, a just society would support the full participation in social and political life of all, whatever their mental and physical capacities. Berridge (2012) sums up these arguments nicely by saying that the Capability Approach normalises interdependence and dependence, which also shows how they accord with Robertson's (1997) arguments.

Nussbaum (2006) additionally argues against any requirements to contribute beyond what is valued by the individual. She argues that "it is the capability or opportunity to engage in such activities that is the appropriate social goal. To dragoon all citizens into functioning in these ways would be dictatorial and illiberal" (p. 171). Thus, Nussbaum argues that the Capability Approach allows us to focus on the support of the valued functionings of all citizens and to argue that the capability to contribute must be supported for all in terms of individual needs and values. It is worth noting here that not all older people wish to actively contribute. The Aotearoa/New Zealand qualitative study drawn on throughout this chapter included examples of older people who had enjoyed participation in social activities but had withdrawn because they were simply too tired to continue. Our work (Breheny & Stephens, 2017) has also highlighted a 'personal time' discourse which older people draw on to prioritise leisure time activities and personal projects. This discourse is used in the context of awareness of the nearness of death and the need to prioritise valued rather than productive activities. This awareness of limited time accords with Carstensen et al.'s (1999) arguments about the withdrawal of older people from broader social participation to focus on familiar experiences and positive emotional states. Tornstam (2005) has used empirical data to develop a theory of 'gerotranscendence' which "describes a developmental pattern beyond the old dualism of activity and disengagement" (p. 4). This life stage emphasises continuous self-discovery, decrease in superficial relationships, and increased need for solitude, material detachment, and renewed interest in nature. Although Tornstam is at pains to differentiate this theory from earlier theories of disengagement, in practice his observations support Carstensen's theory of withdrawal as an adaptive process, and also suggest a tendency for older people to cease active participation in the concerns of the wider society and focus on personal development. From a capabilities perspective, those who choose this path may be recognised as contributing citizens and their roles in society valued.

Conclusion

The Capability Approach highlights contribution to society is an essential aspect of well-being which both organisational and social policy can support. Understanding the benefits of contribution in terms of the moral force of reciprocity recognises that older people do need and want to contribute to their society and these contributions are beneficial for their sense of identity and well-being. One priority for research, practice, and policy must be to understand the many ways older people wish to be involved in their communities and to provide the practical structures necessary to support these preferences.

However, not all older people are able to contribute either physically, mentally, or financially. Without consideration of the inability to contribute, a focus on individual responsibility for active engagement in society, which does not take account of individual circumstances or past contributions, can be harmful. A further practical force of the Capability Approach is the attention drawn to the social environment in which dominant discourses of productivity encourage particular forms of contribution that are not achievable by those who are disabled or excluded in various ways. Discourses of productivity foreground the powerful social norms of reciprocity which demand contribution, while obscuring the broader social value of reciprocal exchanges, and the complex ways in which older people may be seen as contributing members of society. Policies to promote active engagement without concern for the present ability to contribute, reinforce failures to live up to social norms of reciprocity, and may further marginalise those already excluded from engagement by their circumstances.

To support the identity of all older people as making important contributions in various ways, we need more nuanced understandings of the need for and ways in which all older people contribute to their communities and society.

SAVING THE WORLD (VIC AND OPAL, 68 YEARS)

We didn't have jobs once we came here. We both had little part time jobs before, which weren't available when we came here. We work hard voluntarily here.

We, we make sure that the rest of the world knows we're here. So we're trying to save the world and that's a big ask, but you've got to start at the bottom.

Personally though, it gives you satisfaction to know you're doing something. And you are hoping that by your example you're, you try to teach others too. Well, there's a committee of about 10 of us. We had a meeting in town at the town hall and a hundred and six people turned up. So that's a third of the population. So you imagine if Auckland had a meeting to discuss global warming and climate change and a third of the population of Auckland turned up!

So we're teaching within the community, trying to teach sustainability. Different plants to what you can normally get from nurseries that would be far more advantageous to you. Different methods of cooking and preserving foods. All sorts of sustainability things, yeah. We get to meet some very interesting people. And so far it's been a very successful enterprise. We just need to keep the momentum going now. That's the problem.

6

SOCIAL CONNECTIONS

ACCOMMODATING SOCIAL LIFE. (IVY, 72 YEARS)

The place that we are currently living in is very good, we have just shifted in to this place. The place before was not good as it was small and we seemed overcrowded in that place. But this place is very good and I am very happy about it.

The important things in my life right now is to be happy at all times and also going to places, however this is limited due to limited money. Even for people to come and pick me up is rare and difficult as, wherever you go, will cost you money. Even for you to walk is just not possible as places are just too far. Of course I do go to church, the most important thing in my life is church! I am most happy going to community gatherings, funerals or family related events. But at times cannot make it due to no transport as only one car, one driver. So in this case cannot fulfil my wishes and intention.

I like uniting with my children but always restricted as no transport. So mostly I would just stay home. So end up usually never leave the house and just live by myself alone in the house. If my families come around to the house I am very happy!! My life would be content if I stayed together with my children in joy and happiness. If I don't get to see them or be with them often I feel my body is weak. I would like to live with all my children in a big house, however, there is an issue of overcrowding here in New Zealand.

If they do come around, I am always very cheerful as I like being with my children but one thing is that we cannot all be accommodated into one house and live life.

The value of social connections lies in opportunities to engage with friends and family on an everyday basis, to attend regular social activities like club meetings, church services, or social engagements, to contribute to community activities, and to attend special occasions such as family celebrations or funerals. There is a wealth of research which demonstrates the importance of social connections and social integration to the well-being of older people, however, interventions to enhance social support have had disappointing results. Health promotion efforts to encourage older people to be socially engaged have focused on interventions to provide social gatherings or befriending services for older people. Recent suggestions that understanding and supporting naturally occurring social relations in the community may be a more successful approach to enhancing health accord with a capabilities approach. From this perspective, social connections may be understood as a valued and integral aspect of quality of life. Rather than asking how we should prescribe and provide particular levels of social connections, the question becomes, how can society support people's own varied needs for valued social engagement? From this perspective, to enhance the social environment of older people and support the fundamental needs of any person for social engagement, we need sound understandings of how social networks function, and how social integration may be practically supported in the community.

Social connections and well-being

There has been a strong focus on the effects of social connections on the physical, mental and cognitive health of older people. A considerable body of evidence in this paradigm has consistently demonstrated the health benefits of social integration (Holt-Lunstad, Smith, & Layton, 2010), while the risk of premature mortality for those experiencing social isolation and loneliness has been shown to be comparable to other risk factors including lack of physical activity, obesity, substance abuse, injury and violence, and poor access to health care (Holt-Lunstad, Smith, Baker, Harris, & Stephenson, 2015). In particular, social networks and the social support that they offer have been shown to exert significant effects on the health and general functioning of older persons (e.g., Berkman, 2000; Unger, McAvay, Bruce, Berkman, & Seeman, 1999). People who report more social ties have lower mortality risks, and increased social integration and social support has been related to better physical and mental health (e.g., Antonucci, 2001; Giles, Glonek, Luszcz, & Andrews, 2005; Seeman, Lusignolo, Albert, & Berkman, 2001). Conversely, poor social connections, fewer social activities and social disengagement in people over the age of 65 have been shown to predict greater risk of cognitive decline over 4 years of ageing (e.g., Zunzunegui et al., 2005). On a broad scale, Sirven and Debrand (2008) used European survey data to show that higher rates of social participation among people older than 50 years across 11 different countries contributed to higher levels of self-reported health. In a study focused on changes in cognitive functioning in 2,249 US women aged over 78 years, Crooks, Lubben, Petitti, Little, and Chiu (2008) concluded that women engaged in larger social networks were less likely to be diagnosed with dementia 4 years later. Such observations raise many more questions about the basis of these effects. An example of more focused enquiry is a study of 89 older people living in a retirement home, who were followed until death when their brains were autopsied (Bennett, Schneider, Tang, Arnold, & Wilson, 2006). The researchers found that, across different measures of Alzheimer's disease pathology, the size of people's social networks moderated the association between the physical signs of disease and their scores on tests of cognitive functioning. Although many people had developed physical evidence of brain pathology (e.g., tangles in the brain), they retained higher levels of cognitive functioning across time if they had larger networks of friends. Those with similar levels of physical brain changes, but small social networks, showed significant deficits in cognitive functioning over time (particularly for semantic memory and working memory). This study provides some compelling evidence for the importance of social life in regard to functioning well despite physical changes associated with ageing. In general, it has become clear across decades of research that both engagement with social networks and perceived social support is related to better physical and mental health despite any physical changes. However, these studies leave open many questions regarding the nature of beneficial social networks and their relationship to well-being.

Berkman et al. (2000) have drawn upon sociological and psychological theories to develop a public health model that structures the evidence for the relationships of social networks, social engagement, and social support into a causal pathway leading to health. The proposed pathway is based on theoretical understandings of social networks that include both 'upstream' and 'downstream' influences. Upstream, we must take into account the influence of the wider society, and the person's location in that society, which necessarily affects people's networks of social connections. Downstream are the effects of the individual's social connections themselves. Berkman et al. suggest that these downstream effects include several pathways to health provided by social networks, such as social support, social influence, social engagement, close personal contact, and access to material resources. By drawing on sociological explanations, one of Berkman et al.'s contributions has been to highlight the importance of the wider social and physical location of social networks. They specifically suggest paying attention to the culture of the society by including norms and values and the prevalence of stereotypes such as ageism or sexism, socio-economic factors including inequalities and poverty, current social policy, and historical changes across all of these factors.

Social network types

Social networks in this context are understood as webs of social relations and interactions that structure our social lives. Analyses have focused on the structure and composition of the networks surrounding individuals, including their range and size. Research has also shown that differences in the type or makeup of networks (rather than simply network size) are related to both physical and mental health outcomes.

For example, Litwin and Shiovitz-Ezra (2006) explored the association between types of networks (characterised by different types of members) and mortality. They described the social networks of a sample of community dwelling older Israelis as either diverse, friend-focused, neighbour-focused, family-focused, community-clan, or restricted. Among the older members of their sample (aged over 70), those who had diverse, friend-focused and community-clan type networks showed lower risk of all-cause mortality 7 years after assessment.

Wenger (1997) used intensive qualitative research to identify five similar network types that were associated with different strengths and risks for health and health care problems among older adults. Wenger and Tucker (2002) categorised these five types of older adults' social networks based on the presence of close family, the frequency of interaction within the networks, and the degree of involvement in the community. Their typology includes a family-dependent support network focused on close family ties with few neighbourhood and friend links; a locally integrated support network including close relationships with local family, friends, and neighbours; a local self-contained support network with primary reliance on neighbours; a wider community focused network with a high salience of friends; and a private restricted support network which has no relatives, few nearby friends, and low levels of community involvement. Wenger and Tucker (2002) have shown that different networks have different strengths and weaknesses in regard to the health care provision for, and the mental health of, older people living in the community.

Wenger (1997) described older people in family dependent and private restricted networks as those at the highest risk of developing problems with health and with mental health in particular. This has proved to be a useful approach to explaining the effects of social networks on health service use; for example, Naughton et al. (2010) used this typology as one of the factors in an assessment of repeat emergency department visits by hospital patients over 65 years. While decreases in physical ability were only weakly associated with repeat visits over 6 months, the main risk factors were previous hospital admission, anxiety, and being part of one of Wenger's two vulnerable social networks. Those who were part of a vulnerable network were twice as likely as those with stronger networks to revisit the emergency department. The work of Vassilev et al. (2011) also contributes to explanations of how networks support health care. They reviewed literature which assessed the importance of social relationships in the self-care of people with chronic illnesses. The review highlighted several ways in which social embeddedness shapes people's management of their own health needs and use of health services. Vassilev et al. were critical of the work to date, suggesting that the social environment and importance of social networks deserve more sustained and focused attention in health research. Such observations, made from a critical realist perspective, support the Berkman et al. (2000) model which describes how different types of social networks may provide direct routes to health care and well-being through the provision of support, social influence, levels of social participation, and access to material goods and resources.

Berkman et al. (2000) have introduced some important structuring that has helped to untangle concepts such as the conceptual difference between describing the networks of people and understanding the social support they may or may not offer. However, recent work has shown that their proposed linear causal pathway is more complex. Ha, Kahng, and Choi (2017) showed that health has its own effects on social networks. They assessed three different network characteristics: frequency of contact, positive interactions, and negative interactions. When their analysis took into account the bidirectional relationships of these aspects with self-rated health, the social network factors did not affect health. In contrast, poorer health was related to decreased contact and decreased positive interactions with friends and increased negative interactions with adult children and friends. Schafer (2013) examined the formation of connections within social networks to show how these relationships are shaped by physical health. Analysing the social networks within a retirement complex showed that differences in physical well-being affected people's preferences and motivations for being connected with others. Healthier people were less likely to associate with neighbours who had worse health. Although, in general, people living near each other were more likely to form close ties, this was not true for people in poor health. People living near those with poor health were even less likely to include them in their social networks, whereas those with poor health were restricted to associates living nearby. Schafer suggested that health problems may make social relationships themselves more unequal and less supportive. Such findings highlight the negative effects of physical and mental health on social relationships. Researchers finding evidence of linear effects in large population studies, such as Sirven and Debrand (2008), acknowledge that the direction of social participation and health relationships remains to be explored. Meanwhile, it seems reasonable to recognise that there are likely to be reciprocal effects and the needs of those with compromised physical functioning must be taken into account.

Social relationships tend to be regarded as sources of positive support and engagement and positive contributions to well-being. However, there has long been an awareness of the potential for social networks to be harmful and for negative interactions to contribute to poor health. Work focused on the question of whether positive or negative social exchanges have greater impact on older adults' health and well-being has shown a "negativity effect" (Rook, 1997). There is evidence that negative social exchanges have stronger effects on well-being than positive relationships (Rook, 1990). Of particular concern is the outright mistreatment of older people by members of their intimate social networks, commonly known as 'elder abuse'. Although many offenses against older people are committed by those who are close to the victim, denser personal networks, those with more members who are interrelated, seem to provide structural protection against elder mistreatment (Schafer & Koltai, 2015). For those who are physically or cognitively vulnerable, closer networks provide greater protection, as members of the network are able to monitor the behaviour of all those associating with the older person.

Although there is a wealth of evidence to support the importance of social connections to well-being, including both positive and negative effects on well-being, the empirical literature is increasingly highlighting more nuanced understandings of the ways in which social networks and health are bound up together. A capabilities approach suggests that, rather than seeing social relationships as linearly associated with health as an endpoint, or as a causal factor, we consider the evidence for the importance of social relationships as an integral aspect of well-being. From a capabilities perspective, we may build on present recognition of the importance of social interaction, by considering the kinds of social relationships that older people themselves prefer and the ways in which these may be supported.

Valued social relationships

Qualitative work with older people has shown that social connections are highly valued functionings (e.g., Grewal et al. 2006; Stephens et al., 2015a) or aspects of quality of life (Netuveli & Blane, 2008). Work from various perspectives additionally provides perspectives on the important aspects of social connections including their lifelong development, cultural and structural embeddedness, and variations in need among different people.

The "convoy model" (Antonucci, Akiyama, & Takahashi, 2004) has focused attention on the importance of the life course in the development of older people's support networks; most people do not create social networks once they have aged, but rather carry lifelong connections with them.

> These relationships vary in their closeness, their quality (e.g., positive, negative), their function (e.g., aid, affect, affirmation exchanges), and their structure (e.g., size, composition, contact frequency, geographic proximity) . . . while having significant implications for health and well-being.
>
> *(Antonucci et al., 2014, p. 84)*

The major contribution of the convoy model has been to focus attention on the fact that the development of social networks is a lifelong process. A lifelong approach draws attention to the historical influences and the mores and attitudes of different cohorts. It also makes us aware of the importance of contextual influences on the structure of social networks such as age, ethnicity, gender, and socio-economic status.

Older people interviewed in an assisted living facility in the US (Perkins, Ball, Whittington, & Hollingsworth, 2012) were more likely to associate with those who were more similar to themselves, which reflects everyday social life and reinforces the recognition that older people are embedded in a lifetime of cultural expectations which include the nature of relationships. Different types of valued social networks have been described across different countries (e.g., Antonucci et al., 2014; Regidor, Kunst, Rodríguez-Artalejo, & Mackenbach, 2012) and within indigenous colonised cultures (e.g., Kumar & Oakley Browne, 2008; Ranzijn, 2010). For example, Kohli, Hank, and Kunemund (2009) showed significant differences between older people's engagement in formal, informal, and family social activities across 14 European countries. Zunzunegui et al. (2005) have explained that while independence is highly valued in northern Europe, in southern Europe the availability of assistance from family members is highly valued and a source of pride. In Aotearoa/New Zealand, Māori tend to have larger social networks than European New Zealanders, with a different structure focused on extended family relationships; being connected to family is believed to be an integral component of health itself (Kumar & Oakley Browne, 2008). Social networks may also have different meanings for men and women. Certainly patterns of social network support have been consistently shown to vary between men and women. Women generally have larger and more diverse networks than men, report having more friends, and provide and receive more support from network members other than their spouse (Shye, Mullooly, Freeborn, & Pope, 1995).

Social network structures may also be related to age itself. Carstensen's (2006) socio-emotional selectivity theory has been very influential in explaining changes in the structure and size of people's social networks as they age. The theory holds that when we are aware of limited time left in life (as in mortal illness, war, or old age), our motivations are directed away from future-oriented goals towards emotional regulation. Carstensen and colleagues have conducted experimental work to show that when people perceive that time is limited, they choose to interact mainly with emotionally close partners and reduce their contact with those who may provide challenge and interest but require more emotional work. Longitudinal studies (e.g., English & Carstensen, 2014) show that older people reduce the size of their social networks to those with whom they are close (the core convoy), which assists the control of negative emotions and supports older people's preference to focus on the experience of positive emotions. Perkins et al. (2012) conducted more detailed interviews and network analyses with older people living in an assisted living facility in the US. The residents' accounts clearly showed that family connections and other lifelong connections outside the facility were the most valued and that residents were not interested in making new or too many close connections within the setting, saying things like: "I am not close to anyone. I speak and am friendly. I think it is because I have so much family. I don't have any strong ties. I keep up with my four kids and that's a lot" (p. 503). Such reports support suggestions from the convoy model and socio-emotional selectivity theory that people generally prefer to reduce their social connections as they age and focus on more intimate lifelong connections.

Carstensen's work explains some of the changes in network size and composition as people age, but cannot account for the impacts of material constraints on people's social network choices. Kohli et al. (2009) observed that older people across 14 European countries were more likely to reduce their social connections as they aged. However, they also found that poor health and lower socio-economic status were associated with reduced social connections over time. Many people report other material and social changes in their lives that impact on their social connections as highlighted in a longitudinal study of Australian women by McLaughlin, Adams, Vagenas, and Dobson (2011). Many of the older women in this study did tend to reduce their network size over time. Reduction in network size was associated with immigration (loss of language and family connections), moving house (loss of proximity of old friends), and having sight problems (difficulties getting around). When interviewed, women also talked about their loss of close network members like partners and siblings and friends who had died; their network sizes were drastically reduced simply by attrition. Those women who reported larger networks were also enjoying better mental health, adequate financial resources, and no mobility problems, all of which enabled social interaction. Surprisingly, they were also more likely to be widowed or separated; experiencing the death or illness of a family member was associated with the mobilisation of broader support at times of loss.

These explanations indicate the physical, social, and emotional effects on social life in older age. Such effects may be seen most clearly in those who have moved away from lifelong associations (by moving to more suitable housing, or to supported accommodation) or those who have experienced immigration or forced relocation which powerfully affects choices of association. Roos, Kolobe, and Keating (2014) explored the sense of community of a group of African women aged over 70 years who had been forcibly relocated during apartheid. The women, who had lost strong intergenerational connections, described a community of peers who provided support in regard to safety, emotional needs, and instrumental care. These women's stories showed the ongoing need for support and the ways in which people must adapt to circumstances to find it. Social networks change irrevocably when older people lose important members such as spouses or siblings who are close emotional confidantes. In addition, older people's needs for support, particularly support for physical functioning, may change their relationships with important members of their social networks, or introduce needs which cannot be met by their existing connections.

Although networks may change, research shows that older people maintain important social connections as well as they are able. While networks diminish in size with increasing age, older people are more likely to socialise with neighbours, participate in religious groups, and volunteer (Jones, Gilleard, Higgs, & Day, 2016). Register and Scharer (2010) interviewed older people living in communities in the US about the value that they put on connectedness. They identified four main valued aspects of having social connections: having something to do, having relationships, having a stake in the future, and having a sense of continuity. Eighteen older people interviewed in Aotearoa/New Zealand (Ministry of Social Development, 2009) told similar stories. Being involved with other people is about the provision of social support and much more; connectedness with others in different ways provides a vital sense of participation in life.

Accordingly, social connections are powerful aspects of the well-being of older people. In general, there are certain types of preferred connections and these may differ according to nationality, culture, gender, and age. Although network size may reduce to focus on emotionally close relationships as people age, these are the very people (life partners, siblings, and close friends) who are more likely to die, often leaving reliance for close emotional support on children. People who move because of life events, whose families have moved away, or those who move to more suitable housing are more likely to find themselves isolated from these types of connection. At the same time, preferences to restrict social life and difficulties in making new social connections may limit networks further. Those who experience physical illnesses or difficulties such as loss of sight, or poverty, have a great deal more difficulty maintaining social engagement and are not included in new social circles. Living in ageing communities such as retirement complexes can exacerbate these problems. Only those with material and physical resources are able to broaden their support networks at this time. This combination of circumstances increases the likelihood of isolation and loneliness for those who are disadvantaged in modern societies.

Barriers to social connectedness

Loss of social engagement is often considered in terms of feelings of loneliness reported by older people. Loneliness is not the inevitable experience of old age that some media reports may lead us to believe, but it is an artefact of modern society and one that severely impairs the well-being of older people. People value social connections and rather than focus on urging individuals to maintain social activities, a capabilities approach asks us to consider the barriers to social connection in our social and physical environments. Savikko, Routasalo, Tilvis, Strandberg, and Pitkälä (2005) reported that 39% of 6,786 people over 75 years old in Finland suffered from loneliness. The most common causes of loneliness reported by the older people themselves were illness, death of a spouse, and lack of friends. As people aged, they were more likely to report loneliness, which was also associated with poorer health, poorer physical functioning, poor vision, and loss of hearing (cf. McLaughlin et al., 2011; Perkins et al., 2012; Schafer, 2013). Importantly, Savikko et al. also note that in addition to these sorts of physical changes, loneliness seemed to derive from social changes. People who were living in rural areas, living alone or in a residential home, widowed, with a low level of education, and poor income were most likely to be lonely. These risk factors for loneliness are supported by a review in the UK (Bernard, 2013) which added that being from a minority group (ethnic minority or gay or lesbian) and living in deprived areas or those in which crime is an issue enhanced the likelihood of loneliness. These aspects of the social environment of older people work together to isolate people with poorer physical functioning from others, and to keep people immobilised and trapped inside their homes.

Social exclusion may be exacerbated by the loss of lifetime social networks and poor physical functioning, but it is maintained by the social and physical environment. Poverty is one important aspect of the environment that is related to social isolation. Offer (2012) describes the ways in which social inequalities marked by poverty can provide a barrier to the development of social connections and to participation in social exchanges by undermining people's ability to participate in mutual exchanges and leading to social disengagement. In addition to the direct effects of poverty itself, Scharf, Phillipson, Kingston, and Smith (2001) provide a systematic analysis of the different aspects of social exclusion related to social inequalities experienced by older people living in socially deprived inner city areas of England. They focus on three interconnected areas: participation and integration, spatial segregation, and institutional disengagement. Group discussions showed that participation in social networks and integration in local communities was strongly valued. Neighbourhood quality often led to children and other family leaving, while services such as good public transport and the availability of social groups such as churches were very important. Spatial segregation was a key aspect for consideration. Fear of crime and lack of a sense of security kept people confined to limited spaces. Racial segregation also played a role for many groups. Despite good public transport, the costs of engaging in many spaces such as shops and theatres were beyond the reach of older residents. Institutional disengagement was marked by the loss of shops, libraries, cinemas, churches, pubs, and other social facilities for older people. Participants also commented on the absence of visible police presence, difficulties in accessing hospital care, poor upkeep of pavements and lighting, and a general sense of neglect. As institutions withdrew from poorer communities, people felt the stigmatisation of their area by others living in more affluent areas. Institutional disengagement was a very important aspect of exclusion and one immediately open to governmental intervention and support. Together, these very material aspects of social life work together to exclude poorer older people from engagement in their local communities.

Remediating isolation and loneliness

The increasing likelihood of experiencing difficulties with hearing, sight, or other physical functioning means that many older people require support for ongoing social engagement (La Grow, Yeung, Alpass, & Stephens, 2015). Older people may not suffer more from loneliness than younger people, but are more vulnerable to exclusion from society due to life changes, increasing physical disability, and stigma. Those with fewer social and material resources are more at risk of isolation in today's social arrangements in which increasing numbers of people report loneliness (Holt-Lunstad et al., 2015). As recognition of the risks of isolation and loneliness grows, a number of different approaches to alleviating loneliness among older people have been developed.

The most common interventions provided to protect older people from loneliness are individually focused services such as befriending through visiting or phone calling and day centre meetings. Befriending services, often relying on volunteers to visit and spend weekly time with an isolated older person, are a common organisational response. These services aim to provide a 'friend' or 'confidante', for people who are identified or who identify themselves as lonely. Day centres which provide facilities where older people can meet and engage in social activities are also commonly provided by social services and are well used by many older people as a social outing (see Bernard, 2013; Parsons & Dixon, 2004). Both of these approaches to support for isolated older people are usually well received by those who benefit from them, and are understood to support people's ongoing ability to live alone.

There has been little systematic and comprehensive review of such interventions (Bartlett, Warburton, Lui, Peach, & Carroll, 2013; Jopling, 2015; Parsons & Dixon, 2004). Evaluation that has been conducted has noted two general areas of concern. First, these are very individually focused responses often depending on volunteers and social funding which is stretched to meet all needs. For example, befriending services may have waiting lists due to lack of volunteers. Second, such services often fail to include all lonely people in the community for various reasons. Group programmes tend to attract the socially active and many isolated older people are simply not reached; people may be referred by family or health workers, which leaves those more completely isolated not catered for (Parsons & Dixon, 2004). Older people may not seek help because of the stigma attached to loneliness (Victor, Scambler, Bond, & Bowling, 2000), the stigma attached to receiving such specialised services, or because they are not catered for by the culture and activities of the service. Older minority group participants in Wallace, Nazroo, and Bécares's (2016) study on lifetime experiences of racism reported feeling out of place in community settings and services designed for older people generally. Iecovich and Biderman (2013) reviewed the use of day care centres to describe their helpfulness to those who use them, while also noting several barriers to access and use by different groups of frail older people who could benefit. Cattan, Newell, Bond, and White (2003) additionally observed that such services tend to treat older people as a homogenous group, giving little consideration to specific needs of those who are isolated and lonely, or of ways to reach them. These authors conclude that those most in need of services for isolated and lonely older people are excluded by current practices. These types of services also have the potential to mark older people out as different from other age groups with different needs rather than providing intergenerational social integration (Lilburn et al., 2016). Cattan, White, Bond, and Learmouth's (2005) systematic review of loneliness interventions concluded that there was little evidence to support the effectiveness of these practices in reducing loneliness.

Befriending and day care services are reactive solutions. They appear to provide a valuable service, particularly for those suddenly excluded because of bereavement, disability, or illness. However, they cannot cater for the growing need by seeking out lonely people one by one, nor can they prevent the development of exclusion, isolation, and loneliness. Reviews of the efficacy of current interventions to improve loneliness or social isolation by Cattan et al. (2005) and Dickens, Richards, Greaves, and Campbell (2011) came to similar conclusions, that interventions offering social activity within a group format and particularly those in which older people are active participants are more likely to be effective. Earlier, Findlay (2003), while bemoaning the lack of effective evaluation of interventions, had suggested that to be effective, programmes should utilise existing community resources and aim to build community capacity. Berkman (2009) also noted failures of interventions in the US and discussed the need to consider the social and environmental context in which interventions are conducted.

To take this social and environmental approach we need to shift from a risk-based analysis in which being lonely is understood as a risk to certain health outcomes and a problem once it has arisen, to one in which social networks and social connections are understood as an integral part of any community across the life course. A capabilities approach leads us to consider social integration as a valued functioning for all in the community. Moving to community-based approaches shifts our thinking from intervention to support for valued functionings.

Community support for social connectedness

The authors of a meta-analysis demonstrating the beneficial relationship between social relations and well-being (Holt-Lunstad et al., 2010) also pointed to the failures of individually based support projects in which strangers or "hired personnel" are asked to provide support. They point to the importance of the social connection itself shown in their analysis, and suggest that facilitating naturally occurring social relations through community-based interventions may be a more successful approach to enhancing well-being. Other recent literature also suggests the importance of community approaches which involve older people in the development of social integration programmes (Andrews, Gavin, Begley, & Brodie, 2003; Bartlett et al., 2013). A striking example of the popularity of this approach is the 'Men's Shed' movement, in which men gather together to work on practical woodworking and other projects. These projects began in Australia as an approach to health promotion among men in general. They have been very popular with participants and the concept has been taken up in other countries including the UK and Aotearoa/New Zealand. The Men's Shed provides many men with social activities suited to their interests and is valued by many older retired men for the opportunity to engage in practical activity while meeting and sharing skills with others, both old and young (Wilson & Cordier, 2013). However, some critics have anecdotally noted that men who are not interested in working with their hands are excluded which suggests that the underlying concept of shared interests and activities could be broadened (as is occurring today in many Men's Shed groups).

Jopling (2015) described an example of an attempt to provide such shared activities. Open Age, a UK charity, provides opportunities for older Londoners to participate in a very wide range of weekly activities, such as creative and performing arts opportunities, computer classes, dance and physical activity sessions, social groups, trips and lunch groups based in community centres. In addition, Open Age provides phone activities for those who are housebound, activities for carers, and special daily men's sessions. This project is led by the interests of older members and emphasises activity and learning, rather than social contact in itself, as more attractive to older people. Other community-based projects such as a LinkAge Plus Gloucester scheme (Jopling, 2015) develop networks through community agents who provide information and support to assist local people, including immigrants, to participate in existing activities and networks. Such recent programmes have not been systematically evaluated yet, although early reports show good support for their enabling functions.

An important aspect of community-based approaches described by Jopling (2015) is a focus on "structural enablers." Addressing needs at a neighbourhood level is one example of a structural focus. Neighbourhood activities are more likely to take diverse, locally oriented approaches that can include the needs of different groups of people (Collins & Wrigley, 2014). Neighbourhoods are also able to be inclusive so that services and support structures are intergenerational, rather than focusing on older people as a separate group. Intergenerational projects were also a common result in community development programmes taking an asset-based, community development approach (Klee, Mordey, Phuare, & Russell, 2014). These approaches focus on the assets in a community rather than deficits, and engage older people in developing community-based projects. Such community-level approaches also encourage active participation such as volunteering among older people which has been shown to be beneficial for well-being (Dulin et al., 2012; Stephens et al., 2015a). Rather than being seen as the beneficiaries of care, the capability of older people to participate fully in social exchanges is developed from this perspective.

A community approach also informs wider strategic approaches. Neighbourhoods may be the locus of social integration, but broader state and local government policy must provide structural support for such activities and engagement. A recent example of a concerted strategic approach is found in the UK in Manchester's Valuing Older People (VOP) programme (Bernard, 2013). The city of Manchester identified loneliness as a key challenge for the city, through feedback from older people, professionals, and research. Through the VOP programme, addressing loneliness and isolation has been explicitly integrated into local regeneration frameworks within which collective actions and solutions are addressed through local action plans. VOP networks help to co-ordinate provision, provide information, small grants and other support for local areas, so that citywide objectives are enabled to be delivered locally. Manchester is also part of a wider strategic plan developed by the WHO. Manchester has been designated the UK's first age-friendly city and is part of the WHO's global network of age-friendly cities.

Age-friendly communities

The World Health Organization's model of age-friendly communities (WHO, 2007) includes a strong focus on opportunities for social participation which allow older people to contribute their abilities and skills and enjoy the respect of their community. Social connectedness and participation in society is a consistent theme in the age-friendly community literature (Emlet & Moceri, 2012). Wiles et al. (2009) use the term "social space" to describe the integration of social relationships and physical spaces which shape physical and social well-being. This focuses our attention on the importance of environmental support for social functioning.

The current policies in many Western countries of 'ageing-in-place' encourage people to remain in their homes and communities (Schofield, Davey, Keeling, & Parsons, 2006), however, existing physical infrastructures were not designed for the fast-growing ageing population, and suburban areas are poorly designed for the needs of families as they age (Scharlach, 2012). Although interest in the relationship between the physical environment and well-being is growing, social policy for older people focuses on individual behaviours and circumstances, with much less attention given to the material and structural barriers which contribute to unnecessary disablement and poor health (Thomas & Blanchard, 2009). Accordingly, ageing-in-place policies often support older people's ability to remain in what can be unsuitable or socially isolating environments (Sixsmith & Sixsmith, 2008). For those financially able to choose, constructed communities such as retirement villages may provide more socially supportive environments, but these are not available to those without financial resources, and furthermore can segregate elders from the rest of the community (Grant, 2006) or within the retirement complex (Schafer & Koltai, 2015). Cannuscio, Block, and Kawachi (2003) suggest that investment in the ways in which people may 'age in place' within integrated communities are key to delivering the health gains associated with social connections. The age-friendly community movement and associated theories of environmental fit (Scharlach, 2012) highlights the important links between integrated communities, social participation, and the provisions of the local environment including neighbourhood quality, walkability and security, housing arrangements, and services including transport and technology.

Neighbourhoods

Personal activity spaces become smaller as people age so that they spend more time in their neighbourhood, interact more with neighbours, and depend more on local services, resources, and meeting spaces (Cho et al., 2012; Scharlach & Lehning, 2015). If people feel that important resources such as banks, grocery stores, pharmacies, public libraries, community centres, and physical activity centres are more accessible, they are also more likely to report more social participation (Richard, Gauvin, Gosselin, & Laforest, 2009). Richard et al. (2013) also found that in addition to perceived accessibility, actual measures of proximity were related to social participation; the closer the public libraries, community centres, and physical activity centres, the greater the participation. Bowling and Stafford (2007) also noted less social participation if respondents perceived local facilities to be poor, and their local area to be less 'neighbourly'. These were more likely to be people living in less affluent areas. Conversely, those living in more affluent areas had higher levels of social activity, whatever their personal socio-economic circumstances. Concerns about safety, disorder, and crime levels have also been found to contribute to older people's ability to get around (Cho et al., 2012). These findings suggest that neighbourliness itself is associated with better resources in the neighbourhood such as greater walkability, security, and more places to interact. Indeed, De Donder, De

Witte, Buffel, Dury, and Verté (2012) used data from a large-scale Belgian study of older people to link feelings of unsafety with levels of social ties with friends and acquaintances (rather than family) and satisfaction with the neighbourhood.

Social structures and inclusion

The social structures that provide support are important. Small (2009) has used in-depth ethnographic research to provide some insight into how larger social structures shape the context of individual interactions in any populations. Community organisations may support individual social networks, only to the degree that the organisation provides resources that facilitate social interaction. These understandings may be applied to the wider social environment and more research is required to focus on the inclusion of older people within society. An example of this sort of work is an examination of the social capital of a large sample of older people in Belgium conducted by De Donder et al. (2012). They found that membership in social and cultural organisations was related to lower feelings of unsafety, with opportunities for political participation having the strongest effect. They note that policies rarely recognise the importance of having a voice in social affairs and the opportunities to bring solutions to specific problems. Xie and Jaegar (2008) point to the lack of work in this area and the preponderance of quantitative surveys. They suggest that to gain understandings of political engagement among older people we need qualitative methods to explore what political participation means to individuals in particular national, social, and cultural contexts.

Housing

As well as spending more time in the neighbourhood, people spend more time in their home as they age (Iwarsson et al., 2007). Housing can be an important limitation of the capability of older people to engage in society and housing arrangements contribute to the community life of older people. Among very old people, the home itself becomes an important basis for participation (Haak, Ivanoff, Fänge, Sixsmith, & Iwarsson, 2007). As people age and active participation becomes difficult, doing things for others remains centrally important and the home is the site for continuing familiar activities or simply being with others. One of the important contributors to the loss of social networks among older people is moving house in older age (McLaughlin et al., 2011).

Housing has been addressed within environmental gerontology as an important aspect of the environmental impact on ageing (Oswald, Wahl, Martin, & Mollenkopf, 2003), and housing is internationally recognised as important to public health (Howden-Chapman et al., 1999). Research has focused on the meaning of home, housing satisfaction, contributions of housing arrangements to physical activity, or reasons for moving house, which contribute to policies around the development of housing situations and neighbourhood design. However, there has been very little concern with the social provisions of these housing arrangements.

At present housing choices for older people are often constructed in the mainstream literature as a choice between institutional long-term care at one end of a continuum and "an idealized vision of aging in place at the other" (Thomas & Blanchard, 2009). According to Thomas and Blanchard, the challenge is to escape this false dichotomy and move towards an ideal of ageing in community. The development of appropriate housing types and arrangements will be a critical aspect of a society's ability to provide community support for older people in the future. A focus on understanding healthy housing arrangements in terms of both physical protection and their ability to support social integration is a key aspect of supporting the health of an ageing population.

Connecting services

Jopling (2015) identifies the importance of "gateway services" such as transport in supporting community participation by older people. Transport has often been identified as an important aspect of social participation and exclusion of older people (Davey, 2007). Transport, in terms of the availability of good public transport, or the use of private cars is often seen by older people as a crucial support for every day social functioning such as visiting friends and attending meetings. Banister and Bowling (2004) observed that older people who rated local transport highly or had access to a car were more likely to interact socially outside the house. These authors suggest that the positive aspects of this support for neighbourhood resources and social networks are availability, trust, and engagement, while transport issues such as negative perception of traffic and feelings of insecurity are barriers to social participation.

Technology is also highlighted as a connecting service by Jopling (2015). Technology includes the use of devices such as the telephone and internet to maintain social networks (Banister & Bowling, 2004) but today, these technologies are also easily used by older people to access information and contact family at a distance. Stern and Dillman (2006) found that use of the internet is related to higher levels of community participation while supporting social networks outside the local area. We found the same effects among older people in Aotearoa/New Zealand (Stephens et al., 2014). People used the internet to maintain and strengthen existing social networks, rather than making new friends online. They connect with local groups and also use technology to maintain friendships and links with family at a distance and overseas. New technologies provide clear pathways for developing the connections of older people, especially those confined to the home, with local, community, organisational, and political groups.

Conclusion

Social connections and social engagement are valued by older people and are a critical aspect of well-being. The loss of everyday connections with others and resulting isolation and feelings of loneliness are among the most problematic aspects of well-being facing people as they age, particularly for those who lose the ability to get around easily. Attending to the social and physical environments which provide the capability for social engagement valued by older people themselves, provides a direction for supporting valued social engagement. Research in the area of environmental support for social integration is very limited, and a capabilities approach provides a framework for developing more focused investigations into important aspects of the environment. There is innovative work, particularly programmes aimed at developing community-based support, which provide a helpful basis for ongoing evaluation, development, and dissemination. Communities themselves may require support to develop their capability to include all members; a community that isolates some of its own members may not be functioning well. Research must also be aimed at the development of policies to support the broader structural basis of inclusion.

A capabilities approach will focus on developing understandings of the capabilities valued by older people and the need for changes to environmental aspects such as housing arrangements, transport facilities, neighbourhood provisions, community support, and political inclusion, which allow older people to have full access to the social connections that they value.

NOT MISSING OUT (MANAIA, OVER 80 YEARS)

I had been a leader for the Samoan elders group here for a long time. It's good to be involved in groups and different associations, to socialise, share life experience and know other members more. You can also learn something from them. The best I learn from the Samoan elders group is knowing how to humble myself, and not to hurt other members' feelings. I'm also involved in prayer meetings with other ethnic groups like Indian and South Africans, praying for our needs and problems. I go to our Samoan group centre almost every day and only when I'm not well then I'll stay home. We play cards there, dominos, eat, talk and joke and so forth. It shortens the day, and you know you are not missing anything in your life.

I'm old now, but I still have interest in women. This is why. Because without a woman in a house we lose everything. When you are sick, you need a woman to care for you. Your children cannot care for you the way your own wife cares for you. Both of you are committed to each other's body. Look, I'm an old man now, but I cannot avoid looking at beautiful women and I'm still interested in women. It's hard to remove that, its man's nature. I'm happy with my living standard, only that I want a woman companion. But at the same time thinking that the children might read that differently and they might leave me, and I don't want a lonely life without my children.

7

ENJOYMENT

**SEEING THE SUN RISE OVER THE RIVER
(JOSIAH, 63 YEARS)**

Believe it or not I'm a mad fisherman. And shooter. Around weekends we go fishing, I once spent a whole weekend fishing. I'm having a ball, I tell you! [laughs]

Oh another thing I do is the sport for kings. I go spearing flounders at night. There's a wee spot on the Otago peninsula, in the bays down there. I'd spend hours doing it. You'd come out of there with twenty or thirty flounders, it's well worth the trip. I just walk along with a light in one hand and a spear in the other. And it'll shine up an area bigger than this room, you know. And when you see a flounder, it just stands out like a big island. Ah it's marvellous fun. I love it.

My biggest fear is that I might go blind and I can't see these things. You know, you get out in the river sometimes, and the sun was coming up and the steam was coming off the river and I thought what a beautiful sight. I thought it was marvellous. There were some geese flying out of the fog too, but I never had my camera. Story of my life is not having my camera! [laughs]

I went up to a funeral a while back, and we were out the back of the local cemetery, and my younger brother said to me "come and have a look along here" and I went along the headstones and I knew the whole lot. And a lot were younger than me. It was bloody frightening. So I, as I said to the girls when I come in this morning, "It's Friday, we got through another week and we're still on top of the ground." [laughs] I've got no worries unless I can't get up in the morning and watch the sun rise. I love getting up in the morning and watching the sun come up. If a man can't do that there's something wrong.

Older people, like people at any age, value enjoyment. Although enjoyment appears to be a simple matter of taking pleasure in life, research tends to focus on utilising enjoyment for its health and social benefits rather than embracing pleasure as a valued capability in its own right. By linking enjoyment to increased health and improved life expectancy, enjoyment is viewed in terms of the dominant biomedical understandings of successful and healthy ageing. In this way, enjoyment becomes part of the prescription for a good old age and a way of increasing physical functioning. But enjoyment is more than a health promotion opportunity; it is a valued component of well-being in its own right.

A good old age

Enjoyment for its own sake is rarely examined in research, in policy or in media representations of older age. Pleasure and enjoyment in its momentary and anticipatory forms is largely missing from research and policy, which tend to focus on global assessments of life satisfaction. To this end, there is an extensive literature on what constitutes a good old age in terms of subjective well-being, life satisfaction, meaning in life, and happiness. These are overlapping ways of understanding and assessing life quality; subjective well-being is concerned with an evaluation of how well your life is going overall (Dolan, Kudrna, & Stone, 2017) which includes life satisfaction and experienced meaningfulness. Happiness is the emotional component of life satisfaction, which similarly requires people to make an overall assessment of their lives. These have been used to assess the global 'goodness' of one's life.

Much of the research on subjective well-being, life satisfaction, and quality of life focuses on the ability of these assessments to predict health, disability, and mortality. In this way, they focus on ways to protect against poor health, disease, and disability (Shirai et al., 2009; Steptoe, de Oliveira, Demakakos, & Zaninotto, 2014; Steptoe & Wardle, 2012). For example, enjoyment in life is a component of the CASP-19 measure of quality of life. This component has been found to predict survival over a 7-year period, independently of covariates (Steptoe & Wardle, 2012), and to be associated with lower rates of functional decline (Steptoe et al., 2014). Zaninotto, Wardle, and Steptoe (2016) found that sustained enjoyment in life was inversely related to mortality in the English Longitudinal Study of Ageing. Enjoyment of life also predicts incident frailty over a 4-year period (Gale, Baylis, Cooper, & Sayer, 2013).

Although these assessments are linked to objective measures of health, these assessments also reflect the social context in which people live. For older people, happiness is strongly associated with the provision of quality services that support older people to age in place (Hogan et al., 2016). In addition, family situation and health status influence the likelihood that an older person feels happy. Living with family and having good health generally means a much higher level of happiness than for those who lack one or both of these advantages (Hellevik, 2017). These assessments of life satisfaction and happiness therefore reflect broader situational characteristics of older people's lives. Health conditions or disability in later life, or relationship loss, do not preclude the experience of enjoyment. Arguably, living with poor health, chronic pain or the loss of bereavement make the pursuit of enjoyment an imperative.

The focus on global assessments of a good old age and the absence of any sustained interest in enjoyment for its own sake in later life is instructive. Higgs, Hyde, Wiggins, and Blane (2003) state that "It is a feature of much social gerontology that later life is seen through the prism of social and health policy rather than by reference to the circumstances that now constitute 'old age'" (p. 240). When enjoyable activities are promoted as important, it is usually because they go 'beyond mere pleasure' (Nyman & Szymczynska, 2016) and address psychological illness or improve health status. This kind of policy-directed thinking is also evident in research that focuses on the value of pleasant events to alleviate depression or lift mood among older people (Ferreira, Barham & Fontaine, 2015). Enjoyment becomes part of the prescription for a good old age. In this way, enjoyment is part of the medicalisation of later life; another component to be assessed and promoted to improve health outcomes. Focusing on life satisfaction or happiness or the overall quality of one's life is typically justified in light of the concerns of health and social policy.

Policy on pleasure

Although enjoyment seems to be an unadulterated good that should be valued and promoted for older people, there is a tension around the notion of pleasure in research and policy. The difficulty with pleasure in policy is twofold. First, enjoyment in life can trouble the policy account of older age when it directly compete with healthy and productive ageing imperatives. Older people in our Aotearoa/ New Zealand research provided examples of pleasures such as gambling, drinking alcohol and eating treat foods, and watching television. These pleasures were often reported tentatively, with recognition that they were not part of the prescription for healthy ageing and well-being. "I do have a glass of wine every night and I didn't use to but a friend always brings me a flagon." A common pleasure mentioned in our research was gambling in small ways. In the following example, Telila has a sense of the need to justify his gambling and does so in terms of the enjoyment it provides in an uncertain life:

> It's true we lose money when we go to the casino, pokie [gaming] machines around, but what else do we do at home? The good thing is we enjoy life, we don't know how much longer we are going to live.

When the capability to experience pleasure conflicts with other policy-driven motives such as maintaining physical health, increasing social and community contribution, or realising the economic potential of the ageing population, it troubles the policy account of later life. The policy version of later life is about increasing health and well-being and promoting positive ageing; there is no recognition of enjoyable activities that may be detrimental to physical health, financial security, or community contribution.

The second related issue is that even when not health-damaging, pleasure and enjoyment are undertaken for their own sake rather than having any particular purpose. To meet the policy imperatives of sociability and contribution, and to take up the suggestion that older people are a resource that can be used to meet the needs of an ageing population (Peng & Fei, 2013), there has been a tendency to focus on the enjoyment that volunteering can bring. Similarly, policy represents enjoyment in terms of engaging in physical activity. In interviews with older people we found this was reflected in accounts of leisure as productive time, time spent contributing to the community or engaging in health improvement activities (Breheny & Stephens, 2017). These accounts reflect social policy accounts that link leisure time activity to the maintenance of health and the achievement of a valued social identity as an actively ageing citizen. These powerful notions have driven much of both quantitative and qualitative enquiry into determining which activities best promote physical, cognitive, and psychological well-being in later life (Dupuis & Alzheimer, 2008). Although policy intersects with activity and leisure, it provides little account of pleasure or enjoyment as the justification for pursuing later life activities.

Although enjoyment is associated with notions of freedom of choice and pleasurable activity, Wearing (1995) has pointed to the social, moral, and economic constraints on any real freedom to choose. Rojek (2013) suggested that choices are constrained by what is legitimate leisure and what pleasures are morally acceptable today. Rojek's research participants thought that the word 'leisure' meant "things that they 'should' be doing for fitness or health, such as walking or swimming, even though those things were not a part of their lives" (Burden, 1999, p. 32). The meaning of leisure has been shaped by a dominant discourse of healthy ageing which also structures the gerontological literature. For example, a chapter by Dorfman (2013) on "leisure activities in retirement" includes sections on "keeping fit" as well as "giving back." Policy is one way through which government agendas influence which aspects of later life should be encouraged. Policy is designed to ameliorate social ills (Frawley, 2015) and pleasure and enjoyment for their own sake are not a problem to be solved or a solution to be promoted. Discourses of leisure to achieve healthy ageing potentially crowd out the experience of enjoyment as a valued pursuit in its own right. This focus becomes a burden when older people would prefer to focus on self-directed and personally enjoyable activities in later life.

Although community membership includes responsibilities to others, policy needs to actively balance the needs of different citizens (Baglieri, 2012). This balancing includes special recognition of the needs of those who might require additional support due to the experience of "disabilities, misery, oldness, grief and distress" (p. 12). Such balance includes recognising the tensions between government policy agendas that promote responsible conduct and allowing older people to prioritise the capability to experience enjoyment and pleasure in later life. A capabilities approach points us to towards acknowledging pleasure for its own sake as a central human capability. This approach prioritises support for the experience of pleasure by all.

Valuing enjoyment

The experience of joy and pleasure is important to all people and has been identified as a valued capability for older people (Bowling & Gabriel, 2004; 2007; Grewal et al., 2006; Stephens et al., 2015a). Recognising that many quality of life evaluation exercises might not reflect the everyday experience of those whose lives they purport to summarise, Bowling & Gabriel (2007) examined what older people understand quality of life to mean and why they valued these particular domains. The domains included social relationships and activities, leisure activities enjoyed alone, health, and home and neighbourhood. Older people explained that these were important to their quality of life because of freedom to spend their time how they wished, and the pleasure, enjoyment, and satisfaction such activities provide. Grewal's participants similarly described the importance of pleasure and joy, and a sense of satisfaction in undertaking valued activities.

The importance of joy, pleasure, and having something to look forward to was evident from interviews in our research. This involved both taking pleasure in the activities of daily life and having special treats to plan for and look forward to. Older people valued pleasures such as going to the movies or a concert, buying special clothing, having treat foods and restaurant meals, reading, listening to music, or spending time on hobbies. Physical functioning did trouble the experience of pleasure and enjoyment at times, and older people actively negotiated physical changes to continue to experience enjoyment, as Freida illustrates: "books are a great joy, except of course eyesight. But I think these expensive glasses solved that one, for the time being anyway." Other participants in our studies mourned the loss of enjoyable activities such as dancing, drama groups, or playing sports. The recognition that these pleasures may not last meant that older age was viewed as the time to prioritise enjoyment, fulfil personal goals, and focus on pleasure foregone in earlier life.

In response to questions regarding what older people need as they age or what is important in older age, several participants in our interview studies focused on passing the time pleasantly. They viewed pursuit of pleasurable activities as the best use of precious time. Rather than enduring activities for their anticipated long-term gains, older people valued engaging in those activities that brought immediate enjoyment. This finding has also been reported across a range of health and community interventions. Lee, Davidson, and Krause (2016) asked older people why they engaged in a community singing group. A strong motivating factor was the enormous pleasure people experienced in participating in singing. Creech, Hallam, McQueen, and Varvarigou (2013) also found that enjoyment was the main factor in participating in music-making. In our research older people described activities ranging from active pursuits to reflective and creative opportunities in terms of the pleasure and enjoyment they bring (Breheny & Stephens,

2017; Stephens et al., 2015a). Within these descriptions, the focus is on enjoying their time rather than using their time.

Understanding older age as the time for pleasure includes the recognition that time spent in health and activity is limited and physical change is inevitable. Recognition of physical decline and mortality positions pleasure as an immediate priority in later life. Alternative constructions of time as a resource to achieve active ageing deny the inevitably of death and construct a version of ageing in which people may never grow old (Powell & Biggs, 2004).

Pleasure and enjoyment also contribute to positive social identities for older people. In our research, people described their identity in terms of their pleasurable activities. Bruce's self-description as "I'm a lover of jazz" or Vic and Opal's explanation that "we've always been cinema-goers" link enjoyable activities to lifelong identities and associated practices. Often participants explicitly stated that they pursued the preferences that were part of their youth. Guiren described his CD collection and how he was able to buy his preferred style of music cheaply because it was no longer popular. "I love orchestra, Billy Vaughn orchestra, beautiful. That was when I was twenty, nineteen, I used to listen to it. I have a collection, more than a hundred." Thus, many older people relate the pleasures of later life to their past selves, but not in the sense that pleasure is in the past. They link their current enjoyments to lifelong experiences and take pleasure in still being able to enjoy things that have shaped their identity. Similarly Stavridis, Kaprinis, and Tsirogiannis (2015) found that older people took pleasure in dancing because it was a lifelong activity. Creech et al. (2013) found that for older people music-making later in life was embraced in terms of redefining or rediscovering their identity. This has been theorised in terms of continuity theory which proposes that the past is an essential resource, informing and influencing ones adaptation to new situations (Chapman, 2005). In this way, later life is about still being able to enjoy activities that are key to identity, rather than merely remembering past pleasures.

Capability to experience enjoyment

The capability to experience pleasure is about pursuing enjoyment for its own sake; whether that is best conceptualised as enjoying the company of others, or revelling in solitude, whether it is engaging in active sports or passive entertainments, the key to enjoyment is that it is undertaken entirely for the joy it brings. Nussbaum's (2007) list of central human capabilities includes 'Senses, Imagination, and Thought', including being able to have pleasurable experiences, and 'Play', which includes the capability to be able to laugh, to play, and to enjoy recreational activities. Nussbaum views these as central requirements for human flourishing. The centrality of joy is advocated by Creech et al. (2013) in their review of the possibilities of music-making for health and well-being:

> Above all else, music-making is a joyful and creative activity that all humans, regardless of age, have an entitlement to. It is incumbent on music educators,

researchers, and all those with an interest in caring for older people to advocate for high-quality, accessible musical opportunities throughout the life-course.

(p. 98)

This conclusion applies equally to the capability to experience enjoyment in any domain.

Constraints on enjoyment

Enjoyment and pleasure are often represented as equally available to all. But our research suggests that the capability to experience pleasure in later life does depend on the circumstances of one's life. Two aspects that influence access to enjoyment are economic resources and accessibility of activities. Older people at all levels of economic resources describe the pleasure of regular and irregular treats and luxury items, but those living in constrained circumstances described items such as beer, lottery tickets, or treat foods as their single pleasure. Entitlement to small luxuries is described as a way of coping with the harsh realities of financial struggle. Older people living in constrained situations experience regret about the loss of ability to enjoy later life. Outings such as going to a show or ballet, or the movies, gave older people something to anticipate and enjoy. Inability to access these pleasures were mourned and older people narrated the loss of such pleasures or the need to rely on family or friends to access special outings:

> that's something that we don't do that we would like to and that is go to shows or talks or seminars, that sort of thing. We really can't afford to do that anymore. And it's very rare, you see we went, we went to see Malvina Major the other night but that was a birthday present from our daughter. But we would never have been able to go, much as we might have liked to.
>
> *– Vic and Opal*

Older people with significant resources described annual travel to avoid the Aotearoa/ New Zealand winter or regular overseas trips to visit family and friends. Wealthy older people were inclined to suggest that enjoyable experiences were equally available to all older people, as enjoyment did not require money (Mansvelt & Breheny, in press). But older people without significant resources report limitations in many enjoyable activities and anxiety over finances undermines the capability to experience enjoyment in later life (Iwamasa & Iwasaki, 2011; Reichstadt et al., 2007).

Beyond economic resources, characteristics of the home and neighbourhood can structure opportunities for all older people to experience pleasure and enjoyment in later life. Depp, Schkade, Thompson, and Jeste (2010) found that older people are more likely to watch television as they age, even though they report enjoying it less than younger people. These authors argue that this may be because television provides an accessible activity for older people who experience physical changes and mobility limitations or when they cannot afford other activities. Van Cauwenberg et al. (2014) further proposed that the characteristics of the wider neighbourhood such as pavement quality or crime rate would increase television viewing rates. They suggest that neighbourhoods should provide opportunities for older people to participate in their community and provide places for activities that are safe to visit. Similarly, a review pointed to the increase in sedentary activities as people age and the dearth of research investigating the social and ecological correlates of such changes (Rhodes et al., 2012). Support for engagement in a range of activities would support the capability of older people to experience enjoyment. Providing such options would mean that older people could choose sedentary or home-based activities, rather than being restricted by the circumstances of their lives to these activities.

Enhancing access to nature

Across several chapters we have discussed the importance of mobility beyond the home to the lives of older people, in terms of physical functioning, social integration, and to support feelings of security and belonging. But access to the world outside the home is valued, not just for accessing services, socialising, and promoting physical activity (Ashton, 2015), but also for the enjoyment nature brings. Orr et al. (2016) reviewed qualitative studies of older people's experiences of the natural world to conclude that older people derive considerable pleasure and enjoyment from viewing nature as well as being engaged in the natural world. For those who struggled to be physically active, such viewing partially compensated for their reduced opportunities to be outside. Older people also valued the sensory element of being in the fresh air, of feeling the weather, and experiencing sunshine and wind. In terms of doing activities outside, people valued gardening for both its physical and productive nature – moving around outside and the physical benefits of eating produce. But they also noted the other aspects of being immersed in nature, the smell of the soil after rain, the feeling of sitting in the dirt, and experience of being wetted by the rain. Similarly, older people involved in a garden visiting programme focused on the sensory and contemplative aspects of this activity (Leaver & Wiseman, 2016). These sensory experiences are quite apart from physical activity or the health benefits of gardening which have been established (Wang & MacMillan, 2013), rather, they include the sheer enjoyment of being in nature in all its sensory elements.

Access to nature can be improved through simple changes such as improving the accessibility of pavements and providing seating in parks and walkways. Ottoni, Sims-Gould, Winters, Heijnen, and McKay (2016) found that benches enhanced mobility for older people by increasing their access to and enjoyment of green spaces in their communities. In a meta-analytic review of environmental features that promote community participation, Vaughan et al. (2016) found that walkability significantly increased participation. Walkability included places to sit and rest and nice places to walk. Shared community gardens provide another way to increase access to nature that has been found to be particularly relevant for older people (Gasperi, Giorgio Bazzocchi, Bertocchi, Ramazzotti, & Gianquinto, 2015). Accessible spaces provide opportunities for cultural expression and inter-generational engagement (Langegger, 2013) as well as opportunities for respite and reflection. Research on the characteristics of the natural environment tends to focus on increasing physical activity among older people, but engaging with nature is valued for its own sake.

Enjoying eating

There is strong recognition of the importance of enjoying food as a way to main-tain adequate nutrition in later life (Bailly, Maître, & Wymelbeke, 2015; Win-ter & Nowson, 2016; Wylie & Nebauer, 2011). This includes both the sensory pleasure of eating and the promotion of an enjoyable meal environment. Studies have demonstrated that enjoyment and involvement in food is a better predictor of nutritional status in later life than demographic factors (Somers, Worsley, & McNaughton, 2014), and a review of nutritional research on older people (Doets & Kremer, 2016) concluded that interventions to improve nutritional sufficiency need to focus on the pleasure of eating, and the social and situated experiences of eating. Food is pleasurable not only in the eating, but also in the preparation. Par-ticipants in Kullberg, Björklund, Sidenvall, and Åberg's (2011) study described the joy they experienced in cooking as well as the ways that purchase and preparation of food are moments of sociality. Further, taking pleasure in eating has been linked to an enduring identity as a 'food lover' among older people (Plastow, Atwal, & Gilhooly, 2015).

This focus on pleasure has come about largely because of the difficulties in pro-moting nutritional sufficiency in older people; in this way the value of enjoyment in later life is in terms of promoting interventions with health outcomes in mind. Again, the health implications of nutrition are prioritised over the sensual, social, and situated nature of eating. Focusing on the capability to experience pleasure can bring with it other benefits in terms of health, sociability, and engagement with communities. But pleasure should not be focused on because it improves aspects of physical functioning in later life, but because it is a valued capability, and accordingly an aspect of well-being in its own right.

Foregrounding enjoyment

The achievement of other valued goals is a common justification for promoting enjoyment. This is demonstrated in Nyman and Szymczynska's (2016) review that described the importance of meaningful activities for improving the well-being of older people with dementia as "beyond mere pleasure" (p. 99). Although these approaches aim to broaden our understandings of the underpinnings of health, they can work to demean enjoyment and pleasure for its own sake. In contrast, Stavridis et al. (2015) concluded that "dancing is a suitable activity for everyone, and gives the pleasure and satisfaction to the participants without aiming to specific benefits" (p. 535). Skingley, Martin, and Clift (2016) evaluated a community-based singing group for older people to find that enjoyment was by far the most common aspect of the programme mentioned and love for music and singing was the most common reason given for participation. Although the researchers linked the singing programme to wider health and social outcomes, for the participants, the benefit was in terms of sheer enjoyment. A participant in Skingley and Bungay's (2010) study elaborated by saying "Well, if you enjoy anything it's good for your health, isn't it?" (p. 137). The suggestion that enjoyment for its own sake is part of health accords with a focus on the capability to experience enjoyment rather than the health-promoting effects of community interventions. Pleasure and enjoyment are important values irrespective of any relationships they might have to physical functioning, to global assessments of life satisfaction, or to social connection or contribution.

The justification for many social and community interventions is provided in terms of their immediate or downstream health and economic benefits. For example, seniors' clubs are advocated as health promotion opportunities (Fildes, Cass, Wallner, & Owen, 2010; Wilson, Cordier, Doma, Misan, & Vaz, 2015), museums as potential public health interventions (Camic & Chatterjee, 2013), and green spaces as ways to increase physical activity and physical functioning (Ashton, 2015). Adding health education is proposed as a way to increase the health impact of such community interventions. These suggestions often miss the benefit of such groups, in terms of the pleasure such activities bring. Amongst the public policy focus on physical and mental health conditions alone, we need to be alert to the ways in which the explicit focus of such services may undermine their real benefits. For example, an improvement in physical or psychological health may well result from enjoyment of art galleries or museums (Camic & Chatterjee, 2013), but that does not mean we should view museums as health promotion opportunities. Instead of focusing on future health effects, it is possible to consider immediate benefits in terms of the capability to experience pleasure which is an important aspect of well-being, rather than merely a precursor to physical and mental health. Older people recognise the imperative to experience pleasure while there is still time and support for this capability is an essential element of healthy and joyful ageing.

Conclusion

At present, expectations that older people will use their time productively, or that enjoyment is a way to achieve other valued goals such as health promotion or improvements in psychological functioning crowd out the experience of enjoyment in its own right. This reproduces the oppressive ideologies of active ageing and health promotion, as identified in social policy critique. Encouraging productive time and structuring community activities to increase health sounds advantageous for all: the older people who gain in terms of community integration and health benefits, and their wider communities who benefit both from the services older people provide and the societal benefit of increased health among older people. However, this chapter points to some of the ways encouraging older people to use their time productively constrains older people in terms of the types of activities they may legitimately pursue without disparagement and ignores the supports required to enable enjoyment for its own sake. Such accounts reproduce normative expectations that the lives of older people are largely of interest when they are linked to health status, opportunities to promote social contribution, or interventions to limit depression or disability. The Capability Approach provides a different lens for examining enjoyment. The capability to enjoy activities and experience pleasure is a valued capability in its own right, a capability that can be increased with interventions that acknowledge the requirement for economic resources, the need for supportive physical and social environments and inclusive communities. Such communities would recognise the limited time that older people have remaining which makes enjoyment a priority. Acknowledging pleasure as a legitimate pursuit supports participation and pleasure while there is still time.

FINALLY DOING WHAT I LOVE AS THE SUN SETS (HONE, 71 YEARS)

Yes, I've organised my life around the writing that I do. I write novels. I'll eventually get them published and create a legacy for my family, for my children. It's an occupation that I find that I love that in actual fact I should have been doing about 20 or 30 years earlier but my life the way it was it couldn't, couldn't have worked it in.

The hardest to go without now would be losing that computer, or losing the ability to write on the computer because that's what I've always done. And that would affect me the most. There's a chap down Sundale that writes books, as well. He's a writer, but he's got medical problems so he doesn't go around much. He's younger, about 12, 15 years younger than me but he's I think medically he's worse off. But I go and see him and he does pretty well himself.

If I live long enough to sell my books, I will own my own property. For most of my working life I owned my own place. Thirty years of my life I owned my own place. What I would like is a house on this top road here with a good overview and I would, I would have a bedroom downstairs, a good size lounge, but upstairs I would have my bedroom, en suite and my work space. And I would be able to, and I'd have it set up so that I'd look out over the ocean and watch the sunrise and sunset.

8

AUTONOMY

FIERCELY INDEPENDENT (CONNY, 90 YEARS)

I am keeping good health, I am, but I live alone. I've been on my own for about 30 years, and it becomes a habit. Everything I do is just me. I still drive, and I love driving. And I go and see my friends and I take my girlfriend every Friday for coffee and shopping.

I've made my way in my life all by myself. And I became very, very independent. Very independent, and whatever I do is what I do. I'm quite proud of myself really. So I'll be here till I die, I hope, I think. And it is lonely, but you become, oh what should I say? You become independent and stronger in yourself. I still live in my home. I still do my garden. I still do my own shopping. Other than that I stay at home, and I look after my home, and look after my health. I do get help, one hour a week. A girl comes, they give me an hour. She's lovely. Now I'm in the system, if ever I want anything I can ring up but I don't. My doctor said "why don't you?" and "I said I don't need it. Nobody can clean a house like me!"

My friends, they rely too much on their family. One friend has a very steep driveway, and her son comes over to pull the trolley up the driveway. He comes a long way to pull it because they're too old to pull it up. Serves them right for buying a house down in a gully or whatever they've got, you know what I mean? My friends, they ask their daughters to go with them to the doctor and all this nonsense. You can lean on younger people when you're old, but you don't have to. Imagine me, asking family to go with me to the doctor tomorrow. "Would you come with me?" It's not on. You do need somebody to talk to sometimes, but then again I don't get on the phone say "I'm lonely will you talk to me?" Oh no, don't do that. If you're independent, you still stay independent.

Although the dominant narrative of autonomy is that of an independent self-reliant decision maker, this expectation of autonomy does not fit well with the changes typically associated with later life. This chapter will show how the version of independence and self-reliance promoted in social policy and the media makes it hard for older people to accept help as they age. Older people do value autonomy and this is understood in terms of their ability to direct everyday aspects of their lives and to have sufficient resources to fashion such choices. To advance a capabilities approach to autonomy, we need to understand how social and environmental contexts make some identities valued and others denigrated to such a degree that older people may profess a preference for independence that sees them isolated, lonely, and unsupported. Instead we need to support a valued social identity as a participant in interdependent relationships and as the recipient of care, and the services and practical supports that enable physical and social interdependence.

What is autonomy?

Autonomy is often understood as freedom, self-determination, independence, or self-reliance (Agich, 2003). This version of autonomy focuses on "free action – living completely independently, free of coercion and limitation" (Gawande, 2014, p. 140). In this way, achieving autonomy is linked to knowing one's own mind and interests, being free from the coercion of others, and being able to function without the support of others. To achieve this version of autonomy requires individual competence and the ability to make rational choices. Agich (2003) describes this version of autonomy as negative freedom: the freedom to be left alone. Within this account, the value of independence are seen as natural and taken for granted; the state and society are regarded as coercive forces that limit the autonomy of the self-governing individual. This is reflected in Hyde et al.'s (2003, p. 187) definition of autonomy as "the right of an individual to be free from the unwanted interference of others."

Autonomy can be conceptualised in ways that go beyond a focus on freedom from coercion and individual independence. Relational autonomy theorists reject the version of autonomy that "equates the exercise of self-determination with rugged individualism, negative liberty and maximal freedom of choice" (MacKenzie, 2014, p. 42). Instead relational autonomy proposes that autonomy is inherently social. The capacity for autonomy is developed through processes of socialisation, which also frame our social identities in relation to others. Relational autonomy recognises that people are social beings constituted in and by their interpersonal and social environments (Mackenzie, 2008). Social identities frame what is possible, what is valued, and shape the choices available in later life.

Drawing together the notions of autonomy as freedom to choose and the socially embedded nature of our social lives, Gawande (2014) describes the autonomy that people desire at the end of their lives in this way:

All they ask is to keep shaping the story of their life in the world – to make choices and sustain connections to others according to their own priorities. In modern society, we have come to assume that debility and dependence rule out such autonomy.

(p. 140)

Gawande points to modern society as ruling out autonomy in the context of dependence, because autonomy as independence and self-reliance is a valorised cultural ideal that defines our identity (Agich, 2003). Autonomy is inextricably tied to social expectations for personhood. In most Western developed societies, independence is prized and dependence is vilified. Because of this, people display a range of "defences against dependence" (Agich, 2003, p. 7) that are used to resist an identity of dependence. These defences include the denial of need, hostility towards assistance in the face of limitations, and contempt for the weaknesses of others. These defences occur because any acknowledged or perceived dependence on others diminishes one's identity as a self-governing person. Even though the narrow atomistic version of autonomy has been challenged by notions of relational autonomy, the individualistic self-reliant agent is prized.

Maintaining independence

Independence has become the hallmark of social policy accounts of a good older age (Plath, 2002; Secker, Hill, Villeneau, & Parkman, 2003). Independence in social policy is used variously to mean good quality of life, continuing to make a contribution to society, and not accessing residential care or government support (Plath, 2002). All of these policy accounts promote independence and self-reliance as the hallmark of successful ageing (Ranzijn, 2010; Rozanova, 2010) and this may mean it is difficult for some older people to even imagine becoming dependent as they age (Smith et al., 2007). Older people may be strongly self-reliant but the focus on avoidance of dependency has negative consequences when older people face challenges for which they would benefit from support and care.

For older people attempting to maintain an independent identity, accepting help can be worse than not meeting some everyday needs. The desire to maintain an independent identity can mean that older people mask the signs of decline (Ball et al., 2004; Perkins et al., 2012) or refuse to ask for help when it is required (Smith, Braunack-Mayer, Wittert, & Warin, 2007). For example, Ballinger and Payne (2002) found that older people prefer to conceal physical limitations that may bring them to the attention of health and social care professionals or might compromise their identity as capable and independent people. In our research with older people, we found many examples of refusals to accept offers of help or withdrawal from social settings to ensure that others did not view one as needy or dependent. Older people described incidents that showed their ability to manage without the support of others, even when assistance was necessary to manage daily needs. Anna illustrated the lengths to which she went to support a construction of herself as an independent individual by saying:

> I won't let anyone help me. She [my friend] knew that I was in bed and she would come in and make me a cup of coffee and she'd say "do you want to go and have a shower," "I can do it thank you"; and when I get that tone people know leave her alone, let her fall over but leave her alone.

Refusal of assistance allows Anna the freedom to determine the arrangements of her care and a sense of individual control over her decision making, but her account demonstrates the weight of such freedom. Tanner (2001) similarly found that older people made claims of self-reliance and independence when refused social services. Tanner considered such claims as performances to preserve an identity as coping and independent. Without resources, the only recourse older people have to maintaining independence is through a refusal to accept help when they need it.

The possibility of ageing healthily, of achieving well-being in later years, and of having access to options is influenced by economic resources. Older people with greater resources have the choice to purchase care, giving them much greater capability to exercise control in their daily lives. Dependence or need is easier to obscure by paying for services or making adjustments to the home (Breheny & Stephens, 2012). Such resources make independence appear like a personal trait rather than the interplay of a range of physical, social, and environmental resources (Breheny & Stephens, 2010). The difference then is not between those who are independent and those who are dependent in terms of physical capability or need for care, but between those who are able to "render care invisible or normalised and those who are not" (Wiles, 2011, p. 579). Physical functioning is most difficult to achieve for older people who have experienced a lifetime of poor health and low wage insecure employment, and consequently reach later life least physically and financially able to maintain their independence. This is compounded by dependence on the state being stigmatised while purchasing services in the market is a mark of an independent consumer (Leonard, 1997).

The rhetoric in social policy is that independence reflects what older people value and seek. However, this needs to be examined carefully in terms of what alternatives are available for older people. The alternative social identity of dependence is one to be avoided, as it overwhelms all other aspects of identity (Wiles, 2011). Avoiding an identity as dependent determines what support can be requested, or even accepted when offered (Breheny & Stephens, 2009, 2010). People can be judged and judge others in terms of these choices, which have corresponding moral implications. Managing these identities at times become more important than avoiding loneliness, social isolation and struggle, however, the social environment that supports particular choices can be changed. Tanner (2001) argues that a hostile social environment encourages a mask of independent coping whereas a compassionate environment will support connection and disclosure of need.

The tyranny of independence

Maintaining an independent identity enables freedom to determine the arrangements of life circumstances and a sense of individual control over decision making. When this is achieved by refusing needed assistance from friends or family, independence can be burdensome. At this point, independence is no longer about what older people can do without help, but rather about claims that older people make to not needing others; dependence and independence are not bodily states, but social identities (Fine & Glendinning, 2005). These claims may be achieved in ways that are detrimental to physical capability.

Although the social value of independence has a long history, its dominance has increased in recent social policy accounts of healthy and active ageing. Fears regarding large numbers of older people overwhelming health and social services are transformed and taken up by older people as personal fears of becoming a burden in old age (Kemp & Denton, 2003; Portacolone, 2011). Some older people deal with this by maintaining geographical and relational distance with those who could provide support. Andrew illustrates this by claiming that moving closer to family members would only be necessary if you were ill, and illness itself was a justification for avoiding support:

> Int: Have you ever considered that perhaps you might move to be closer to your sister when you are much older? Andrew: No. I mean the only reason you'd do that is if you were really ill and then you'd be a burden.
>
> *(Breheny & Stephens, 2012)*

As needing support is viewed as burdensome, it is justification enough to avoid others. This illustrates what Hoagland (1988) referred to when she described autonomy as a noxious concept which encourages the view that connecting with others somehow limits us. Viewing autonomy and relations of need in this way has significant implications for relationships of care as people age. Many older people will become unavoidably less able to manage on their own and may be at risk of refusing help or legitimate social support. Many indicate that they would rather go without support than become a burden to others.

Technologies of independence

In the context of expectations for self-reliance and a corresponding denial of need, independence can be achieved through the promotion of technology to enable older people to rely less on family and friends, health and social care agencies (see Wang, Redington, Steinmetz, & Lindeman, 2011). Such technologies include personal alarm systems and home monitoring devices. Home monitoring systems enable remote surveillance of smoke, CO_2 levels, and movement throughout the house, and can sense falls. Personal alarm systems enable older people to maintain living alone even when at risk of falls. Electronic pill boxes support accurate and timely medication regimens (Sorell & Draper, 2014). Such technologies enable older people to live alone for longer, and provide security for family members that elders are safe from a distance, rather than providing intimacy and regular interactions. Sorell and Draper argue that technologies can enable people to 'look in' on older family members without travelling. Technological solutions enable older people to be safer without support, rather than supported to age well. More sophisticated devices such as robot animals and care robots have been developed to enable the benefits of touch and social interactions for older people who are isolated. This focus on independence in an age of technology leads to the promotion of strategies by which older people may be supported to rely less on others, rather than in terms of autonomy to maintain their preferences for supportive care. Technologies of independence frame older people as separate from society, 'other', to be cared for, segregated, monitored, and controlled (Johnson, 1995). Further, such approaches exploit older people's desires to avoid burdening others or being viewed as dependent. Together, these imperatives account for the popularity of technological solutions to address increased social care needs of an ageing population.

Embracing interdependence

This sort of technological response can be understood in terms of the absence of any valued identity as the recipient of care in older age. Achieving self-reliance presents particular challenges as people age and experience changes in health, social networks, and physical environments. Although self-reliance and individualism are damaging across the life course, they are particularly constraining in later life, when changes in physical functioning, social networks, and social identities impact independence. When individual worth is tied to self-reliance, ageing has the potential to undermine identity and value. As age-related changes occur, different conceptualisations of autonomy are required if older people are to achieve autonomy.

Relations of need can be understood as part of a normal process of mutual interdependence as people develop and grow in interaction with each other (Motenko & Greenberg, 1995). Seeking and accepting help can be viewed as maintaining connectedness between people (Fine & Glendinning, 2005) which acknowledges the fundamental interdependence of all people (Robertson, 1999): "All people, young and old, are dependent on each other through a variety of social systems in order for physical and emotional needs to be met" (Plath, 2008, pp. 1353–1354). Rather than focusing on dependence as linked with decline and disengagement, interdependence may be constructed as part of reciprocity and connectedness throughout life. Sánchez and Hatton-Yeo (2012) in their axioms for active ageing claim that interdependence, and not autonomy or independence, must be the priority if we intend to age well.

A key aspect of interdependence is that it strengthens intergenerational bonds. In spite of the rhetoric suggesting the demise of the family and the rise of intergenerational conflict and inequity (Binstock, 2010), there is evidence that intergenerational bonds remain strong. Many older people maintain close ties with their family members, and family continue to provide primary relationships for older people. Family members value being able to provide care, and view caring relationships as freely chosen expressions of their emotional ties to each other (Horrell et al., 2015). Support and connectedness are not restricted to intergenerational family support. Childless older people also report networks of support that have been established over the life course that provide ways to accept help as they age (Allen & Wiles, 2013). In contrast to discourse around the importance of maintaining independence and the burden of care to others, care relationships strengthen bonds and deepen relationships. From these perspectives, avoiding interdependence and refusing care is not an ideal to be aimed for.

Autonomy in later life

Older people, like people of any age, draw upon understandings of autonomy from the wider social world. Accordingly, many older people claim to have choices and be independent even when the alternatives are limited (Tanner, 2001). Many use dominant individualistic understandings of autonomy and independence as synonymous and constructed in terms of managing alone (see Plath, 2008). However, there are more nuanced versions of autonomy provided by research with older people.

Research on what older people value has consistently found that notions of autonomy are endorsed as important in later life. Grewal et al. (2006) found that older people valued control, which was described as being independent and able to make one's own decisions. In their analysis, the experience of control was undermined by poor health and limited finances. Fisk and Abbott (1998) similarly found that older people value deciding things for themselves, having financial resources, and being able to receive help without burdening others. In our interviews with older people on their living standards and experience of ageing, autonomy was identified as a valued capability (Stephens et al. 2015a). This was very similar to control as conceptualised by Grewal et al., encompassing the ability to make decisions about how to spend one's time, where to live, and what to buy. Our analysis also demonstrated that experiences of autonomy are interconnected. For example, restrictions in transport undermined autonomy by severely limiting the options that older people had for how they spent their time. Availability of transport also structured housing choices and lack of transport altered relationships with family, friends, and neighbours. Wiles et al. (2012) found that notions of independence and autonomy were identified as important in decisions about where to age. Being able to choose how to spend one's time, determine the daily patterns of one's life, and make ordinary choices about alterations in the home were all viewed as aspects of autonomy. The desire for autonomy in aspects of daily life has been seen as important to older people with dementia as well; interviews with people with dementia demonstrated the importance of the capacity to make as many personal decisions for as long as possible (Fetherstonhaugh, Tarzia, & Nay, 2013). The support of others was valued, but older people with dementia wished to be central players in the decisions that affected them, rather than feeling marginalised and excluded from their own lives.

Independence is more than individual; environmental factors such as accessible bus services and timely health services and sufficient economic resources enable independence, while family and interpersonal relationships are also viewed as important to maintaining independence (Fetherstonhaugh et al., 2013). Wiles et al. (2012) found that people differed in how they discussed independence, with some emphasising independence "from" family as opposed to independence "through" family. This willingness to be independent through family parallels dependence on place and people as enabling ageing well for older Māori in Aotearoa/New Zealand (Butcher & Breheny, 2016). The older people in Wiles et al.'s study also described autonomy as freedom from the constraining influence of others who might "push you" to make unwelcome decisions. Tanner (2001) found that people could feel stifled by family support that was emotionally nurturing but too focused on limiting risk. One older man in Tanner's study reported feeling "caged" by his family's efforts to keep him safe. Similarly, the childless older people in Allen and Wiles (2013) study valued the support they received from others, but support with an absence of autonomy was described as 'smothering support'. This happened when there was insufficient negotiation regarding needs for support or when people assumed that support was by definition required because someone was 'old' or would be lonely because they were childless. Older people wanted to be in control of when they asked for help, rather than having help pressed or foisted upon them (Allen & Wiles, 2013).

While people may value independent decision making, many also express apprehension regarding their future ability to make their own decisions. Rather than defining the self-governing autonomous individual in later life, decision making can be burdensome (Agich, 2003). Plath's (2008) interview study found that older people at times found being faced with decisions an isolating and frightening experience. Older people expressed needing help and support to make decisions, particularly when facing a crisis or when viable options were limited. Tanner (2001) found that older people accessing in-home services may need support to articulate and address their needs; even the process of identifying needs and requesting services can exhaust their resources. Even though health decisions are often viewed as highly individual, older people may prefer to defer to family members in matters of health decision making (Ho, 2008). Shared decision making spreads the responsibility for the outcome and recognises that decision making does impact on others; the atomistic independent individual is at odds with the socially integrated older person. Instead of aiming for self-reliance, older people may benefit from negotiating decision making within reliable relationships and networks, while being "respected, valued and supported by others in their decision making" (Plath, 2008, p. 1366).

Focusing on environmental and social versions of autonomy also supports the inclusion of accounts of autonomy from non-Western cultures. In Aotearoa/New Zealand, analysis of interviews with older Māori found that drawing on land and family enabled autonomy in later life (Butcher & Breheny, 2016). Rather than dependence being viewed as a state to be avoided, older people narrated a comfortable dependence on land and relationships as the foundation of a good older age. In addition, Māori tend to have larger social networks than European New Zealanders, and the structure of these networks is focused on extended family relationships; being connected to family is valued. Similarly Ranzijn (2010) notes the narrow and exclusionary nature of successful ageing models that promote independence and points to the ways that they exclude Australian Aboriginal elders from achieving what they value in later life. Rather than striving for independence, Aboriginal elders see later life as a time of custodianship, of renewing links with spiritually significant places, and strengthening intergenerational relationships (Ranzijn, 2010). These values are not undermined by changes in physical functioning or reliance on others; arguably, these later life changes strengthen intergenerational bonds. Asian models of harmonious ageing are based on the importance of recognising balance in relationships, and the interconnectedness of the body and the mind. In particular, harmonious ageing emphasises the interdependence of people and the gains and losses of older age (Liang & Luo, 2012). Older Japanese Americans also emphasised group harmony rather than the expression of individual needs in later life (Iwamasa & Iwasaki, 2011). Independence was viewed in terms of adjusting needs and focusing on the needs of others. In southern Europe, assistance from family members is highly valued and a source of pride rather than a sign of dependence (Zunzunegui et al., 2005), and among older Puerto Ricans in America, the overwhelming priority was to age in connection with others (Todorova et al., 2015). Fears were not about becoming a burden in later life, but were centred on loneliness, abandonment, and being unable to have people to rely on.

Although approaches to ageing that emphasise independence and self-reliance are compatible with Western neo-liberal and rational worldviews, they do not necessarily serve Western elders any better than older people from other cultural contexts (Ranzijn, 2010). A more nuanced version of autonomy would recognise that people are seldom (if ever) in a situation of total dependence or independence, and always require both protection and nurturing (Agich, 2003). Being in receipt of protection and nurturance from others need not require accepting a position of dependence or loss of dignity. Protection and nurturance can be viewed in terms of evidence of one's value to and interconnection with others (Allen & Wiles, 2013). "Human beings attain autonomy only through human relationships and the exercise of autonomy requires supportive relationships throughout one's life" (Agich, 2003, p. 50).

Autonomy as a capability

Autonomy is a key governing idea from the Capability Approach. It is understood by Sen as the freedom to choose the most valued amongst a set of possible capabilities. Freedom within the Capability Approach is not negative freedom from restraint, but a positive freedom, the capability of achieving something (Alkire,

2005a). Sen's Capability Approach is part of the liberal tradition that values individual freedom, but it also acknowledges the role of social influences and personal history on individual choices (Robeyns, 2005a). Individualistic accounts of autonomy and vulnerability suggest that these are characteristics of the individual, reflecting inherent capabilities or weaknesses. But vulnerability and need are not necessarily properties of the individual, but rather reflect the intersection of social and political structures and individual characteristics (Mackenzie, 2014). Older people do not become vulnerable in isolation; they become vulnerable in response to lifelong processes of economic, social, and ethnic inequalities.

The Capability Approach enables us to examine what we can make of autonomy at the intersection of socially sanctioned possibilities, environmental resources, and interpersonal relationships. If prevailing social norms of independence and self-reliance mean that making a choice to depend on others for social support and practical tasks of daily living undermines one's self-identity as a competent person, then such choices are not realistically available for older people. In such a context, the only reasonable choice may be to refuse help. Although this might be conceptualised as a choice, it is at best a constrained choice, which compounds the health and disability issues that created it. In this context, choosing to refuse help and continue to suffer from disabling conditions in older age is not an expression of autonomy but an assault on autonomy (Agich, 2003). Choices can be tragic choices that demonstrate the scarcity of alternative viable options (Nussbaum, 2011). Consequently, we need to interrogate autonomy, and examine the context of people's choices to ensure they reflect a fair distribution of opportunities (Robeyns, 2005a). Autonomy can be defined in terms of having both the power to choose and access to the resources to realise that choice (Tanner, 2001). Within a capabilities approach, a focus on independence and self-reliance is revealed as misplaced if it correspondingly undermines the capability to experience autonomy, in terms of the freedom to choose the support of others.

From a capability perspective, autonomy is about command over physical, social, psychological, and environmental resources and the possibilities that such resources make available to a person. Equally autonomy is freedom from the constraining influence of environmental factors that limit choices of how and where to age. A capabilities approach shifts the focus from the responsibility of the individual to maintain independence, and improve personal situations, to a consideration of the provisions of the social and physical environment to support the values of healthy ageing. Imperatives to age well must be underpinned by the policies, structures, and spaces which enable this for all. Constraining social identities and culturally narrow alternatives limit the possibilities for social, political, and economic interventions which will secure ageing well. Earlier we examined the ways that individualistic versions of independence make sensible technological solutions to population ageing that support older people to manage alone. From a capability perspective, such solutions support one version of ageing and limit options based on social connectedness and interdependence.

The predominant challenges to autonomy in later life are physical functionings, social identities and the social isolation they bring, and insufficient resources.

Interventions can be focused on mitigating these challenges to autonomy by acknowledging autonomy as the capability to make viable choices in the context of supportive conditions.

Interdependent identities

Policy is one realm in which language can shape both services and identities for older people. There has been sustained critique of the socially exclusionary nature of the current policy approaches to promoting independence among older people (Breheny & Stephens, 2010, 2017; Fine & Glendinning, 2005; Laliberte Rudman, 2006; Plath, 2002, 2008). To support the capability to achieve autonomy in later life, it is necessary to be alert to the social identities available to older people when they face reductions in physical functioning or social isolation. In these circumstances in particular, independence and self-reliance provide very limited and damaging versions of autonomy.

To achieve a well-supported and well-resourced older age, ageing policy would need to "go beyond promoting the self-reliance of older people surviving alone in their own homes and aim to promote community responsibility for socially and emotionally rewarding lives in old age" (Plath, 2002, p. 46). Rather than encouraging physical and relational independence, policy could equally increase support for community members to care (Portacolone, 2011). One way this can be enacted is through supporting a range of care options rather than naturalising self-reliance and family obligation. The availability of both family carers and paid carers provides the greatest autonomy for older people requiring support, not just because of the increased provision of instrumental care, but because the presence of both sources enables older people to view themselves as not reliant on home help or dependent on family members (Hammarström & Torres, 2010). Autonomy need not be the autonomy of the individual decision maker, but can include relational autonomy distributed through the participants in the care relationship, across social structures, and enacted through social networks (Schwanen, Banister, & Bowling, 2012). Viewing care in terms of interdependence and autonomy provides broader support for older people and their carers, and may assist us to provide appropriate material and community support for members of an ageing population, many of whom will face some degree of decline and need.

Everyday autonomy

Supporting the capability to experience autonomy is also achieved by viewing autonomy in terms of the ordinary, everyday activities that older people wish to engage in as part of maintaining their place in social life (Agich, 2003). Plath (2008) suggests that services must be mindful of how older people define their own needs and provide services that meet these needs without stigmatising the receipt of service. An everyday example of this may be seen in the provision of meal services for older people. When older people report that meal services provide no choice regarding what is delivered, and yet they are expected to be thankful (Plath, 2008), this points to the ways that 'independence' is shaped. The policy version of independence is being achieved by preventing the need to move into residential care. The autonomy of older people to achieve dominion over the very ordinary activities of their daily lives has not. Yet these everyday decisions are what are valued by older people, and what contributes to their experience of autonomy and quality of life.

Rather than accepting the inevitability of social isolation and designing technological solutions to enable older people to manage alone, there are a number of ways to enable autonomy and interdependence. Sorell and Draper (2014) note that for autonomy to co-exist with dependence among older people, "the choices of older people can often need to be realized through the efforts of others" (p. 190), particularly to address increasing support needs as people age. Assisted living facilities are one way to provide this distributed autonomy. Typically, these community-based facilities that provide housing, food service, personal services, and 24-hour availability of care staff to support frail elders (Ball et al., 2004) are based on the principle of enabling older people to have autonomy over their own space and privacy from staff and other residents (Carder, 2002). As far as possible, residents' preferences are honoured and support is provided to implement those preferences. These principles map on closely to the aspects of autonomy that older people value.

Assisted living facilities have also been developed in specific contexts to meet particular needs. Elder co-housing shares the principles of assisted living, but is distinguished from it in that residents manage and run the co-housing community themselves. Glass (2013) examined how older people in an elder co-housing community provided mutual support and increased acceptance of the experience of ageing. They felt safe and supported. Even those who enjoyed privacy and solitude reported that they welcomed the security of neighbours who cared. Such age-segregated and age-focused communities provide an option that acknowledges the primacy of ageing identity for some older people and enables supported social lives as physical functioning changes.

The basic principles of self-determination and autonomy can also be found in other residential alternatives. Humanitas housing developments advanced by Becker focus on supporting quality of life and enabling older people to do what they value even with chronic conditions. The values promoted in this approach are self-determination, continuing valued activities in later life, and an expectation that residents' requests will be met if possible. Whatever assistance is required by a resident, including nursing level care, is brought to them in their own apartment (Glass, 2014). Similarly, the 'Eden Alternative' is a model of residential care which seeks to maximise the role of older people in decision making that effects them and foster autonomy and self-determination (Bergman-Evans, 2004; Brownie, 2011; Downes, 2013). Evidence suggests that the Eden Alternative is associated with increased health and well-being outcomes, and reductions in loneliness, boredom, and helplessness (Brownie, 2011). All these housing alternatives attempt to meet the range of needs of people as they age. Such recent approaches to housing arrangements have significant potential to alter how we understand the intersection of care and autonomy in later life.

Conclusion

The dominant policy narrative of independence promotes a positive social identity for older people who age without accepting support. This limits the capacity for older people to ask for or accept help when they face physical changes as they age. To address this we need broader understandings of relational autonomy that acknowledge the interrelated nature of all community members across the life course. Rather than achieving autonomy through self-reliance and denying need, it is possible to conceptualise autonomy in terms of accepting welcome assistance and acknowledging interdependence. The Capability Approach acknowledges the desire that people have to make decisions about aspects that influence their lives, whilst recognising that such decisions are fraught with social and physical implications. To recognise the empowering possibilities of autonomy requires that it be expanded as far as possible with genuine choices representing viable alternatives. Autonomy as a value needs to be subject to careful scrutiny to ensure it does not serve broader social and political purposes and ultimately burden older people rather than enable options for lives of value, care, and social integration.

DECIDING YOUR OWN FUTURE (URSULA, 80 YEARS)

I used to get very achy knees and I thought if I could find a place that was on one level I'd be alright. There's a bus stop right outside the gate that you can get the bus into town if you wish to. Otherwise you can go down a quarter of an hour walk to the station and get the train in which is very quick. I've very good neighbours here. When they come back from their holiday they are going to help me prune the trees. They've got a son who's very good, helps me take the rubbish bins in and out and things, you know, which is good. But I should go and do it myself. I can still walk. I'm still capable.

I think, long term plan, if I can't drive, well neither will my friends be able to drive. Then I'll have to make a decision what I do. And it may be that I have, I go to live where I've got two sons. So it's one of those big question marks hanging over your head and I don't really want to make a great big decision about it yet, that's just awful. And I know you should do but . . . My sons, they would prefer me to be closer, but they also realise and they say "well you know it's your decision. You keep going as long as you can. As long as you want to." I'd like to be independent for as long as possible.

And as I get older I probably will have to give up things, will give up choir. Things that I do, once I know I can't do them anymore well that'll be the end of that part of my life. My life will change and I'm not looking forward to that but I hope that it keeps going as long as I can. I have good health at the present moment, yes. I think that's the most important thing. If you're in good health well then you can do things like take yourself to a film or say well I'll have a little holiday because I can manage and I can do this. But if you aren't in good health you're stuck at home, or in a hospital, or in some, you know. And I've seen it with other people, it shrinks your world.

9
RESEARCH UTILISING THE CAPABILITY APPROACH

Sen's Capability Approach is a theory of social justice which also provides a framework for research, practice, and social policy. Using the Capability Approach would involve evaluations of what people value, and work to increase their ability to be the sort of people and do the things that are valued by them and their society. From a capabilities perspective, intervention and policy would focus on all older people being capable of achieving the values of healthy ageing rather than being responsible to actively produce physical health (as a sort of commodity). Accordingly, focusing on capabilities shifts research questions towards a focus on the social and material provisions that support these aspects of well-being. While economists and public health theorists grapple with the problems of operationalising and measuring capabilities, we suggest that other social scientists can bring additional theories and methodologies to support the practical development of a capabilities approach to inform different aspects of inquiry. In this chapter we outline a basis for methodological development, and provide examples of frameworks for research that have been utilised using the topic of housing as an example.

Methodological development within the capability framework

The Capability Approach is a theoretical perspective rather than a fully realised theory of development, justice, social policy, or economics. Sen's general response to criticisms of under-theorisation has been to describe it as an approach to the "evaluation of effective freedom" (Wells, 2016). As such it remains an open, under-developed, and often contested framework that can be used for a variety of aims (Robeyns, 2005a). Comim (2001) described it as "a framework for evaluating and assessing social arrangements, standards of living, inequality, poverty, justice, quality of life or well-being" rather than a "substantive theory of these issues" (p. 4). The main contribution of the Capability Approach, then, as often recognised by commentators such as Comim, Alkire, or Robeyns, is the shift away from institutionally prescribed achievements to a focus on evaluating the things that people are able to be or to do and their freedom or capability to achieve those valued functionings. This means that those engaged in researching development, public health, or social justice issues from a capability perspective must bring additional theoretical and particularly methodological perspectives to enable the inclusion of the plurality of contexts, heterogeneity of values, and what Comim (2001) terms the counterfactual nature of the focus on capability (rather than on actual functioning).

Capability research questions are often based on the needs of particular groups in particular contexts, as in research examining the needs of people with disabilities (Allmark & Machaczek, 2015; Saleeby, 2007) or conducting drug and alcohol therapy (Sharma, 2004). Sen's (2004) focus on identifying capabilities through deliberative democracy and context-driven enquiry suggests the use of qualitative and participatory approaches among particular groups. However, Robeyns (2005a) notes that Sen's own work on the Capability Approach is based on his roots in formal economic reasoning with quantitative empirical applications, while Nussbaum's work is closer to traditions such as narrative approaches which are more suited to understanding people's hopes, desires, and values.

There are several different methodological frameworks which could be employed to flesh out aspects of a capabilities approach and provide additional explanations for specific directions of research. Narrative approaches are already well used in gerontological research to understand the meaning and coherence of the lives of older people (Kenyon, Clark, & De Vries, 2001; Phoenix, Smith, & Sparkes, 2010; Severinsen et al., 2016). Other qualitative approaches such as phenomenology (Kolb, 2014) and ethnomethodology (Dewsbury et al., 2004) used to understand the experiences of ageing, or discourse analysis (Rozanova, 2010) to reveal social and power relations, are available. In the following sections, we will describe examples of different approaches and the issues and opportunities that they provide in developing further research.

Capabilities are intertwined

Lists of capabilities, however derived, can suggest that capabilities are separate entities. In this book, to describe examples of different capabilities that have been identified as of value to older people, we have discussed physical functioning, social connectedness, contribution, enjoyment, security, and autonomy as if they are separate capabilities, when of course they are also interrelated and often inextricably entwined.

The interconnected nature of capabilities was first brought home to us in a study of caregivers of older people (Horrell et al., 2015). The use of Nussbaum's list of central human capabilities as a template for the analysis of qualitative data gathered in an online forum, highlighted important aspects of the caregiving experience such as physical functioning, financial hardship, and social isolation, which were readily interpreted using Nussbaum's capability categories. The information provided by the caregivers in this study endorsed the use of Nussbaum's list. The study identified several instances where using Nussbaum's list highlighted particular capability restrictions in the context of caring informally for older people. Some capabilities on Nussbaum's list were more likely to be supported than others; however, the chief finding was that the capabilities were inextricably connected in a web.

Kimberley et al. (2012) also used Nussbaum's list as the basis for identifying valued capabilities among older people receiving care services in Australia. The researchers chose to use this existing list after noting similarities between several capability sets identified in previous research. As in the study of carers (Horrell et al., 2015), they noted that some of Nussbaum's identified capabilities were more likely than others to be endorsed by respondents to their survey and in focus groups. They also noted the interdependence of capabilities; participants often described opportunities for developing capability in terms of clusters of capabilities. Spending time with family and friends, being active, being well informed, and getting out and about were seen as interdependent. Physical functioning and health were important to social engagement or control over the environment. Health overlapped with independence, security, and social connections. In the context of aged care services, Kimberley and colleagues suggested that these might be termed 'enabling capabilities'. For example, a very large part of the value of good physical health was what it enabled people to be and to do. Similarly, financial capabilities also enabled other capabilities. "For many people, the nexus of adequate means, good health and social engagement enabled them to live in ways they highly valued" (p. 42). These authors concluded that capabilities should be seen as a complex web when considering service provision.

In the Horrell et al. (2015) study of caregivers, a further conclusion was that the web of capabilities was connected by emotions which play a significant role in caregivers' lives, across the capability set identified. Although services such as respite care and home help were available, many caregivers resisted the help that was offered based on feelings of commitment to their role and concern for the wishes of the person being cared for. These findings suggested that a capability to care was an important aspect underlying informal family care and that all the capabilities related to the caregivers' well-being were linked by emotional commitment to that care. Supporting the well-being of informal caregivers by providing extra resources to support isolated capabilities may be inadequate. Nussbaum (2011) argues that "the crucial good societies should be promoting is a set of opportunities, or substantial freedoms, which people may or may not exercise in action" (p. 18). However, the findings from this study suggested that when resistance to these 'opportunities' affects well-being, we need to look more closely at the interaction of capabilities and personal relationships. Understanding the interaction of capabilities and personal relationships in this context will enable moves beyond simplistic notions of care as being either burdensome or rewarding. Choices about the provision of care are made in a relational context, in which the well-being of the person being cared for is also important to the well-being of the caregiver. Being able to care for a loved one is a valued capability and emotional attachment informs the decision to provide care, as well as how care is managed in conjunction with the caregivers' own needs. As Collins (2004) has observed, "values are cognitions infused with emotion" (p. 102).

In this example, Horrell et al. (2015) concluded that emotional tensions in informal caregiving may be a crucial place to focus institutional support for caregivers. This requires acknowledgement of the interdependent nature of shared bonds and that respite from the 'burden' of care is not always appropriate support for caregivers. It requires support for the role of caregiving, which could include finding practical ways to strengthen bonds and relationships, not only between caregiver and care recipient, but within families and wider society, including formal health care services and health professionals. This would necessitate working more closely with families to identify their particular needs and strengths, and valuing their knowledge of the person being cared for. Informal caregivers need to be treated as an integral part of the caregiving process, not simply as a convenient provider to contain the cost of eldercare.

Supporting integrated capabilities

When we move from a concern with listing capabilities to ways in which we can support those capabilities as in the previous example, the Capability Approach leads to a focus on the social and material environment. Housing is an important feature of the environment, shown by its recurrence across the previous chapters as a critical focus for the support of different capabilities. Housing is an important aspect of the environment for any person, and is an obvious focus for achievable social, economic, and health policy change. Housing may also be usefully understood in terms of an integrated approach to capabilities; in general it has been noted that appropriate living situations have implications for older people's physical functioning, social integration, identity, pleasure, security, and autonomy together (Carr et al., 2013; Peace et al., 2011).

Housing is internationally recognised as important to public health (Howden-Chapman et al., 1999), and much of the international research and intervention in regard to housing and health focuses on the provision of affordable, warm, healthy housing (Pearson, Barnard, Pearce, Kingham, & Howden-Chapman, 2014), and repairs, maintenance, and economic issues in retirement (Preiser & Ostroff, 2001). Housing has been more broadly addressed within environmental gerontology as a major example of the environmental impact on ageing and health (Oswald et al., 2003). The age-friendly community movement and associated theories of environmental fit (Scharlach, 2012) highlight the important links between built space provision, social connections, and social participation as important aspects of health supporting communities. Wiles et al. (2009) use the term 'social space' to describe this integration of social relationships and physical spaces which shapes all aspects of well-being. Morris (2012) used the Capability Approach in qualitative research to highlight the ways in which the material environment, in terms of accommodation costs, security of tenure, and the neighbourhood, affected older people's capability to engage in social life. Older private renters, with higher rents and low security of tenure, did not have the capability to participate in neighbourhood activities and were isolated. In contrast, older social housing interviewees, who had lower rents, guaranteed tenure, and longevity of residence reported stronger social ties and were able to engage in social activities outside the home. In general, researchers have begun to explore the implications of home for the quality of life of older people, by describing the objective (housing type and housing conditions) and subjective (control and autonomy) aspects of housing in relation to health, conceptualised more broadly in terms of autonomy, participation and well-being (Sixsmith et al., 2014).

Home and self

Like caregiving, housing is also infused with emotion; the multiple meanings of 'home' (Wiles et al., 2012) are recognised as an important aspect of older people's well-being. Theories about place attachment and identity (Neisser, 1988), emphasise the transformation of 'space' into 'place' (Rowles & Watkins, 2003), describing how people form affective, cognitive, behavioural, and social bonds to the environment (Peace, Wahl, Mollenkopf, & Oswald, 2007). Concepts such as the meaning of home are directly related to place attachment (Oswald & Wahl, 2005). In the process of reflecting on the past, social, cognitive, and emotional links are more likely to become manifest, symbolically represented by certain places and cherished objects within the home (Wiles et al., 2012). Meanings of home and attachment to place are particularly important for older people, especially for preserving a sense of identity and independence in older age (Peace et al., 2011).

Housing may be an important support for maintaining valued identities, or valued ways of 'being and doing', across many different situations. Severinsen et al. (2016) interviewed a wide range of older people in Aotearoa/New Zealand to explore the reasons that some older people choose to age in "unsuitable places." Their analysis of personal and public narratives showed that people drew on different types of identities to describe their preferences. People who were described as "practical planners" described their decisions to move house to age in places with appropriate conditions and good access to services. Other older people lived proudly in unsuitable places and did not wish for support to move or accommodations made to their housing. These older people draw upon narratives of place as foundational to their identity, of relationships with people both living and dead as social relationships that are part of their identity, and of their house as an important character in situated lifelong narratives. Both the situation of their home and the condition of the home provide the backdrop to different narrative identities that require them to remain in housing because of, or irrespective of, its unsuitability. These stories exemplified the strong identities that have been developed in and through housing and place over the life course.

In an in-depth qualitative study of older people and housing across five countries in Europe, Sixsmith et al. (2014) also found that many older people resisted changes to their housing to resist ageing identities and maintain their lifelong selves. Some participants preferred a less than ideal living environment because of the importance of the symbolic qualities of the home. Maintaining the use of challenging aspects of the house such as stairs provided a sense of achievement. Others resisted adaptations, such as ramps and rails, because they suggested a new identity of frailty. These people chose support for their familiar identity, rather than support for physical functioning.

Different cultural, political, and economic contexts provide different views of the important aspects of housing and place. The findings of Sixsmith and colleagues (2014) emphasise the value of the home in supporting and facilitating well-being. In particular, the relationship between their participants' sense of identity and the physical spaces and provisions experienced in their homes contributed to their constructions of healthy ageing. In contrast, research from developing countries which provide more tenuous living situations for older people, showed a focus on the importance of basic household amenities, income adequacy, safety, and multi-generation households (van der Pas et al., 2015).

Nevertheless, in-depth enquiry has shown that identity remains a significant aspect of housing situations, even in the most difficult circumstances. Becker (2003) explored the experience of place among three groups of older immigrants living in the US. These people were often living in situations of considerable hardship, with insecurity, overcrowding, and poverty. Despite the novelty and transience of many living situations, Becker observed the importance of creating a sense of home as a place of comfort and a haven. The process of finding and investing new homes with significance was interpreted in terms of identity-making. Even in later life, people work to re-establish valued, albeit disrupted, identities.

Viewed in terms of valued beings and doings, research has already shown that housing provides a complex web of capabilities (in terms of multiple meanings of home, the physical nature of housing, support for health services, social relationships, social integration, and personal identities) that are also important to different groups of people in different ways.

Diversity

Burchardt and Vizard (2011) have highlighted the importance of maintaining the visibility of at-risk and vulnerable groups. In generalising experiences, differences in sexuality, gender, ethnicity, or socio-economic status may be ignored, leading to the further disempowerment of those groups already marginalised in society. Housing is a significant area within which inequalities and their effects on well-being continue to manifest in regard to the experiences of many different groups such as minority ethnic groups (Logie, Jenkinson, Earnshaw, Tharao, & Loutfy, 2016; Roscigno, Karafin, & Tester, 2009) or older lesbian, gay, bisexual, and transgender (LGBT) adults (Addis, Davies, Greene, MacBride Stewart, & Shepherd, 2009). As a specific example we focus on differences between men and women in housing experiences.

Culturally, research suggests that Western homes are characterised by gendered roles and obligations. For example, Sixsmith et al. (2014) reported that the women and men in their study of older people in Europe talked about home in very different ways. For women, the home was a centre for focusing on nutrition and diet and for maintaining an active social and family life. For the men, home-based activities (such as decorating and gardening) were important more as ways to maintain active lifestyles. Russell (2007) also found that the men and women in her study in Australia reported quite different meanings of home. Both men and women characterised the home as a woman's space and as important for a woman's identity. Women were more likely to be attached to the particular home of their family and social life, and also noted that the men were not as involved in the local community. Russell comments on the implications of these sorts of findings for supportive service provision for older people, which currently tend to be functional substitutes for "women's work" (2007, p. 187).

From a broader social perspective in Australia, Darab and Hartman (2013) point out that the assumptions behind men's and women's roles in the home have created housing difficulties for women in later life. Women's traditional roles in society have led to housing insecurity for many older women. Not all women live in the secure position described in many studies; for women who do not own their home, ageing and single status together place them at higher risk of homelessness or inappropriate housing. Darab and Hartman describe the social and economic conditions of the mid-20th century that have led to this situation.

Understanding that housing provides a complex web of capabilities that are also affected by different social and economic locations, demands the development of systematic approaches to combining these aspects to understand the needs of diverse groups.

Integrating capabilities

The Capability Approach requires that we attend to multiple capabilities and their interdependence and interactivity. "One of the greatest challenges for its application is to incorporate this multidimensionality and complexity into any operational framework" (Kimberley et al., 2012, p. 8). Gilroy (2008) has suggested that a capabilities approach is a valuable way to examine how living environments can support the quality of life of older people. She cited quality of life research showing that the important features of well-being according to older people include accessibility in the home, security of tenure, feelings of being in control, environmental quality of the neighbourhood, availability of transport, and strength of social support. To develop a framework for understanding how housing supports older people's needs (by addressing the interconnected issues that older people themselves believe contribute to their quality of life), Gilroy used the Capability Approach to analyse results from eight studies of quality of life viewed by older people and provide a list of identified capabilities and functionings. She argues that the emphasis of the Capability Approach on "actual beings and doings provides a robust empirical approach to consider how places may support or deny older adults' quality of life as they define it" (p. 345).

Drawing on the Capability Approach, Saleeby (2007) has provided a model of the relationships between the kinds of determinants of well-being that were identified by Gilroy (2008). In this model, capabilities are a reflection of a person's life situation (e.g., physical functioning and environmental factors). Personal factors (e.g., economic well-being and disability or chronic illnesses) and environmental factors (e.g., health care accessibility, stigma, and attitude) play integral roles in facilitating or limiting functionings. By focusing on capability, attention is turned to the ways personal and environmental factors interact to influence the achievement of functionings, and in turn to identify interventions to promote capability development. Gilroy also noted the importance of the interdependence of capabilities in older people's assessment of their quality of life, and further stressed the essential role of agency. The Capability Approach emphasises the need to assess individuals' abilities or capacities within their specific life environment and their freedom to achieve valued capabilities. With a supportive and enabling environment, older people can achieve high levels of well-being on their own terms, even while experiencing chronic conditions and physical health challenges.

Saleeby's (2007) development of the Capability Approach for use in research and practice in disability support maps on to a model of ageing well developed specifically in terms of housing and well-being by Wahl, Iwarsson, and Oswald (2012). This model suggests the simultaneous consideration of the environment (housing), individual agency, and sense of belonging to understand ageing well. By focusing on the person-environment interaction, their model is able to include the interactions of different capabilities supported by housing, neighbourhood, and technological environments. Wahl et al.'s model includes consideration of the environment in terms of practical supports in the home and neighbourhood including housing and technological support for physical functioning, social engagement, and autonomy. The sense of belonging or sense of home includes people's emotional and social bonds to the environment and opens questions about support for personal identity needs. Agency encompasses important broader aspects of power, including control of the physical and social environment and the ability to make changes to the house or one's housing situation.

In the sphere of housing, this model can be used to enquire into the ways in which any housing situation supports or fails to support important capabilities such as physical functioning, social connectedness, contribution, enjoyment, security, and autonomy. The important aspect of belonging introduces the emotional threads which bind the web of capabilities together. The inclusion of agency maintains our awareness of the social location of different people (as in Saleeby's model) and their freedom to make choices about valued functionings that is an essential aspect of Sen's Capability Approach.

Capabilities and the physical environment

A capabilities approach to well-being highlights the neglect of the environment in research on well-being for older people. Wahl et al. (2012) have expressed their dismay that despite early environmental theorising, the role of the immediate physical, spatial, and technical environment has largely been neglected in gerontological research. Furthermore, important ecological theories are omitted from current handbooks of theories of ageing, and classic theories such as the Selection, Optimisation and Compensation model (Baltes & Baltes, 1990) have not been developed to specify the environment well. Sixsmith et al. (2014) add that, although the housing environment is important to older people in particular, the home itself is an under-researched aspect of quality of life amongst old people. From a capabilities perspective, understanding healthy housing arrangements in terms of both physical protection and their ability to support social integration is highlighted as important supports for the health of an ageing population.

Neglect in research feeds in to social policy. Although interest in the physical environment and health is growing, social policy for older people focuses on individual behaviours and circumstances, with much less attention given to the material and structural barriers which contribute to unnecessary disablement and poor health (Thomas & Blanchard, 2009). The current policies of 'ageing-in-place' in many Western countries encourage people to remain in their current homes and communities (Schofield et al., 2006). This reflects both older people's preferences as well as the economic advantages of caring for older people in the community (Wiles et al., 2012).

However, ageing-in-place social policies are also based on simple assumptions regarding the link between ageing in place and healthy ageing. As Smith (2009) states, "the optimality of ageing in place has generally assumed that there is a particular quality to the environments in which people age" (p. 3). In fact, existing physical infrastructures were not designed for the fast-growing ageing population, and suburban areas are poorly designed for the needs of families as they age (Scharlach, 2012). Accordingly, ageing-in-place policies often support older people's ability to remain in what can be unsuitable or socially isolating environments (Sixsmith & Sixsmith, 2008; van der Pas et al., 2015). The support needed to maintain these policies and the physical characteristics of the houses themselves, requires more attention while communities vary considerably in the resources they have to support people as they age (Keating et al., 2013; Roos et al., 2014; Walsh, Scharf, & Shucksmith, 2014). As an example of older people ageing in place without appropriate consideration, Tuohy and Stephens (2011) describe the experiences of older people in Aotearoa/New Zealand, living in social housing built near a flood-prone river on the outside of town. These people were neglected in disaster planning, and consequently almost completely forgotten in a flood emergency and not warned about the flooding until the water was lapping at their doors and entering their houses. They had no time to protect or gather their possessions as they were hastily evacuated. For those financially able to choose, constructed communities such as retirement villages may provide more socially and physically supportive environments, but these are not available to those without financial resources, and furthermore can segregate elders from the rest of the community (Cannuscio et al., 2003; Grant, 2006).

In addition to segregation, the provision of supportive housing and care for older people raises further issues in regard to the neglect of valued capabilities. Research with older people in the community has shown that housing arrangements are important aspects of people's sense of identity and place in society as contributing citizens. Unfortunately, modern nursing homes, for reasons of institutional convenience or to comply with safety regulations, tend to deny people who need specialised care the freedom to make choices about their daily lives. Such institutionalisation disrupts the autonomy and identity of residents, and also shapes relations between carers and those receiving care. For example, Dunn and Moore (2016) used a qualitative study of carers in a nursing home in the UK to describe how the institutional routines, medically based working practices, and staff shortages resulted in the institutionalisation of daily life so that the psychosocial importance of activities such as meals was neglected. Focusing on dietary and care requirements led to the segregation of friends and loss of pleasure for residents at institutionalised mealtimes, and anxiety for staff, so that residents' risk of malnutrition was actually heightened. Despite the carers' good intentions, the relational aspects of care were constrained by legislative and medical requirements.

Several new models of care have been developed across the world including different types of assisted living arrangements to allow for more autonomy with care, and communal apartments such as Humanitas Apartments for Life (see Glass, 2014), which stresses freedom and community integration. The Netherlands has also provided De Hogeweyk (Glass, 2014) as a model for a village situation which supports identity and freedom for those with dementia. This style of care has attracted international attention and some similar developments in other countries. However, there is a great need for more research to evaluate and share these models of care.

Without the support of a concerted research programme, prevailing policies and models of care can shape the provision of such care. Across time and space, different conditions and legislative environments have shaped the realisation of assisted living facilities which were originally based on the principles of autonomy and support. Kane, Wilson, and Spector (2007) tracked the legislative and industry pressures on the development of the concept of assisted living and on the use of the term to mean many different styles of provision. They call for a new research agenda focused on the original ideals of assisted living. Perkins et al. (2012) have more recently provided a relational model of autonomy in assisted living which is based on grounded theory research among older people. This model develops the original principles to include race, class, and cultural differences, and social and institutional change. Their research shows the importance of place to people's identity and also the importance of maintaining links to past aspects of identity. They also point to the importance of relationships, including for people with dementia, in supporting the maintenance of the sense of self. Such examples of research remain isolated and fragmented while other ideals of ageing well, such as a focus on medical constructions of health and denial of death, dominate the discursive landscape.

Currently, there is resistance to support for older people which includes valued ways of being and doing. Care arrangements that provide autonomy for older people are often resisted in the first place because of the attitudes of families who have become responsible for the older person's welfare. Advertisements for nursing homes are largely aimed at family members and not the older person themselves and focus on protection and care for loved ones. Gawande (2014) has quoted Keren Browne Wilson, a pioneer in supportive care, as saying:

> We want autonomy for ourselves and safety for those we love. That remains the main problem and paradox for the frail. Many of the things that we want for those we care about are things that we would adamantly oppose for ourselves because they would infringe upon our sense of self.
>
> *(p. 106)*

However, the constructions of appropriate health care for older people are dominated by policy requirements which create serious tensions in nursing homes between perceptions of what is safe and good for health and the freedom to realise valued capabilities (e.g., Dunn & Moore, 2016). Perkins et al. (2012) who provide a model for relational care based on empirical research, also briefly discuss issues of legislation designed to protect the safety of residents of nursing homes, particularly those with dementia, which effectively marginalises those facilities that do provide support for autonomy and thus risks increasing health disparities. They hope that focused research will contribute to policy debates and increase support for assisted living facilities that support older people's capabilities. Kimberley et al. (2012) also describe the way in which aversion to risk among care providers in Australia "undermines older adults' rights and independence and insinuates itself not only into care programs and relationships between professional carers and service users but also into restricting the choices that older adults are able to make" (p. 3). In response to presentations about the Humanitas model in Aotearoa/New Zealand, nursing home operators noted that such a style would not fit with current regulations or the demands of families, investors, and shareholders. For older people to achieve autonomy in many societies today, research is required to challenge ageist assumptions and practices that work to actively constrain the rights of older people.

There are several good examples of research that support the development of housing arrangements for older people that would foster well-being. However, serious obstacles to the implementation of these understandings remain. There is a need for more research focusing on the ways in which environmental influences, both social and material, support well-being. A capabilities approach to well-being provides a broad conceptual framework for an integrated programme of research into the well-being and quality of life of all older people. A research focus on supporting capabilities to age well, can shift attention from a narrow policy focus on physical health and safety to attend to the valued capabilities supported by the environment in general.

132 Research utilising the Capability Approach

Conclusions

The Capability Approach shifts the focus of concerns about healthy ageing from individually achieved success to the ways in which the social and material environment can support quality of life. This shift includes a broader conceptualisation of health itself in terms of quality of life or the capability to achieve a variety of valued functionings. Physical functioning is an important capability from this perspective, but one among other valued capabilities such as social integration, contribution, autonomy, security, and enjoyment of life.

This framework for a broader approach to health is able to include the diversity of older people's lives and current capability, while acknowledging agency. A capabilities approach allows for the inclusion of differing needs by taking into account varying social contexts. Accordingly, minority groups are included and inequalities are recognised. It enables the values of older people, whatever their physical or cognitive capacity or whatever their current living situation, to be included. Agency is recognised in the democratic and inclusive principles inherent in the Capability Approach. By focusing on the values of older people themselves, it asks for knowledge from the older person's perspective and requires their active participation in the generation of knowledge and decision making. By focusing on what makes life worthwhile, it takes a human approach to understanding the needs of the people it serves.

By including diversity and agency, the Capability Approach can make significant contributions to policies that support healthy ageing. First, the Capability Approach can usefully broaden the policy focus from one on elders as dependent to one which supports autonomy and well-being. These are 21st century policy aims, and the Capability Approach provides a social justice perspective and a framework for change in accord with these aims. Second, using a capability framework can highlight gaps between the values and the actual experiences of older adults. This broader focus requires researchers to develop those methods which involve older people and establish their particular needs. Third, Sen's focus on 'capability', or the extent to which a person is able to function in a valued way, rather than on the functionings themselves, supports the core value of agency and recognises diversity. Thus, the Capability Approach supports a move away from policies that have oppressive or homogenising effects towards those that increase people's ability to be the sort of people they want to be and do the things that are valued in their society.

Kimberley et al. (2012) have provided a useful summary of the ways in which the Capability Approach has been used in policy. According to these authors, it has been influential in international development and increasingly popular among policy analysts for evaluation of progress. In the European Union and Australia, the Capability Approach has influenced a shift from a narrow focus on income to broader factors that constitute well-being, a focus on what people value, and increasing interest in disadvantage and social inclusion. However, these applications of the Capability Approach have been evaluative only and focused on functionings rather than capabilities, omitting assessment of agency or opportunity.

Furthermore, Kimberley et al. (2012) noted that policies and programs for older people in Australia remain

> generally underpinned by the traditional welfarist tenet of trying to "equalise" or "fairly" distribute quantities of resources. There is no explicit government recognition of the heterogeneity of older adults in the provision of services, nor recognition that equal allocation of resources (inputs) will often result in unequal outcomes in respect of achieved functionings (outputs) because people do not have access to the same "central human capabilities" due to the different constraints of their individual circumstances and their different values and ideas about what constitutes "a good life."
>
> *(p. 10)*

The World Health Organization's Global Report on Ageing and Health (2015) will be influential in developing global policies for healthy ageing. Drawing considerably on Sen's Capability Approach, the report defines "healthy ageing" as

> the process of developing and maintaining the functional ability that enables well-being in older age. Functional ability comprises the health related attributes that enable people to be and to do what they have reason to value. It is made up of the intrinsic capacity of the individual, relevant environmental characteristics and the interactions between the individual and these characteristics . . . Well-being is considered in the broadest sense and includes domains such as happiness, satisfaction and fulfilment.
>
> *(p. 29)*

Keating and Phillips (2017) suggest that this is a good beginning towards a focus on the environment, however, these broad suggestions for policy require development. In regard to the physical environment, Keating and Phillips have drawn on the notion of a good fit between a person and their environment in terms of critical human ecological theories which suggest that well-being itself is an indication of "'goodness of fit' between persons and contexts" (p. 7). They propose the development of the concept of 'liveability', saying that the "WHO definition of 'environment' requires refinement to incorporate liveability if it is to succeed in recognizing the opportunities and constraints of environments in which people live" (p. 13). Such an approach will enable recognition of diversity (of both people and places), challenge ageism, and include older people as active citizens, and reduce inequities while accounting for societal beliefs and structures.

The WHO policy framework and Keating and Phillips's (2017) work towards developing the environmental focus, by drawing on ecological theorising, provides good examples of the scope for application of the Capability Approach. In this book we have described the Capability Approach as a solution to the problems raised by popular frameworks that have had unintended effects of oppression, individualising responsibility, and denial of physical decline and death. We have provided examples of the ways in which the multiple aspects of quality of life in older age may be further understood in terms of relevant theoretical perspectives. Within the broad framework for social change that a capabilities approach offers, new and old ways of understanding the valued aspects of older people's lives may be drawn upon to inform research. The focus of research will be on identifying what people actually value, and the focus of policy and practice that follows will be to ensure that all older people are capable of achieving their values of healthy ageing.

REFERENCES

Addis, S., Davies, M., Greene, G., MacBride-Stewart, S., & Shepherd, M. (2009). The health, social care and housing needs of lesbian, gay, bisexual and transgender older people: A review of the literature. *Health & Social Care in the Community, 17*(6), 647–658.

Agich, G. J. (2003). *Dependence and autonomy in old age: An ethical framework for long term care.* Cambridge: Cambridge University Press.

Akiyama, H., Antonucci, T. C., & Campbell, R. (1997). Exchange and reciprocity among two generations of Japanese and American women. In J. Sokolovsky (Ed.), *The cultural context of aging: Worldwide perspectives.* (pp. 127–138). New York: Bergin and Garvey.

Albrecht, G. L., & Devlieger, P. J. (1999). The disability paradox: High quality of life against all odds. *Social Science & Medicine, 48*(8), 977–988.

Alkire, S. (2002). *Valuing freedoms: Sen's Capability Approach and poverty reduction.* Oxford: Oxford University Press.

Alkire, S. (2005a). *Capability and functionings: Definition and justification.* HDCA Briefing Note. Retrieved from www.capabilityapproach.com/pubs/HDCA_Briefing_Concepts.pdf

Alkire, S. (2005b). Why the Capability Approach? *Journal of Human Development, 6*(1), 115–135.

Alkire, S. (2007). Measuring freedoms alongside wellbeing. In I. Gough & J. A. McGregor (Eds.), *Wellbeing in developing countries: From theory to research* (pp. 93–108). Cambridge: Cambridge University Press.

Allen, R.E.S., & Wiles, J. L. (2013). The utility of positioning theory to the study of ageing: Examples from research with childless older people. *Journal of Aging Studies, 27*(2), 175–187.

Allmark, P., & Machaczek, K. (2015). Financial capability, health and disability. *BMC Public Health, 15*(1), 1–5.

Alstott, A. L. (2017). The new inequality of old age: Implications for law. *Theoretical Inquiries in Law, 18*(1), 111–124. https://doi.org/10.1515/til-2017-0007

Anand, P., & Van Hees, M. (2006). Capabilities and achievements: An empirical study. *The Journal of Socio-Economics, 35*(2), 268–284.

Anderson, N. D., Damianakis, T., Kröger, E., Wagner, L. M., Dawson, D. R., Binns, M. A., . . . Cook, S. L. (2014). The benefits associated with volunteering among seniors: A critical review and recommendations for future research. *Psychological Bulletin, 140*(6), 1505–1533.

Andrews, G. J., Gavin, N., Begley, S., & Brodie, D. (2003). Assisting friendships, combating loneliness: Users' views on a "befriending" scheme. *Ageing and Society, 23*(3), 349–362.

Andrews, M. (2009). The narrative complexity of successful ageing. *International Journal of Sociology and Social Policy, 29*(1/2), 73–83.

Angus, J., & Reeve, P. (2006). Ageism: A threat to "aging well" in the 21st century. *Journal of Applied Gerontology, 25*(2), 137–152.

Antonovsky, A. (1993). *The salutogenic approach to ageing.* Address to University of California, Berkeley, January 21. Retrieved from www.angelfire.com/ok/soc/a-berkeley.html

Antonucci, T. C. (2001). Social relations: An examination of social networks, social support, and sense of control. In J. E. Birren & K. W. Schaie (Eds.), *Handbook of the psychology of ageing* (pp. 427–453). San Diego: Academic Press.

Antonucci, T. C., Ajrouch, K. J., & Birditt, K. S. (2014). The convoy model: Explaining social relations from a multidisciplinary perspective. *The Gerontologist, 54*(1), 82–92.

Antonucci, T. C., Akiyama, H., & Takahashi, K. (2004). Attachment and close relationships across the life span. *Attachment & Human Development, 6*(4), 353–370.

Antonucci, T. C., Fuhrer, R., & Jackson, J. S. (1991). Social support and reciprocity: A cross-ethnic and cross-national perspective. *Journal of Social & Personal Relationships, 7,* 519–530.

Arneson, R. (2007). Distributive justice and basic capability equality. In A. Kaufman (Ed.), *Capabilities equality: Basic issues and problems* (pp. 17–43). New York and London: Routledge.

Ashton, J. (2015). Plants and green spaces provide more than just aesthetic benefits. *Perspectives in Public Health, 135*(4), 178–179.

Atchley, R. C. (1989). A continuity theory of normal aging. *The Gerontologist, 29*(2), 183–190. https://doi.org/10.1093/geront/29.2.183

Baglieri, M. (2012). Emotions, fear and security in Sen Nussbaum's Capability Approach. *Governare la Paura: Journal of Interdisciplinary Studies, 5*(1).

Bailly, N., Maître, I., & Wymelbeke, V. V. (2015). Relationships between nutritional status, depression and pleasure of eating in aging men and women. *Archives of Gerontology and Geriatrics, 61*(3), 330–336.

Baker, T. A., Buchanan, N. T., Mingo, C. A., Roker, R., & Brown, C. S. (2015). Reconceptualizing successful aging among black women and the relevance of the strong black woman archetype. *The Gerontologist, 55*(1), 51–57.

Balandin, S., Llewellyn, G., Dew, A., Ballin, L., & Schneider, J. (2006). Older disabled workers' perceptions of volunteering. *Disability & Society, 21*(7), 677–692.

Ball, M. M., Perkins, M. M., Whittington, F. J., Hollingsworth, C., King, S. V., & Combs, B. L. (2004). Independence in assisted living. *Journal of Aging Studies, 18*(4), 467–483. https://doi.org/10.1016/j.jaging.2004.06.002

Ballinger, C., & Payne, S. (2002). The construction of the risk of falling among and by older people. *Ageing and Society, 22*(3), 305–324.

Baltes, P. B. (1997). On the incomplete architecture of human ontogeny: Selection, optimization, and compensation as foundation of developmental theory. *American Psychologist, 52,* 366–380.

Baltes, P. B., & Baltes, M. M. (1990). Psychological perspectives on successful aging: The model of selective optimization with compensation. In P. B. Baltes & M. M. Baltes (Eds.), *Successful aging: Perspectives from the behavioral sciences* (Vol. 1, pp. 1–34). New York: Cambridge University Press.

Bamberg, M. (2011). Who am I? Narration and its contribution to self and identity. *Theory & Psychology, 21*(1), 3–24.

Banister, D., & Bowling, A. (2004). Quality of life for the elderly: The transport dimension. *Transport Policy, 11*(2), 105–115.

Bartlett, H., Warburton, J., Lui, C.-W., Peach, L., & Carroll, M. (2013). Preventing social isolation in later life: Findings and insights from a pilot Queensland intervention study. *Ageing and Society, 33*(7), 1167–1189.

Battaglia, A. M., & Metzer, J. (2000). Older adults and volunteering: A symbiotic association. *Australian Journal on Volunteering, 5*(1), 5–12.

BBC Business News (2013). Retirement 'harmful to health', study says. Retrieved from www.bbc.com/news/business-22550536

Becker, G. (2003). Meanings of place and displacement in three groups of older immigrants. *Journal of Aging Studies, 17*(2), 129–149.

Bennett, D. A., Schneider, J. A., Tang, Y. X., Arnold, S. E., & Wilson, R. S. (2006). The effect of social networks on the relation between Alzheimer's disease pathology and level of cognitive function in old people: A longitudinal cohort study. *Lancet Neurology, 5*(5), 406–412.

Berg, A. I., Hassing, L. B., Thorvaldsson, V., & Johansson, B. (2011). Personality and personal control make a difference for life satisfaction in the oldest-old: Findings in a longitudinal population-based study of individuals 80 and older. *European Journal of Ageing, 8*(1), 13–20.

Bergman-Evans, B. (2004). Beyond the basics: Effects of the Eden Alternative model on quality of life issues. *Journal of Gerontological Nursing, 30*(6), 27–34.

Berkman, L. F. (2000). Social support, social networks, social cohesion and health. *Social Work in Health Care, 31*(2), 3–15.

Berkman, L. F. (2009). Social epidemiology: Social determinants of health in the United States: Are we losing ground? *Annual Review of Public Health, 30*, 27–41.

Berkman, L. F., Glass, T., Brissette, I., & Seeman, T. E. (2000). From social integration to health: Durkheim in the new millennium. *Social Science & Medicine, 51*(6), 843–857.

Berks, J., & McCormick, R. (2008). Screening for alcohol misuse in elderly primary care patients: A systematic literature review. *International Psychogeriatrics, 20*(6), 1090–1103.

Bernard, S. (2013). *Loneliness and social isolation among older people in North Yorkshire: Stage 1 report.* SPRU Working Paper, WP256. Social Policy Research Unit, York. Retrieved from http://eprints.whiterose.ac.uk/77335/

Berridge, C. (2012). Envisioning a gerontology-enriched theory of care. *Affilia, 27*(1), 8–21.

Biggs, S. (2001). Toward critical narrativity: Stories of aging in contemporary social policy. *Journal of Aging Studies, 15*(4), 303–316.

Biggs, S. (2005). Beyond appearances: Perspectives on identity in later life and some implications for method. *Journals of Gerontology: Series B Psychological Sciences and Social Sciences, 60*(3), S118–S128.

Biggs, S., McGann, M., Bowman, D., & Kimberley, H. (2017). Work, health and the commodification of life's time: Reframing work-life balance and the promise of a long life. *Ageing & Society, 37*(7), 1458–1483.

Bin-Sallik, M. A., & Ranzijn, R. (2001). *Report on a scoping study into the needs of indigenous aged care in South Australia.* Adelaide: The College of Indigenous Education, University of South Australia. Retrieved from www.sapo.org.au

Binstock, R. H. (2010). From compassionate ageism to intergenerational conflict? *Gerontologist, 50*(5), 574–585.

Birkbeck, D. (2014). "Happy meals": Finding happiness with Hans Becker and the Humanitas care model. *Architectural Design, 84*(2), 94–101.

Bowling, A. (2007). Aspirations for older age in the 21st century: What is successful aging? *International Journal of Aging & Human Development, 64*(3), 263–297.

Bowling, A., & Dieppe, P. (2005). What is successful ageing and who should define it? *British Medical Journal, 331*(7531), 1548–1551.

Bowling, A., & Gabriel, Z. (2004). Integrational model of quality of life in older age: Results from the ESRC/MRC HSRC quality of life survey in Britain. *Social Indicators Research, 69*(1), 1–36.

Bowling, A., & Gabriel, Z. (2007). Lay theories of quality of life in older age. *Ageing and Society, 27*(6), 827–848.

Bowling, A., Seetai, S., Morris, R., & Ebrahim, S. (2007). Quality of life among older people with poor functioning: The influence of perceived control over life. *Age and Ageing, 36*(3), 310–315.

Bowling, A., & Stafford, M. (2007). How do objective and subjective assessments of neighbourhood influence social and physical functioning in older age? Findings from a British survey of ageing. *Social Science & Medicine, 64*(12), 2533–2549.

Breheny, M. (2017). Older people, inequalities and the lessons of universality. In S. Groot, C. Van Ommen, B. Masters-Awatere, & N. Tassell-Matamua (Eds.), *On shaky ground: Precariat lives in Aotearoa New Zealand*. Auckland: Massey University Press.

Breheny, M., & Stephens, C. (2009). "I sort of pay back in my own little way": Managing independence and social connectedness through reciprocity. *Ageing and Society, 29*(8), 1295–1313.

Breheny, M., & Stephens, C. (2010). Ageing in a material world. *New Zealand Journal of Psychology, 39*(2), 41–48.

Breheny, M., & Stephens, C. (2012). Negotiating a moral identity in the context of later life care. *Journal of Aging Studies, 26*(4), 438–447.

Breheny, M., & Stephens, C. (2017). Spending time: The discursive construction of leisure in later life. *Annals of Leisure Research, 20*(1), 39–54.

Brownie, S. (2011). A culture change in aged care: The Eden Alternative(TM). *Australian Journal of Advanced Nursing, 29*(1), 63–68.

Bryant, L. L., Corbett, K. K., & Kutner, J. S. (2001). In their own words: A model of healthy aging. *Social Science & Medicine, 53*(7), 927–941.

Buffel, T., Phillipson, C., & Scharf, T. (2012). Ageing in urban environments: Developing "age-friendly" cities. *Critical Social Policy, 32*(4), 597–617.

Burchardt, T., & Vizard, P. (2011). "Operationalizing" the capability approach as a basis for equality and human rights monitoring in twenty-first century Britain. *Journal of Human Development and Capabilities, 12*(1), 91–119.

Burden, J. (1999). Leisure as process and change: What do older people say? *Annals of Leisure Research, 2*(1), 28–43.

Burr, J. A., Caro, F. G., & Moorhead, J. (2002). Productive aging and civic participation. *Journal of Aging Studies, 16*(1), 87–105.

Burr, J. A., Tavares, J., & Mutchler, J. E. (2011). Volunteering and hypertension risk in later life. *Journal of Aging and Health, 23*(1), 24–51.

Butcher, E., & Breheny, M. (2016). Dependence on place: A source of autonomy in later life for older Māori. *Journal of Aging Studies, 37*, 48–58.

Buys, L., & Miller, E. (2006). *The meaning of "active ageing" to older Australians: Exploring the relative importance of health, participation and security*. Paper presented at the 39th Australian Association of Gerontology Conference, Sydney.

Calasanti, T. (1999). Feminism and gerontology: Not just for women. *Hallym International Journal of Aging, 1*(1), 44–55.

Calasanti, T. (2007). Bodacious berry, potency wood and the aging monster: Gender and age relations in anti-aging ads. *Social Forces, 86*(1), 335–355.

Calvo, E., & Williamson, J. B. (2008). Old-age pension reform and modernization pathways: Lessons for China from Latin America. *Journal of Aging Studies, 22*(1), 74–87.

Camic, P. M., & Chatterjee, H. J. (2013). Museums and art galleries as partners for public health interventions. *Perspectives in Public Health, 133*(1), 66–71.

Cannuscio, C., Block, J., & Kawachi, I. (2003). Social capital and successful aging: The role of senior housing. *Annals of Internal Medicine, 139*(5), 395–399.

Carder, P. C. (2002). The social world of assisted living. *Journal of Aging Studies, 16*(1), 1–18.

Carr, K., Weir, P. L., Azar, D., & Azar, N. R. (2013). Universal design: A step toward successful aging. *Journal of Aging Research*, Article ID 324624, 8 pages. https://doi.org/10.1155/2013/324624

Carstensen, L. L. (1995). Evidence for a life-span theory of socioemotional selectivity. *Current Directions in Psychological Science, 4*(5), 151–156.

Carstensen, L. L. (2006). The influence of a sense of time on human development. *Science, 312*(5782), 1913–1915.

Carstensen, L. L., Isaacowitz, D. M., & Charles, S. T. (1999). Taking time seriously: A theory of socioemotional selectivity. *American Psychologist, 54*(3), 165–181.

Cattan, M., Hogg, E., & Hardill, I. (2011). Improving quality of life in ageing populations: What can volunteering do? *Maturitas, 70*(4), 328–332.

Cattan, M., Newell, C., Bond, J., & White, M. (2003). Alleviating social isolation and loneliness among older people. *International Journal of Mental Health Promotion, 5*(3), 20–30.

Cattan, M., White, M., Bond, J., & Learmouth, A. (2005). Preventing social isolation and loneliness among older people: A systematic review of health promotion interventions. *Ageing & Society, 25*(1), 41–67.

Chan, C.M.A., & Liang, J.S.E. (2013). Active aging: Policy framework and applications to promote older adult participation in Hong Kong. *Ageing International, 38*(1), 28–42.

Chandola, T., Ferrie, J., Sacker, A., & Marmot, M. (2007). Social inequalities in self reported health in early old age: Follow-up of prospective cohort study [see comment]. *BMJ, 334*(7601), 990.

Chapman, S. A. (2005). Theorizing about aging well: Constructing a narrative. *Canadian Journal on Aging, 24*(1), 9–18.

Cho, J., Cook, C., & Bruin, M. J. (2012). Functional ability, neighborhood resources and housing satisfaction among older adults in the US. *Journal of Housing for the Elderly, 26*(4), 395–412.

Clarke, L. H., Griffin, M., & Team, P. R. (2008). Failing bodies: Body image and multiple chronic conditions in later life. *Qualitative Health Research, 18*(8), 1084–1095.

Clarke, P., & Nieuwenhuijsen, E. R. (2009). Environments for healthy ageing: A critical review. *Maturitas, 64*, 14–19.

Coburn, D. (2000). Income inequality, social cohesion and the health status of populations: The role of neo-liberalism. *Social Science & Medicine, 51*(1), 135–146.

Coleman, M. T., Looney, S., O'Brien, J., Ziegler, C., Pastorino, C. A., & Turner, C. (2002). The Eden Alternative: Findings after 1 year of implementation. *The Journals of Gerontology Series A: Biological Sciences and Medical Sciences, 57*(7), M422–M427.

Colic-Peisker, V., Ong, R., & Wood, G. (2015). Asset poverty, precarious housing and ontological security in older age: An Australian case study. *International Journal of Housing Policy, 15*(2), 167–186.

Collings, P. (2001). "If you got everything, it's good enough": Perspectives on successful aging in a Canadian Inuit community. *Journal of Cross-Cultural Gerontology, 16*(2), 127.

Collins, A. B., & Wrigley, J. (2014). *Can a neighbourhood approach to loneliness contribute to people's wellbeing*? York: Joseph Rowntree Foundation.

Collins, R. (2004). *Interaction ritual chains*. Princeton, NJ: Princeton University Press.

Comim, F. (2001). *Operationalizing Sen's Capability Approach*. Paper presented at Conference, *Justice and Poverty*, Cambridge, June 5–7. Retrieved from http://192.203.177.38/humanismocristiano/seminario_capability/pdf/7.pdf

Costa-Font, J., Mascarilla-Miró, O., & Elvira, D. (2009). Ageing in place? Exploring elderly people's housing preferences in Spain. *Urban Studies, 46*(2), 295–316.

Craciun, C., & Flick, U. (2015). "I want to be 100 years old, but I smoke too much": Exploring the gap between positive aging goals and reported preparatory actions in different social circumstances. *Journal of Aging Studies, 35*, 49–54.

Craciun, C., & Flick, U. (2016). Aging in precarious times: Exploring the role of gender in shaping views on aging. *Journal of Women and Aging, 28*(6), 530–539.

Crawford, R. (1980). Healthism and the medicalization of everyday life. *International Journal of Health Services, 10*(3), 365–388.

Crawford, R. (2006). Health as a meaningful social practice. *Health, 10*(4), 401–420.

Creech, A., Hallam, S., McQueen, H., & Varvarigou, M. (2013). The power of music in the lives of older adults. *Research Studies in Music Education, 35*(1), 87–102.

Crocker, D. A. (2007). Deliberative participation in local development. *Journal of Human Development, 8*(3), 431–455.

Crooks, V. C., Lubben, J., Petitti, D. B., Little, D., & Chiu, V. (2008). Social network, cognitive function, and dementia incidence among elderly women. *American Journal of Public Health, 98*(7), 1221–1227.

Crowther, M. R., Parker, M. W., Achenbaum, W. A., Larimore, W. L., & Koenig, H. G. (2002). Rowe and Kahn's model of successful aging revisited: Positive spirituality – The forgotten factor. *The Gerontologist, 42*(5), 613–620.

Cummins, R. A. (1997). Assessing quality of life *Quality of life for people with disabilities: Models, research and practice* (Vol. 2, pp. 116–150). Cheltenham, UK: Stanley Thornes.

Dale, B., Söderhamn, U., & Söderhamn, O. (2012). Life situation and identity among single older home-living people: A phenomenological–hermeneutic study. *International Journal of Qualitative Studies on Health and Well-Being, 7*(1), 18456.

Darab, S., & Hartman, Y. (2013). Understanding single older women's invisibility in housing issues in Australia. *Housing, Theory and Society, 30*(4), 348–367.

Davey, J. A. (2006). "Aging in Place": The views of older homeowners on maintenance, renovation and adaptation. *Social Policy Journal of New Zealand, 27*, 128–141.

Davey, J. A. (2007). Older people and transport: Coping without a car. *Ageing and Society, 27*(1), 49–65.

Dean, H. (2009). Critiquing capabilities: The distractions of a beguiling concept. *Critical Social Policy, 29*(2), 261–278.

De Donder, L., De Witte, N., Buffel, T., Dury, S., & Verté, D. (2012). Social capital and feelings of unsafety in later life a study on the influence of social networks, place attachment, and civic participation on perceived safety in Belgium. *Research on Aging, 34*(4), 425–448.

Department of Work & Pensions. (2012). *Pension Reform*. Retrieved from www.dwp.gov.uk/policy/pensions-reform/

Depp, C. A., & Jeste, D. V. (2006). Definitions and predictors of successful aging: A comprehensive review of larger quantitative studies. *American Journal of Geriatric Psychiatry, 14*(1), 6–20.

Depp, C. A., Schkade, D. A., Thompson, W. K., & Jeste, D. V. (2010). Age, affective experience, and television use. *American Journal of Preventive Medicine, 39*(2), 173–178.

Devins, G. M. (2010). Using the Illness Intrusiveness Ratings Scale to understand health-related quality of life in chronic disease. *Journal of Psychosomatic Research, 68*(6), 591–602.

Dewsbury, G., Clarke, K., Randall, D., Rouncefield, M., & Sommerville, I. (2004). The anti-social model of disability. *Disability & Society, 19*(2), 145–158.

Dickens, A. P., Richards, S. H., Greaves, C. J., & Campbell, J. L. (2011). Interventions targeting social isolation in older people: A systematic review. *BMC Public Health, 11*(1). Retrieved from www.biomedcentral.com/1471-2458/1411/1647

Dixey, R. (2013). *Health promotion: Global principles and practice.* London: CABI.

Doets, E. L., & Kremer, S. (2016). The silver sensory experience: A review of senior consumers' food perception, liking and intake. *Food Quality and Preference, 48,* 316–332.

Dolan, P., Kudrna, L., & Stone, A. (2017). The measure matters: An investigation of evaluative and experience-based measures of wellbeing in time use data. *Social Indicators Research, 134*(1), 57–73.

Dorfman, L. T. (2013). Leisure activities in retirement. In M. Wang (Ed.), *The Oxford handbook of retirement* (pp. 339–353). New York: Oxford University Press.

Downes, S. (2013). The Eden Principles in dementia respite care: Carers' experience. *Quality in Ageing and Older Adults, 14*(2), 105–115.

Downs, M. (2015). *Person centred care in the community* (No. 978-1-907711-33-6). GENIO. Retrieved from http://hdl.handle.net/10147/612287

Draper, H., & Sorell, T. (2016). Ethical values and social care robots for older people: An international qualitative study. *Ethics and Information Technology,* 1–20.

D'Souza, J. C., James, M. L., Szafara, K. L., & Fries, B. E. (2009). Hard times: The effects of financial strain on home care services use and participant outcomes in Michigan. *The Gerontologist, 49*(2), 154–165.

Duay, D. L., & Bryan, V. C. (2006). Senior adults' perceptions of successful aging. *Educational Gerontology, 32*(6), 423–445.

Dulin, P. L., Gavala, J., Stephens, C., Kostick, M., & McDonald, J. (2012). Volunteering predicts happiness among older Maori and non-Maori in the New Zealand health, work, and retirement longitudinal study. *Aging & Mental Health, 16*(5), 617–624.

Dunn, H., & Moore, T. (2016). "You can't be forcing food down 'em": Nursing home carers' perceptions of residents' dining needs. *Journal of Health Psychology, 21*(5), 619–627.

Dupuis, S. L., & Alzheimer, M. (2008). Leisure and ageing well. *World Leisure Journal, 50*(2), 91–107.

Durie, M. H. (1985). A Maori perspective of health. *Social Science & Medicine, 20*(5), 483–486.

Durie, M. H. (1999). Kaumātautanga Reciprocity: Māori elderly and whānau. *New Zealand Journal of Psychology, 28*(2), 102–106.

Dyall, L., Kepa, M., Teh, R., Mules, R., Moyes, S. A., Wham, C., . . . Kerse, N. (2014). Cultural and social factors and quality of life of Maori in advanced age: Te puawaitanga o nga tapuwae kia ora tonu – Life and living in advanced age: A cohort study in New Zealand (LiLACS NZ). *New Zealand Medical Journal, 127*(1393), 62–79.

Edwards, W. (2010). *Taupaenui: Maori positive ageing.* (PhD thesis), Massey University, Palmerston North.

Ekerdt, D. J. (2004). Born to retire: The foreshortened life course. *The Gerontologist, 44*(1), 3–9.

Emlet, C. A., & Moceri, J. T. (2012). The importance of social connectedness in building age-friendly communities. *Journal of Aging Research,* 9.

English, T., & Carstensen, L. L. (2014). Selective narrowing of social networks across adulthood is associated with improved emotional experience in daily life. *International Journal of Behavioral Development, 38*(2), 195–202.

Estes, C. L., Biggs, S., & Phillipson, C. (2003). *Social theory, social policy and ageing: A critical introduction.* Maidenhead: Open University Press.

Estes, C. L., & Binney, E. A. (1989). The biomedicalization of aging: Dangers and dilemmas. *The Gerontologist, 29*(5), 587–596.

Estes, C. L., Swan, J. H., & Gerard, L. E. (1982). Dominant and competing paradigms in gerontology: Towards a political economy of ageing. *Ageing and Society, 2*(2), 151–164.

Evans, G. W., Kantrowitz, E., & Eshelman, P. (2002). Housing quality and psychological well-being among the elderly population. *The Journals of Gerontology: Series B, 57*(4), P381–P383.

Evans, S., Fear, T., Means, R., & Vallelly, S. (2007). Supporting independence for people with dementia in extra care housing. *Dementia, 6*(1), 144–150.

Fabbre, V. D. (2015). Gender transitions in later life: A queer perspective on successful aging. *The Gerontologist, 55*(1), 144–153.

Fang, M. L., Woolrych, R., Sixsmith, J., Canham, S., Battersby, L., & Sixsmith, A. (2016). Place-making with older persons: Establishing sense-of-place through participatory community mapping workshops. *Social Science and Medicine, 168*, 223–229.

Farquhar, M. (1995). Elderly peoples definitions of quality-of-life. *Social Science & Medicine, 41*(10), 1439–1446.

Fealy, G., McNamara, M., Treacy, M. P., & Lyons, I. (2012). Constructing ageing and age identities: A case study of newspaper discourses. *Ageing and Society, 32*, 85–102.

Ferreira, H. G., Barham, E. J., & Fontaine, A.M.G.V. (2015). A measure to assess elderly Brazilians' involvement in pleasant activities: Initial evidence of internal and external validity. *Clinical Gerontologist, 38*(5), 375–394.

Fetherstonhaugh, D., Tarzia, L., & Nay, R. (2013). Being central to decision making means I am still here!: The essence of decision making for people with dementia. *Journal of Aging Studies, 27*(2), 143–150.

Fildes, D., Cass, Y., Wallner, F., & Owen, A. (2010). Shedding light on men: The Building Healthy Men Project. *Journal of Men's Health, 7*(3), 233–240.

Findlay, R. A. (2003). Interventions to reduce social isolation amongst older people: Where is the evidence? *Ageing and Society, 23*(5), 647–658.

Fine, M., & Glendinning, C. (2005). Dependence, independence or inter-dependence? Revisiting the concepts of "care" and "dependency." *Ageing and Society, 25*(4), 601–621.

Fischer, L. R., Mueller, D. P., & Cooper, P. W. (1991). Older volunteers: A discussion of the Minnesota senior study. *The Gerontologist, 31*(2), 183–194.

Fisk, M., & Abbott, S. (1998). Older people and the meaning of independence. *Generations Review, 8*(2), 9–11.

Foster, L., & Walker, A. (2015). Active and successful aging: A European policy perspective. *The Gerontologist, 55*(1), 83–90.

Fox O'Mahony, L. (2012). *Home equity and ageing owners: Between risk and regulation.* Oxford: Bloomsbury Publishing.

Foye, C., Clapham, D., & Gabrieli, T. (2017). Home-ownership as a social norm and positional good: Subjective wellbeing evidence from panel data. *Urban Studies.* https://doi.org/10.1177/0042098017695478

Franco, O. H., Karnik, K., Osborne, G., Ordovas, J. M., Catt, M., & van der Ouderaa, F. (2009). Changing course in ageing research: The healthy ageing phenotype. *Maturitas, 63*(1), 13–19.

Frawley, A. (2015). Happiness research: A review of critiques. *Sociology Compass, 9*(1), 62–77.

Friedan, B. (1994). *The Fountain of Age.* London: Vintage.

Funk, L. M. (2012). "Returning the love," not "balancing the books": Talk about delayed reciprocity in supporting ageing parents. *Ageing and Society, 32*, 634–654.

Gabriel, Z., & Bowling, A. (2004). Quality of life from the perspectives of older people. *Ageing and Society, 24*(5), 675–691.

Gale, C. R., Baylis, D., Cooper, C., & Sayer, A. A. (2013). Inflammatory markers and incident frailty in men and women: The English Longitudinal Study of Ageing. *Age, 35*(6), 2493–2501.

Galvin, R. (2002). Disturbing notions of chronic illness and individual responsibility: Towards a genealogy of morals. *Health, 6*(2), 107–137.

Gasper, D., & van Staveren, I. (2003). Development as freedom: And as what else? *Feminist Economics, 9*(2–3), 137–161.

Gasperi, D., Giorgio Bazzocchi, G., Bertocchi, I., Ramazzotti, S., & Gianquinto, G. (2015). The multifunctional role of urban gardens in the twentieth century: The Bologna case study. *Acta Horticulturae, 1093*, 91–98.

Gawande, A. (2014). *Being mortal: Medicine and what matters in the end* (1st ed.). New York: Metropolitan Books, Henry Holt & Company.

Gerrans, P., Clark-Murphy, M., & Speelman, C. (2010). Asset allocation and age effects in retirement savings choices. *Accounting & Finance, 50*(2), 301–319.

Giddens, A. (1991). *Modernity and self-identity: Self and society in the late modern age.* Cambridge: Polity Press.

Gilbert, T., & Powell, J. L. (2005). Family, caring and aging in the UK. *Scandinavian Journal of Caring Sciences, 41*(2), 41–48.

Gilbertson, J., Stevens, M., Stiell, B., & Thorogood, N. (2006). Home is where the hearth is: Grant recipients' views of England's Home Energy Efficiency Scheme (Warm Front). *Social Science and Medicine, 63*(4), 946–956.

Giles, L. C., Glonek, G.F.V., Luszcz, M. A., & Andrews, G. R. (2005). Effect of social networks on 10 year survival in very old Australians: The Australian longitudinal study of aging. *Journal of Epidemiology and Community Health, 59*(7), 574–579.

Gilleard, C., & Higgs, P. (2000). *Cultures of ageing: Self, citizen and the body.* Harlow, England: Pearson Education Ltd.

Gilroy, R. (2008). Places that support human flourishing: Lessons from later life. *Planning Theory and Practice, 9*(2), 145–163.

Glass, A. P. (2013). Lessons learned from a new elder cohousing community. *Journal of Housing for the Elderly, 27*(4), 348–368.

Glass, A. P. (2014). Innovative seniors housing and care models: What we can learn from the Netherlands. *Seniors Housing & Care Journal, 22*(1), 74–81.

Gouldner, A. W. (1960). The norm of reciprocity: A preliminary statement. *American Sociological Review, 25*(2), 161–178.

Graham, V., & Tuffin, K. (2004). Retirement villages: Companionship, privacy and security. *Australasian Journal on Ageing, 23*(4), 184–188.

Grant, B. C. (2006). Retirement villages: An alternative form of housing on an ageing landscape. *Social Policy Journal of New Zealand, 27*, 100–113.

Greenfield, E. A., & Marks, N. F. (2004). Formal volunteering as a protective factor for older adults' psychological well-being. *The Journals of Gerontology Series B: Psychological Sciences and Social Sciences, 59*(5), S258–S264.

Grewal, I., Lewis, J., Flynn, T., Brown, J., Bond, J., & Coast, J. (2006). Developing attributes for a generic quality of life measure for older people: Preferences or capabilities? *Social Science & Medicine, 62*(8), 1891–1901.

Grimm, R., Spring, K., & Dietz, N. (2007). *The health benefits of volunteering: A review of recent research.* New York, NY: Corporation for National & Community Service, Office of Research and Policy Development.

Grohmann, B., Gucciardi, E., & Espin, S. (2015). Patients' perspectives of the integration of diabetes self-management training in primary care using principles of person centred care. *Canadian Journal of Dietetic Practice & Research, 76*(3), 8–9.

Ha, J.-H., Kahng, S. K., & Choi, N. (2017). Reciprocal effects between health and social support in older adults' relationships with their children and friends. *Research on Aging, 39*(2), 300–321.

Haak, M., Ivanoff, S. D., Fänge, A., Sixsmith, J., & Iwarsson, S. (2007). Home as the locus and origin for participation: Experiences among very old Swedish people. *OTJR: Occupation, Participation and Health, 27*(3), 95–103.

Hagemann, S., & Scherger, S. (2016). Increasing pension age: Inevitable or unfeasible? Analysing the ideas underlying experts' arguments in the UK and Germany. *Journal of Aging Studies, 39*, 54–65.

Hammarström, G., & Torres, S. (2010). Being, feeling and acting: A qualitative study of Swedish home-help care recipients' understandings of dependence and independence. *Journal of Aging Studies, 24*(2), 75–87.

Hanratty, B., Lowson, E., Holmes, L., Grande, G., Addington-Hall, J., Payne, S., & Seymour, J. (2012). Funding health and social services for older people: A qualitative study of care recipients in the last year of life. *Journal of the Royal Society of Medicine, 105*(5), 201–207.

Harris, A. H., & Thoresen, C. E. (2005). Volunteering is associated with delayed mortality in older people: Analysis of the longitudinal study of aging. *Journal of Health Psychology, 10*(6), 739–752.

Health Canada. (2002). Workshop on healthy aging 2001. Ottawa: Minister of Public Works and Government Services Canada.

Heenan, D. (2011). How local interventions can build capacity to address social isolation in dispersed rural communities: A case study from Northern Ireland. *Ageing International, 36*(4), 475–491.

Hellevik, O. (2017). The U-shaped age-happiness relationship: Real or methodological artifact? *Quality & Quantity, 51*(1), 177–197.

Herd, A., Street, A., & Wells, Y. (2016). *Hearing older people's voices: What matters in housing design?* Paper presented at the International Federation on Ageing 13th Global Conference on Ageing, Brisbane, Australia. Retrieved from www.ifa-fiv.org/wp-content/uploads/2016/07/Tue-P2-1130-Herd.pdf

Hershey, D. A., Henkens, K., & van Dalen, H. P. (2010). What drives retirement income worries in Europe? A multilevel analysis. *European Journal of Ageing, 7*(4), 301–311.

Higgs, P., Hyde, M., Wiggins, R., & Blane, D. (2003). Researching quality of life in early old age: The importance of the sociological dimension. *Social Policy & Administration, 37*(3), 239–252.

Hillcoat-Nallétamby, S., & Ogg, J. (2014). Moving beyond "ageing in place": Older people's dislikes about their home and neighbourhood environments as a motive for wishing to move. *Ageing and Society, 34*(10), 1771–1796.

Hilton, J. M., Gonzalez, C. A., Saleh, M., Maitoza, R., & Anngela-Cole, L. (2012). Perceptions of successful aging among older Latinos, in cross-cultural context. *Journal of Cross-Cultural Gerontology, 27*(3), 183–199.

Hiscock, R., Kearns, A., MacIntyre, S., & Ellaway, A. (2001). Ontological security and psycho-social benefits from the home: Qualitative evidence on issues of tenure. *Housing, Theory and Society, 18*(1–2), 50–66.

Ho, A. (2008). Relational autonomy or undue pressure? Family's role in medical decision-making. *Scandinavian Journal of Caring Sciences, 22*(1), 128–135.

Hoagland, S. L. (1988). *Lesbian ethics: Towards new values.* Palo Alto, CA: Institute of Lesbian Studies.

Hodgetts, D., Chamberlain, K., & Bassett, G. (2003). Between television and the audience: Negotiating representations of ageing. *Health (London), 7*(4), 417–438.

Hogan, M. J., Leyden, K. M., Conway, R., Goldberg, A., Walsh, D., & McKenna-Plumley, P. E. (2016). Happiness and health across the lifespan in five major cities: The impact of place and government performance. *Social Science and Medicine, 162*, 168–176.

Holstein, M. B., & Minkler, M. (2003). Self, society, and the "new gerontology." *The Gerontologist, 43*(6), 787–796.

Holt-Lunstad, J., Smith, T. B., Baker, M., Harris, T., & Stephenson, D. (2015). Loneliness and social isolation as risk factors for mortality a meta-analytic review. *Perspectives on Psychological Science, 10*(2), 227–237.

Holt-Lunstad, J., Smith, T. B., & Layton, J. B. (2010). Social relationships and mortality risk: A meta-analytic review. *PLoS Med, 7*(7), e1000316.

Hong, S.-I., Morrow-Howell, N., Tang, F., & Hinterlong, J. (2009). Engaging older adults in volunteering: Conceptualizing and measuring institutional capacity. *Nonprofit and Voluntary Sector Quarterly, 38*(2), 200–219.

Horrell, B., Stephens, C., & Breheny, M. (2015). Capability to care: Supporting the health of informal caregivers for older people. *Health Psychology, 34*(4), 339–348.

Houben, P.P.J. (2000). Towards a conceptual framework for "ageing in place" in frail older adults. *European Journal of Social Quality, 2*(1), 47–66.

Houben, P.P.J. (2001). Changing housing for older people and co-ordination issues in Europe. *Housing Studies, 16*(5), 651–673.

Howden-Chapman, P., Signal, L., & Crane, J. (1999). Housing and health in older people: Ageing in place. *Social Policy Journal of New Zealand, 13*, 14–30.

Hughes, B., & Paterson, K. (1997). The social model of disability and the disappearing body: Towards a sociology of impairment. *Disability & Society, 12*(3), 325–340.

Huisman, M., Kunst, A. E., Andersen, O., Bopp, M., Borgan, J.-K., Borrell, C., . . . Mackenbach, J. P. (2004). Socioeconomic inequalities in mortality among elderly people in 11 European populations. *Journal of Epidemiology and Community Health, 58*(6), 468–475.

Humpage, L. (2007). Models of disability, work and welfare in Australia. *Social Policy & Administration, 41*(3), 215–231.

Hurley, K., Breheny, M., & Tuffin, K. (2015). Intergenerational inequity arguments and the implications for state-funded financial support of older people. *Ageing and Society, 37*(3), 561–580.

Hyde, M., Wiggins, R. D., Higgs, P., & Blane, D. B. (2003). A measure of quality of life in early old age: the theory, development and properties of a needs satisfaction model (CASP-19). *Aging & Mental Health, 7*(3), 186–194.

Iecovich, E., & Biderman, A. (2013). Attendance in adult day care centers of cognitively intact older persons: Reasons for use and nonuse. *Journal of Applied Gerontology, 32*(5), 561–581.

International Federation on Ageing. (1999). *International Federation on Ageing.* The Montreal Declaration. Retrieved from www.ifa-fiv.org/wp-content/uploads/2012/11/057_IFA-Montreal-Declaration.pdf

Iwamasa, G., & Iwasaki, M. (2011). A new multidimensional model of successful aging: Perceptions of Japanese American older adults. *Journal of Cross-Cultural Gerontology, 26*(3), 261–278.

Iwarsson, S., Wahl, H.-W., Nygren, C., Oswald, F., Sixsmith, A., Sixsmith, J., . . . Tomsone, S. (2007). Importance of the home environment for healthy aging: Conceptual and methodological background of the European ENABLE–AGE project. *The Gerontologist, 47*(1), 78–84.

James, I., Ardeman-Merten, R., & Kihlgren, A. (2014). Ontological security in nursing homes for older persons: Person-centred care is the power of balance. *The Open Nursing Journal, 8*, 79–87.

James, J. B., Matz-Costa, C., & Smyer, M. A. (2016). Retirement security: It's not just about the money. *American Psychologist, 71*(4), 334–344.

Jatrana, S., & Blakely, T. (2008). Ethnic inequalities in mortality among the elderly in New Zealand. *Australian and New Zealand Journal of Public Health, 32*(5), 437–443.

Johnson, T. F. (1995). Aging well in contemporary society: Introduction. *American Behavioral Scientist, 39*(2), 120–130.

Jones, I. R., Gilleard, C., Higgs, P., & Day, G. (2016). *Connectivity, place and elective belonging: Community and later life.* Arts and Humanities Research Council, UK: AHRC. Retrieved from www.ahrc.ac.uk/documents/project-reports-and-reviews/connected-communities/connectivity-place-and-elective-belonging-community-and-later-life/

Jopling, K. (2015). *Promising approaches to reducing loneliness and isolation in later life.* London: Age UK.

Kane, R. A., Wilson, K. B., & Spector, W. (2007). Developing a research agenda for assisted living. *The Gerontologist, 47*(suppl 1), 141–154.

Kastenbaum, R. J. (2015). *Death, society, and human experience.* London and New York: Routledge.

Katz, S., & Calasanti, T. (2015). Critical perspectives on successful aging: Does it "appeal more than it illuminates"? *The Gerontologist, 55*(1), 26–33.

Katz, S., & Marshall, B. (2003). New sex for old: Lifestyle, consumerism, and the ethics of aging well. *Journal of Aging Studies, 17*(1), 3–16.

Keating, N., Eales, J., & Phillips, J. E. (2013). Age-friendly rural communities: Conceptualizing "best-fit." *Canadian Journal on Aging/La Revue canadienne du vieillissement, 32*(4), 319–332.

Keating, N., & Phillips, J. E. (2017). *Global issues in ageing and health: Policy challenges from the World Health Organization.* Retrieved from www.massey.ac.nz/?sccc13309s

Kemp, C. L., & Denton, M. (2003). The allocation of responsibility for later life: Canadian reflections on the roles of individuals, government, employers and families. *Ageing & Society, 23*(6), 737–760.

Kenyon, G. M., Clark, P. G., & De Vries, B. (2001). *Narrative gerontology: Theory, research, and practice.* New York: Springer Publishing Company, Inc.

Kimberley, H., Gruhn, R., & Huggins, S. (2012). *Valuing capabilities in later life: The capability approach and the Brotherhood of St Laurence aged services.* Fitzroy, VA Australia: Brotherhood of St Laurence.

Kinnvall, C. (2017). Feeling ontologically (in)secure: States, traumas and the governing of gendered space. *Cooperation and Conflict, 52*(1), 90–108.

Klee, D., Mordey, M., Phuare, S., & Russell, C. (2014). Asset based community development—enriching the lives of older citizens. *Working with Older People, 18*(3), 111–119.

Klein, D. (2012). *Travels with Epicurus: A journey to a Greek island in search of an authentic old age.* The Text Publishing Company. Kindle Edition.

Koh, L. (Producer). (2016, October 16). *Old strategies to fund retirement won't cut it anymore.* Retrieved from www.stuff.co.nz/business/83990150/old-strategies-to-fund-retirement-wont-cut-it-anymore

Kohli, M., Hank, K., & Kunemund, H. (2009). The social connectedness of older Europeans: Patterns, dynamics and contexts. *Journal of European Social Policy, 19*(4), 327–340.

Kolb, P. (2014). *Understanding aging and diversity: Theories and concepts.* New York: Routledge.

Komter, A. E. (1996). Reciprocity as a principle of exclusion: Gift giving in the Netherlands. *Sociology, 30*(2), 299–316.

Krause, N., Newsom, J. T., & Rook, K. S. (2008). Financial strain, negative social interaction, and self-rated health: Evidence from two United States nationwide longitudinal surveys. *Ageing and Society, 28*(7), 1001–1023.

Kullberg, K., Björklund, A., Sidenvall, B., & Åberg, A. C. (2011). "I start my day by think-ing about what we're going to have for dinner": A qualitative study on approaches to food-related activities among elderly men with somatic disease. *Scandinavian Journal of Caring Sciences, 25*(2), 227–234.

Kumar, S., & Oakley Browne, M. A. (2008). Usefulness of the construct of social network to explain mental health service utilization by the Maori population in New Zealand. *Transcultural Psychiatry, 45*(3), 439–454.

La Grow, S. J., Yeung, P., Alpass, F., & Stephens, C. (2015). The relationship between loneliness and perceived quality of life among older persons with visual impairments. *Journal of Visual Impairment & Blindness, 109*(6), 478–499.

Laliberte Rudman, D. (2006). Shaping the active, autonomous and responsible modern retiree: An analysis of discursive technologies and their links with neo-liberal political rational-ity. *Ageing and Society, 26*(2), 181–201. https://doi.org/10.1017/S0144686X05004253

Laliberte Rudman, D. (2015). Embodying positive aging and neoliberal rationality: Talking about the aging body within narratives of retirement. *Journal of Aging Studies, 34*, 10–20.

Lamb, S. (2014). Permanent personhood or meaningful decline? Toward a critical anthro-pology of successful aging. *Journal of Aging Studies, 29*, 41–52.

Langegger, S. (2013). Emergent public space: Sustaining Chicano culture in North Denver. *Cities, 35*, 26–32.

Latimer, J. (1997). Figuring identities: Older people, medicine and time. In A. Jamieson, S. Harper, & C. Victor (Eds.), *Critical approaches to ageing and later life* (pp. 143–159). Buckingham: Open University Press.

Latimer, J. (1999). The dark at the bottom of the stair: Participation and performance of older people in hospital. *Medical Anthropology Quarterly, 13*(2), 186–213.

Lawler, K. (2015). Age-friendly communities: Go big or go home. *Public Policy & Aging Report, 25*(1), 30–33.

Lawton, M. P., & Nahemow, L. (1973). Ecology and the aging process. In C. Eisdorfer & M. P. Lawton (Eds.), *The psychology of adult development and aging* (pp. 619–674). Wash-ington, DC: American Psychological Association.

Leaver, R., & Wiseman, T. (2016). Garden visiting as a meaningful occupation for people in later life. *British Journal of Occupational Therapy, 79*(12), 768–775.

Lee, J., Davidson, J. W., & Krause, A. E. (2016). Older people's motivations for participat-ing in community singing in Australia. *International Journal of Community Music, 9*(2).

Leonard, P. (1997). *Postmodern welfare: Reconstructing an emancipatory project.* London: Sage.

Liang, J., & Luo, B. (2012). Toward a discourse shift in social gerontology: From successful aging to harmonious aging. *Journal of Aging Studies, 26*(3), 327–334.

Lilburn, L.E.R., Breheny, M., & Pond, R. (2016). "You're not really a visitor, you're just a friend": How older volunteers navigate home visiting. *Ageing and Society*, 1–22.

Lindsay, S. (2014). *Ageism, gender and the positive ageing strategy: The portrayal of the elderly population within newspaper articles between 2000 and 2009.* (MA thesis), Massey Univer-sity, Palmerston North.

Litwin, H., & Meir, A. (2013). Financial worry among older people: Who worries and why? *Journal of Aging Studies, 27*(2), 113–120.

Litwin, H., & Shiovitz-Ezra, S. (2006). Network type and mortality risk in later life. *The Gerontologist, 46*(6), 735–743.

Löckenhoff, C. E., & Carstensen, L. L. (2004). Socioemotional selectivity theory, aging, and health: The increasingly delicate balance between regulating emotions and making tough choices. *Journal of Personality, 72*(6), 1395–1424.

Logie, C. H., Jenkinson, J. I., Earnshaw, V., Tharao, W., & Loutfy, M. R. (2016). A struc-tural equation model of HIV-related stigma, racial discrimination, housing insecurity and wellbeing among African and Caribbean black women living with HIV in Ontario, Canada. *PloS One, 11*(9), e0162826.

Lui, C.-W., Everingham, J.-A., Warburton, J., Cuthill, M., & Bartlett, H. (2009). What makes a community age-friendly: A review of international literature. *Australasian Journal on Ageing, 28*(3), 116–121.

Lunney, J. R., Lynn, J., Foley, D. J., Lipson, S., & Guralnik, J. M. (2003). Patterns of functional decline at the end of life. *Jama, 289*(18), 2387–2392.

Lupton, D. (1995). *The imperative of health: Public health and the regulated body.* London: Sage.

Lyons, M., & Hocking, S. (2000). Australia's highly committed volunteers. In J. Warburton & M. Oppenheimer (Eds.), *Volunteers and volunteering* (pp. 44–55). Sydney: The Federation Press.

Mackenzie, C. (2008). Relational autonomy, normative authority and perfectionism. *Journal of Social Philosophy, 39*(4), 512–533.

Mackenzie, C. (2014). The importance of relational autonomy and capabilities for an ethics of vulnerability. In W. Rogers, C. Mackenzie, & S. Dodds (Eds.), *Vulnerability: New essays in ethics and feminist philosophy.* Oxford: Oxford University Press.

Maguire, M., Peace, S., Nicolle, C., Marshall, R., Sims, R., Percival, J., & Lawton, C. (2014). Kitchen living in later life: Exploring ergonomic problems, coping strategies and design solutions. *International Journal of Design, 8*(1), 73–91.

Maher, P. (1999). A review of "traditional" Aboriginal health beliefs. *Australian Journal of Rural Health, 7*(4), 229–236.

Mansvelt, J. (2012). Consumption, ageing and identity: New Zealander's narratives of gifting, ridding and passing on. *New Zealand Geographer, 68*(3), 187–200.

Mansvelt, J., & Breheny, M. (in press) "I choose to go without everything really": Moral imperatives, economic choice and ageing. *The Australian Journal of Anthropology, Special Issue: Moralities of Care in Later Life.*

Mansvelt, J., Breheny, M., & Stephens, C. (2014). Pursuing security: Economic resources and the ontological security of older New Zealanders. *Ageing and Society, 34*(10), 1666–1687.

Mansvelt, J., Breheny, M., & Stephens, C. (2017). Still being "Mother"? Consumption and identity practices for women in later life. *Journal of Consumer Culture, 17*(2), 340–358.

Marengoni, A., Angleman, S., Melis, R., Mangialasche, F., Karp, A., Garmen, A., . . . Fratiglioni, L. (2011). Aging with multimorbidity: A systematic review of the literature. *Ageing Research Reviews, 10*(4), 430–439.

Marmot, M., Allen, J., & Goldblatt, P. (2010). A social movement, based on evidence, to reduce inequalities in health. *Social Science & Medicine, 71*(7), 1254–1258.

Martin, P., Kelly, N., Kahana, B., Kahana, E., Willcox, B. J., Willcox, D. C., & Poon, L. W. (2015). Defining successful aging: A tangible or elusive concept? *The Gerontologist, 55*(1), 14–25.

Martin, R., Williams, C., & O'Neill, D. (2009). Retrospective analysis of attitudes to ageing in the Economist: Apocalyptic demography for opinion formers? *BMJ, 339,* b4914. https://doi.org/10.1136/bmj.b4914

Martin, W. (2007). *Embodying "active" ageing: Bodies, emotions and risk in later life.* (Doctoral thesis), University of Warwick, Coventry.

Martinez, I. L., Crooks, D., Kim, K. S., & Tanner, E. (2011). Invisible civic engagement among older adults: Valuing the contributions of informal volunteering. *Journal of Cross-Cultural Gerontology, 26*(1), 23–37.

Martinson, M., & Berridge, C. (2015). Successful aging and its discontents: A systematic review of the social gerontology literature. *The Gerontologist, 55*(1), 58–69.

Martinson, M., & Halpern, J. (2011). Ethical implications of the promotion of elder volunteerism: A critical perspective. *Journal of Aging Studies, 25*(4), 427–435.

Matthews, T., & Stephens, C. (2017). Constructing housing decisions in later life: A discursive analysis of older adults' discussions about their housing decisions in New Zealand. *Housing, Theory and Society, 34*(3), 343–358.

McLaughlin, D., Adams, J.O.N., Vagenas, D., & Dobson, A. (2011). Factors which enhance or inhibit social support: A mixed-methods analysis of social networks in older women. *Ageing & Society, 31*(1), 18–33.

McMunn, A., Nazroo, J., Wahrendorf, M., Breeze, E., & Zaninotto, P. (2009). Participation in socially-productive activities, reciprocity and wellbeing in later life: Baseline results in England. *Ageing and Society, 29*(5), 765–782.

Midlarsky, E., & Kahana, E. (2007). Altruism, well-being, and mental health in late life. In S. G. Post (Ed.), *Altruism and health: Perspectives from empirical research* (pp. 56–69). New York, NY: Oxford University Press.

Ministry of Social Development. (2009). *"In a place I call my own": Support networks of older people ageing in the community.* Wellington, New Zealand: Ministry of Social Development.

Ministry of Social Development. (2014). *2014 report on positive ageing strategy.* Wellington, New Zealand: Office for Senior Citizens.

Minkler, M. (1996). Critical perspectives on ageing: New challenges for gerontology. *Ageing & Society, 16*(4), 467–487.

Minkler, M., & Estes, C. L. (1999). *Critical gerontology: Perspectives from political and moral economy.* Amityville, NY: Baywood.

Montgomery, S. M., Netuveli, G., Hildon, Z., & Blane, D. (2007). Does financial disadvantage at older ages eliminate the potential for better health? *Journal of Epidemiology and Community Health, 61*(10), 891–895.

Moody, H. R. (2005). From successful aging to conscious aging. In H. R. Moody, P. J. Whitehouse, & D. L. Morris (Eds.), *Successful aging through the life span: Intergenerational issues in health* (pp. 55–68). New York, NY: Springer Publishing Company, Inc.

Moody, M. (2008). Serial reciprocity: A preliminary statement. *Sociological Theory, 26*(2), 130–151.

Morris, A. (2012). Older social and private renters, the neighbourhood, and social connections and activity. *Urban Policy and Research, 30*(1), 43–58.

Morrow-Howell, N., Hinterlong, J., Rozario, P. A., & Tang, F. (2003). Effects of volunteering on the well-being of older adults. *The Journals of Gerontology Series B: Psychological Sciences and Social Sciences, 58*(3), S137–S145.

Morrow-Howell, N., Hong, S., & Tang, F. (2009). Who benefits from volunteering? Variations in perceived benefits. *The Gerontologist, 49*(1), 91–102.

Morrow-Howell, N., Tang, F., Kim, J., Lee, M., & Sherraden, M. (2005). Maximizing the productive engagement of older adults. In M. L. Wykle, P. J. Whitehouse, & D. L. Morris (Eds.), *Successful aging through the life span: Intergenerational issues in health* (pp. 19–54). New York: Springer Publishing Company, Inc.

Motenko, A. K., & Greenberg, S. (1995). Reframing dependence in old age: A positive transition for families. *Social Work, 40*(3), 382–390.

Murray, M., Pullman, D., & Rodgers, T. H. (2003). Social representations of health and illness among "baby boomers" in Eastern Canada. *Journal of Health Psychology, 8*(5), 485–499.

Musick, M. A., Herzog, A. R., & House, J. S. (1999). Volunteering and mortality among older adults: Findings from a national sample. *The Journals of Gerontology Series B: Psychological Sciences and Social Sciences, 54*(3), S173–S180.

Nagalingam, J. (2007). Understanding successful aging: A study of older Indian adults in Singapore. *Care Management Journals, 8*(1), 18–25.

Narushima, M. (2005). "Payback time": Community volunteering among older adults as a transformative mechanism. *Ageing and Society, 25*(4), 567–584.

Naughton, C., Drennan, J., Treacy, P., Fealy, G., Kilkenny, M., Johnson, F., & Butler, M. (2010). The role of health and non-health-related factors in repeat emergency department visits in an elderly urban population. *Emergency Medicine Journal, 27*(9), 683–687.

Neisser, U. (1988). Five kinds of self-knowledge. *Philosophical Psychology, 1,* 35–59.

Netuveli, G., & Blane, D. (2008). Quality of life in older ages. *British Medical Bulletin, 85*(1), 113–126.

Noone, J., & Bohle, P. (2017). Enhancing the health and employment participation of older workers. In K. O'Loughlin, C. Browning, & H. Kendig (Eds.), *Ageing in Australia: Challenges and opportunities* (pp. 127–146). New York, NY: Springer Publishing Company, Inc.

Nussbaum, M. (2006). *Frontiers of justice.* Cambridge, MA: Harvard University Press.

Nussbaum, M. (2007). Human rights and human capabilities. *Harvard Human Rights Journal, 20,* 21–24.

Nussbaum, M. (2011). *Creating capabilities: The human development approach.* Cambridge, MA, USA: Belknap and Harvard University Press.

Nyman, S. R., & Szymczynska, P. (2016). Meaningful activities for improving the wellbeing of people with dementia: Beyond mere pleasure to meeting fundamental psychological needs. *Perspectives in Public Health, 136*(2), 99–107. https://doi.org/10.1177/175791391 5626193

Offer, S. (2012). The burden of reciprocity: Processes of exclusion and withdrawal from personal networks among low-income families. *Current Sociology, 60*(6), 788–805.

Okun, M. A. (1994). The relation between motives for organizational volunteering and frequency of volunteering by elders. *Journal of Applied Gerontology, 13*(2), 115–126.

Okun, M. A., Yeung, E. W., Brown, S. (2013). Volunteering by older adults and risk of mortality: A meta-analysis. *Psychology and Aging, 28*(2), 564–577.

O'Loughlin, K., & Kendig, H. (2017). Attitudes to ageing. In K. O'Loughlin, C. Browning, & H. Kendig (Eds.), *Ageing in Australia: Challenges and opportunities* (pp. 29–45). New York, NY: Springer Publishing Company, Inc.

Oman, D. (2007). Does volunteering foster physical health and longevity? In S. G. Post (Ed.), *Altruism and health: Perspectives from empirical research* (pp. 15–32). New York, NY: Oxford University Press.

Oosterlaken, I. (2009). Design for development: A capability approach. *Design Issue, 25*(4), 91–102.

Orr, N., Wagstaffe, A., Briscoe, S., & Garside, R. (2016). How do older people describe their sensory experiences of the natural world? A systematic review of the qualitative evidence. *BMC Geriatrics, 16*(1), 116. https://doi.org/10.1186/s12877-016-0288-0

Orrell, A., McKee, K., Torrington, J., Barnes, S., Darton, R., Netten, A., & Lewis, A. (2013). The relationship between building design and residents' quality of life in extra care housing schemes. *Health & Place, 21,* 52–64.

O'Sullivan, J., & Ashton, T. (2012). A minimum income for healthy living (MIHL): Older New Zealanders. *Ageing & Society, 32*(5), 747–768.

Oswald, F., & Wahl, H.-W. (2005). Dimensions of the meaning of home. In G. D. Rowles & H. Chaudhury (Eds.), *Home and identity in late life: International perspectives* (pp. 21–46). New York: Springer Publishing Company, Inc.

Oswald, F., Wahl, H.-W., Martin, M., & Mollenkopf, H. (2003). Toward measuring pro-activity in person-environment transactions in late adulthood: The housing-related Control Beliefs Questionnaire. *Journal of Housing For the Elderly, 17*(1–2), 135–152.

Oswald, F., Wahl, H.-W., Schilling, O., Nygren, C., Fänge, A., Sixsmith, A., . . . Iwarsson, S. (2007). Relationships between housing and healthy aging in very old age. *The Gerontologist, 47*(1), 96–107.

Ottoni, C. A., Sims-Gould, J., Winters, M., Heijnen, M., & McKay, H. A. (2016). "Benches become like porches": Built and social environment influences on older adults' experiences of mobility and well-being. *Social Science and Medicine, 169*, 33–41.

Parsons, M., & Dixon, R. (2004). *An evaluation of befriending services in New Zealand.* Ministry of Health: Ministry of Health. Retrieved from www.health.govt.nz/system/files/documents/pages/an-evaluation-of-befriending-services.pdf

Peace, S., Holland, C., & Kellaher, L. (2011). "Option recognition" in later life: Variations in ageing in place. *Ageing and Society, 31*(5), 734–757.

Peace, S., Wahl, H.-W., Mollenkopf, H., & Oswald, F. (2007). Environment and ageing. In J. Bond, S. M. Peace, F. Dittmann-Kohli, & G. Westerhof (Eds.), *Ageing in society* (pp. 209–234). Thousand Oaks, CA: Sage.

Pearson, A. L., Barnard, L. T., Pearce, J., Kingham, S., & Howden-Chapman, P. (2014). Housing quality and resilience in New Zealand. *Building Research & Information, 42*(2), 182–190.

Peel, N. M., McClure, R. J., & Bartlett, H. P. (2005). Behavioral determinants of healthy aging. *American Journal of Preventive Medicine, 28*(3), 298–304.

Peng, D., & Fei, W. (2013). Productive ageing in China: Development of concepts and policy practice. *Ageing International, 38*(1), 4–14.

Perkins, M. M., Ball, M. M., Whittington, F. J., & Hollingsworth, C. (2012). Relational autonomy in assisted living: A focus on diverse care settings for older adults. *Journal of Aging Studies, 26*(2), 214–225.

Perry, B. (2016). *The material wellbeing of NZ households: Overview and key findings.* Wellington, NZ: Ministry of Social Development.

Petersen, A. R. (1996). Risk and the regulated self: The discourse of health promotion as politics of uncertainty. *Journal of Sociology, 32*(1), 44–57.

Phillipson, C. (1982). *Capitalism and the construction of old age.* London: Macmillan.

Phillipson, C. (2011). Developing age-friendly communities: New approaches to growing old in urban environments. In R. A. Settersten & J. L. Angel (Eds.), *Handbook of sociology of aging* (pp. 279–293). New York: Springer Publishing Company, Inc.

Phillipson, C. (2012). Globalisation, economic recession and social exclusion: Policy challenges and responses. In T. Scharf & N. Keating (Eds.), *From exclusion to inclusion in old age: A global challenge.* Bristol, UK: The Policy Press.

Phillipson, C., & Buffel, T. (2016). *Can global cities be age-friendly cities? Urban development and ageing populations.* Paper presented at the International Federation on Ageing 13th Global Conference on Ageing Brisbane, Australia. Retrieved from www.ifa-fiv.org/wp-content/uploads/2016/07/Tue-P1-1545-Phillipson.pdf

Phillipson, C., Leach, R., Money, A., & Biggs, S. (2008). Social and cultural constructions of ageing: The case of the baby boomers. *Sociological Research Online, 13*(3), 5.

Phoenix, C., Smith, B., & Sparkes, A. C. (2010). Narrative analysis in aging studies: A typology for consideration. *Journal of Aging Studies, 24*(1), 1–11.

Piliavin, J. A., & Siegl, E. (2007). Health benefits of volunteering in the Wisconsin longitudinal study*. *Journal of Health and Social Behavior, 48*(4), 450–464.

Plastow, N. A., Atwal, A., & Gilhooly, M. (2015). Food activities and identity maintenance among community-living older adults: A grounded theory study. *American Journal of Occupational Therapy, 69*(6).

Plath, D. (2002). Independence in old age: Shifting meanings in Australian social policy. *Just Policy: A Journal of Australian Social Policy, 26*, 40.

Plath, D. (2008). Independence in old age: The route to social exclusion? *The British Journal of Social Work, 38*(7), 1353–1369.

Plouffe, L., & Kalache, A. (2010). Towards global age-friendly cities: Determining urban features that promote active aging. *Journal of Urban Health, 87*(5), 733–739.

Pond, R., Stephens, C., & Alpass, F. (2010). Virtuously watching one's health older adults' regulation of self in the pursuit of health. *Journal of Health Psychology, 15*(5), 734–743.

Portacolone, E. (2011). The myth of independence for older Americans living alone in the Bay area of San Francisco: A critical reflection. *Ageing & Society, 31*(5), 803–828.

Portacolone, E. (2013). The notion of precariousness among older adults living alone in the U.S. *Journal of Aging Studies, 27*(2), 166–174.

Portacolone, E. (2015). Older Americans living alone: The influence of resources and intergenerational integration on inequality. *Journal of Contemporary Ethnography, 44*(3), 280–305.

Powell, J., & Biggs, S. (2000). Managing old age: The disciplinary web of power, surveillance and normalization. *Journal of Aging and Identity, 5*(1), 3–13.

Powell, J., & Biggs, S. (2004). Ageing, technologies of self and bio-medicine: A Foucauldian excursion. *International Journal of Sociology and Social Policy, 24*(6), 17–29.

Preiser, W. F., & Ostroff, E. (2001). *Universal design handbook.* New York: McGraw Hill.

Quandt, S. A., Arcury, T. A., Bell, R. A., McDonald, J., & Vitolins, M. Z. (2001). The social and nutritional meaning of food sharing among older rural adults. *Journal of Aging Studies, 15*(2), 145–162.

Quinn, J. F., & Cahill, K. E. (2016). The new world of retirement income security in America. *American Psychologist, 71*(4), 321–333.

Ranzijn, R. (2010). Active ageing: Another way to oppress marginalized and disadvantaged elders?: Aboriginal elders as a case study. *Journal of Health Psychology, 15*(5), 716–723.

Reed, J., & Clarke, C. L. (1999). Nursing older people: Constructing need and care. *Nursing Inquiry, 6*(3), 208–215.

Regidor, E., Kunst, A. E., Rodríguez-Artalejo, F., & Mackenbach, J. P. (2012). Small socioeconomic differences in mortality in Spanish older people. *European Journal of Public Health, 22*(1), 80–85.

Register, M. E., & Scharer, K. M. (2010). Connectedness in community-dwelling older adults. *Western Journal of Nursing Research, 32*(4), 462–479.

Reichstadt, J., Depp, C. A., Palinkas, L. A., & Jeste, D. V. (2007). Building blocks of successful aging: A focus group study of older adults' perceived contributors to successful aging. *The American Journal of Geriatric Psychiatry, 15*(3), 194–201.

Rhodes, R. E., Mark, R. S., & Temmel, C. P. (2012). Adult sedentary behavior: A systematic review. *American Journal of Preventive Medicine, 42*(3), e3–e28. https://doi.org/10.1016/j.amepre.2011.10.020

Richard, L., Gauvin, L., Gosselin, C., & Laforest, S. (2009). Staying connected: Neighbourhood correlates of social participation among older adults living in an urban environment in Montreal, Quebec. *Health Promotion International, 24*(1), 46–57.

Richard, L., Gauvin, L., Kestens, Y., Shatenstein, B., Payette, H., Daniel, M., . . . Mercille, G. (2013). Neighborhood resources and social participation among older adults results from the VoisiNuage study. *Journal of Aging and Health, 25*(2), 296–318.

Rios, R., & Zautra, A. J. (2011). Socioeconomic disparities in pain: The role of economic hardship and daily financial worry. *Health Psychology, 30*(1), 58–66.

Roberts, L. R., Schuh, H., Sherzai, D., Belliard, J. C., & Montgomery, S. B. (2015). Exploring experiences and perceptions of aging and cognitive decline across diverse racial and ethnic groups. *Gerontology and Geriatric Medicine.* https://doi.org/10.1177/2333721415596101

Robertson, A. (1997). Beyond apocalyptic demography: Towards a moral economy of interdependence. *Ageing & Society, 17*(4), 425–446.

Robertson, A. (1999). Beyond apocalyptic demography: Toward a moral economy of interdependence. In M. Minkler & C. L. Estes (Eds.), *Critical gerontology: Perspectives from political and moral economy* (pp. 75–90). New York: Baywood.

Robeyns, I. (2005a). The capability approach: A theoretical survey. *Journal of Human Development, 6*(1), 93–117.

Robeyns, I. (2005b). Selecting capabilities for quality of life measurement. *Social Indicators Research, 74*(1), 191–215.

Robeyns, I. (2006). The capability approach in practice. *Journal of Political Philosophy, 14*(3), 351–376.

Rohe, W. M., & Basolo, V. (1997). Long-term effects of homeownership on the self-perceptions and social interaction of low-income persons. *Environment and Behavior, 29*(6), 793–819.

Rojek, C. (2013). *Capitalism and leisure theory.* New York: Routledge.

Rook, K. S. (1990). Stressful aspects of older adults' social relationships: Current theory and research. In M.A.P. Stephens, J. H. Crowther, S. E. Hobfoll, & D. L. Tennenbaum (Eds.), *Stress and coping in later-life families* (pp. 173–192). Washington, DC: Hemisphere.

Rook, K. S. (1997). Positive and negative social exchanges: Weighing their effects in later life. *Journal of Gerontology: Social Sciences, 52B*(4), S167–S169.

Roos, V., Kolobe, P. S., & Keating, N. (2014). (Re)creating community: Experiences of older women forcibly relocated during apartheid. *Journal of Community & Applied Social Psychology, 24*(1), 12–25.

Roscigno, V. J., Karafin, D. L., & Tester, G. (2009). The complexities and processes of racial housing discrimination. *Social Problems, 56*(1), 49–69.

Rose, N. (2001). The politics of life itself. *Theory, Culture & Society, 18*(6), 1–30.

Rowe, J. W., & Kahn, R. L. (1987). Human aging: Usual and successful. *Science, 237*(4811), 143–149.

Rowe, J. W., & Kahn, R. L. (1997). Successful aging. *The Gerontologist, 37*(4), 433–440.

Rowe, J. W., & Kahn, R. L. (2015). Successful aging 2.0: Conceptual expansions for the 21st century. *The Journals of Gerontology Series B: Psychological Sciences and Social Sciences, 70*(4), 593–596.

Rowles, G. D., & Watkins, J. F. (2003). History, habit, heart and hearth: On making spaces into places. In K. W. Schaie, H.-W. Wahl, H. Mollenkopf, & F. Oswald (Eds.), *Aging independently: Living arrangements and mobility* (pp. 77–96). New York: Springer Publishing Company, Inc.

Rozanova, J. (2010). Discourse of successful aging in The Globe & Mail: Insights from critical gerontology. *Journal of Aging Studies, 24*(4), 213–222.

Rubinstein, R. L., & de Medeiros, K. (2015). "Successful aging," Gerontological theory and neoliberalism: A qualitative critique. *The Gerontologist, 55*(1), 34–42.

Russell, C. (2007). What do older women and men want?: Gender differences in the "lived experience" of ageing. *Current Sociology, 55*(2), 173–192.

Ryff, C. D. (1989). Beyond Ponce de Leon and life satisfaction: New directions in quest of successful ageing. *International Journal of Behavioral Development, 12*(1), 35–55.

Ryff, C. D., & Singer, B. (2009). Understanding healthy aging: Key components and their integration. In D.G.V. Bengtson, N. M. Putney, & M. Silverstein (Eds.), *Handbook of theories of aging* (2nd ed., pp. 117–144). New York: Springer Publishing Company, Inc.

Safiliou-Rothschild, C. (2009). Are older people responsible for high healthcare costs? *CESifo Forum, 10*(1), 57–64.

Saleeby, P. W. (2007). Applications of a capability approach to disability and the international classification of functioning, disability and health (ICF) in social work practice. *Journal of Social Work in Disability & Rehabilitation, 6*(1–2), 217–232.

Sánchez, M., & Hatton-Yeo, A. (2012). Active ageing and intergenerational solidarity in Europe: A conceptual reappraisal from a critical perspective. *Journal of Intergenerational Relationships, 10*(3), 276–293.

Savikko, N., Routasalo, P., Tilvis, R. S., Strandberg, T. E., & Pitkälä, K. H. (2005). Predictors and subjective causes of loneliness in an aged population. *Archives of Gerontology and Geriatrics, 41*(3), 223–233.

Scanlon, K., Fernández Arrigoitia, M., & Whitehead, C.M.E. (2015). Social housing in Europe. *European Policy Analysis, 17*, 1–12.

Schafer, M. H. (2013). Structural advantages of good health in old age: Investigating the health-begets-position hypothesis with a full social network. *Research on Aging, 35*(3), 348–370.

Schafer, M. H., & Koltai, J. (2015). Does embeddedness protect? Personal network density and vulnerability to mistreatment among older American adults. *The Journals of Gerontology: Series B, 70*(4), 597–606.

Scharf, T., Phillipson, C., Kingston, P., & Smith, A. E. (2001). Social exclusion and older people: Exploring the connections. *Education and Ageing, 16*(3), 303–320.

Scharf, T., Phillipson, C., & Smith, A. E. (2002). *Growing older in socially deprived areas: Social exclusion in later life*. London, UK: Help the Aged. Retrieved from www.opengrey.eu/item/display/10068/515507

Scharf, T., Phillipson, C., & Smith, A. E. (2004). Poverty and social exclusion: Growing older in deprived urban neighbourhoods. In A. Walker & C. H. Hennessey (Eds.), *Growing older: Quality of life in old age* (pp. 81–106). Maidenhead: Open University Press.

Scharlach, A. (2012). Creating aging-friendly communities in the United States. *Ageing International, 37*(1), 25–38.

Scharlach, A., & Lehning, A. (2015). *Creating aging-friendly communities*. Oxford: Oxford University Press.

Schofield, V., Davey, J. A., Keeling, S., & Parsons, M. (2006). Ageing in place. In J. Boston & J. A. Davey (Eds.), *Implications of population ageing: Opportunities and Risks* (pp. 275–306). Wellington, NZ: Institute of Policy Studies.

Schokkaert, E. (2009). The capabilities approach. In P. Anand, P. Pattanaik, & C. Puppe (Eds.), *The handbook of rational and social choice* (pp. 542–566). Oxford: Oxford University Press.

Schultz, J. H. (1997). The real crisis of the century: Growing inequality, not stealing from our children. *The Gerontologist, 37*(1), 130–131.

Schwanen, T., Banister, D., & Bowling, A. (2012). Independence and mobility in later life. *Geoforum, 43*(6), 1313–1322.

Seaman, P. M. (2012). Time for my life now: Early boomer women's anticipation of volunteering in retirement. *The Gerontologist, 52*(2), 245–254.

Secker, J., Hill, R., Villeneau, L., & Parkman, S. (2003). Promoting independence: But promoting what and how? *Ageing and Society, 23*(3), 375–391.

Seeman, T. E., Crimmins, E., Huang, M.-H., Singer, B., Bucur, A., Gruenewald, T., . . . Reuben, D. B. (2004). Cumulative biological risk and socio-economic differences in mortality: MacArthur Studies of Successful Aging. *Social Science & Medicine, 58*(10), 1985–1997.

Seeman, T. E., Lusignolo, T. M., Albert, M., & Berkman, L. (2001). Social relationships, social support, and patterns of cognitive aging in healthy, high-functioning older adults: MacArthur Studies of Successful Aging. *Health Psychology, 20*(4), 243–255.

Sen, A. (1983). *Choice, welfare, and measurement*. Oxford: Basil Blackwell.

Sen, A. (1985). *Commodities and capabilities*. Professor Dr P. Hennipman Lectures in Economics 7. Amsterdam: North-Holland.

Sen, A. (1987). *The standard of living (The Tanner lectures)* (G. Hawthorne, Ed.). Cambridge: Cambridge University Press.

Sen, A. (1992). *Inequality reexamined*. New York: Russell Sage Foundation.

Sen, A. (1993). Capability and well-being. In M.C.N.A. Sen (Ed.), *The quality of life* (pp. 30–53). Oxford: Clarendon Press.

Sen, A. (1999). *Development as freedom*. New York: Oxford University Press.

Sen, A. (2002a). *Rationality and freedom*. Cambridge, MA: Harvard University Press.

Sen, A. (2002b). Why health equity? *Health Economics, 11*(8), 659–666.

Sen, A. (2004). Capabilities, lists, and public reason: Continuing the conversation. *Feminist Economics, 10*(3), 77–80.

Sen, A. (2010a). *The idea of justice*. Harmondsworth: Penguin.

Sen, A. (2010b). The place of capability in a theory of justice. In H. Brighouse & I. Robeyns (Eds.), *Measuring justice: Primary goods and capabilities* (pp. 239–253). Cambridge, UK: Cambridge University Press.

Severinsen, C., Breheny, M., & Stephens, C. (2016). Ageing in unsuitable places. *Housing Studies, 31*(6), 714–728.

Sharam, A., Ralston, L., & Parkinson, S. (2016). *Security in retirement: The impact of housing and key critical life events*. Melbourne: Swinburne Institute for Social Research. Retrieved from http://apo.org.au/resource/security-retirement-impact-housing-and-key-critical-life-events

Sharma, M. (2004). Capability theory for use in alcohol and drug education research. *Journal of Alcohol and Drug Education, 48*(1), 1–4.

Shirai, K., Iso, H., Ohira, T., Ikeda, A., Noda, H., Honjo, K., . . . Tsugane, S. (2009). Perceived level of life enjoyment and risks of cardiovascular disease incidence and mortality. *The Japan Public Health Center-Based Study, 120*(11), 956–963.

Shye, D., Mullooly, J. P., Freeborn, D. K., & Pope, C. R. (1995). Gender differences in the relationship between social network support and mortality: A longitudinal study of an elderly cohort. *Social Science & Medicine, 41*(7), 935–947.

Siegrist, J., von dem Knesebeck, O., & Pollack, E. C. (2004). Social productivity and well-being of older people: A sociological exploration. *Social Theory & Health, 2*(1), 1–17.

Sims, R., Marshall, R., Maguire, M., Nicolle, C., Lawton, C., Peace, S., & Percival, J. (2012). Design of kitchens for independence: Lessons from history for the future. In M. Anderson (Ed.), *Contemporary ergonomics and human factors* (pp. 39–46). London, UK: Taylor & Francis.

Sirven, N., & Debrand, T. (2008). Social participation and healthy ageing: An international comparison using SHARE data. *Social Science & Medicine, 67*(12), 2017–2026.

Sixsmith, A., & Sixsmith, J. (2008). Ageing in place in the United Kingdom. *Ageing International, 32*(3), 219–235.

Sixsmith, J., Sixsmith, A., Fänge, A. M., Naumann, D., Kucsera, C., Tomsone, S., . . . Woolrych, R. (2014). Healthy ageing and home: The perspectives of very old people in five European countries. *Social Science & Medicine, 106*, 1–9.

Skey, M. (2010). "A sense of where you belong in the world": National belonging, ontological security and the status of the ethnic majority in England. *Nations and Nationalism, 16*(4), 715–733.

Skingley, A., & Bungay, H. (2010). The Silver Song Club project: Singing to promote the health of older people. *British Journal of Community Nursing, 15*(3), 135–140.

Skingley, A., Martin, A., & Clift, S. (2016). The contribution of community singing groups to the well-being of older people: Participant perspectives from the united kingdom. *Journal of Applied Gerontology, 35*(12), 1302–1324.

Small, M. L. (2009). *Unanticipated gains: Origins of network inequality in everyday life*. New York: Oxford University Press.

Smith, A. E. (2009). *Ageing in urban neighbourhoods: Place attachment and social exclusion*. Bristol, UK: The Policy Press.

Smith, A. E., Sim, J., Scharf, T., & Phillipson, C. (2004). Determinants of quality of life amongst older people in deprived neighbourhoods. *Ageing & Society, 24*(5), 793–814.

Smith, J. A., Braunack-Mayer, A., Wittert, G., & Warin, M. (2007). "I've been independent for so damn long!": Independence, masculinity and aging in a help seeking context. *Journal of Aging Studies, 21*(4), 325–335.

Smith, S. J., Cigdem, M., Ong, R., & Wood, G. (2017). Wellbeing at the edges of ownership. *Environment and Planning A., 49*(5), 1080–1098. https://doi.org/10.1177/0308518X16688471

Somers, J., Worsley, A., & McNaughton, S. A. (2014). The association of mavenism and pleasure with food involvement in older adult. *International Journal of Behavioral Nutrition and Physical Activity, 11*, 60. https://doi.org/10.1186/1479-5868-11-60

Sommers, D. K., & Rowell, K. R. (1992). Factors differentiating elderly residential movers and non-movers: A longitudinal analysis. *Population Research and Policy Review, 11*, 249–262.

Sorell, T., & Draper, H. (2014). Robot carers, ethics, and older people. *Ethics and Information Technology, 16*(3), 183–195.

Spitzer, W. J., Neuman, K., & Holden, G. (2004). The coming of age for assisted living care. *Social Work in Health Care, 38*(3), 21–45.

Sprangers, M.A.G., De Regt, E. B., Andries, F., Van Agt, H.M.E., Bijl, R. V., De Boer, J. B., . . . De Haes, H.C.J.M. (2000). Which chronic conditions are associated with better or poorer quality of life? *Journal of Clinical Epidemiology, 53*(9), 895–907.

Stavridis, A., Kaprinis, S., & Tsirogiannis, I. (2015). Participation's motives in dancing activities: Gender and age as differentiation factors. *Mediterranean Journal of Social Sciences, 6*(3 S1), 535.

Stenner, P., McFarquhar, T., & Bowling, A. (2011). Older people and "active ageing": Subjective aspects of ageing actively. *Journal of Health Psychology, 16*(3), 467–477.

Stephens, C. (2016). From success to capability for healthy ageing: Shifting the lens to include all older people. *Critical Public Health*, 1–9.

Stephens, C., Alpass, F., & Stevenson, B. (2014). *Inclusion, contribution and connection: A study of ageing in Aotearoa: Summary report.* Massey University, New Zealand. Retrieved from www.massey.ac.nz/?p697c3241c

Stephens, C., Alpass, F., & Towers, A. (2010). Economic hardship among older people in New Zealand: The effects of low living standards on social support, loneliness, and mental health. *New Zealand Journal of Psychology, 39*(2), 49–55.

Stephens, C., Alpass, F., Towers, A., & Stevenson, B. (2011). The effects of types of social networks, perceived social support, and loneliness on the health of older people: Accounting for the social context. *Journal of Aging and Health, 23*(6), 887–911.

Stephens, C., Breheny, M., & Mansvelt, J. (2015a). Healthy ageing from the perspective of older people: A capability approach to resilience. *Psychology & Health, 30*(6), 715–731.

Stephens, C., Breheny, M., & Mansvelt, J. (2015b). Volunteering as reciprocity: Beneficial and harmful effects of social policies to encourage contribution in older age. *Journal of Aging Studies, 33*, 22–27.

Stephens, C., & Flick, U. (2010). Health and ageing: Challenges for health psychology research. *Journal of Health Psychology, 15*(5), 643–648.

Steptoe, A., de Oliveira, C., Demakakos, P., & Zaninotto, P. (2014). Enjoyment of life and declining physical function at older ages: A longitudinal cohort study. *Canadian Medical Association Journal, 186*(4), E150–E156.

Steptoe, A., & Wardle, J. (2012). Enjoying life and living longer. *Archives of Internal Medicine, 172*(3), 273–275.

Stern, M. J., & Dillman, D. A. (2006). Community participation, social ties, and use of the internet. *City & Community, 5*(4), 409–424.

St John, S. (2016). Can older citizens lead the way to a universal basic income? In G.M.J. Mays & J. Tomlinson (Eds.), *Basic income in Australia and New Zealand: Perspectives from the neoliberal frontier.* New York: Palgrave Macmillan.

Stowe, J. D., & Cooney, T. M. (2015). Examining Rowe and Kahn's concept of successful aging: Importance of taking a life course perspective. *The Gerontologist, 55*(1), 43–50.

Strawbridge, W. J., Wallhagen, M. I., & Cohen, R. D. (2002). Successful aging and well-being: Self-rated compared with Rowe and Kahn. *The Gerontologist, 42*(6), 727–733.

Szabo, A., Allen, J., Alpass, F., & Stephens, C. (2017). Longitudinal trajectories of quality of life and depression by housing tenure status. *The Journals of Gerontology Series B Psychological Sciences and Social Sciences.* https://doi.org/10.1093/geronb/gbx028

Tang, F., Morrow-Howell, N., & Choi, E. (2010). Why do older adult volunteers stop volunteering? *Ageing and Society, 30*(5), 859–878.

Tannenbaum, C., Ahmed, S., & Mayo, N. (2007). What drives older women's perceptions of health-related quality of life? *Quality of Life Research, 16*(4), 593–605.

Tanner, D. (2001). Sustaining the self in later life: Supporting older people in the community. *Ageing and Society, 21*(3), 255–278.

Taylor, P., & Walker, A. (1994). The ageing workforce: Employers' attitudes towards older people. *Work, Employment & Society, 8*(4), 569–591.

Theurer, K., & Wister, A. (2009). Altruistic behaviour and social capital as predictors of well-being among older Canadians. *Ageing and Society, 30*(1), 157–181.

Thoits, P. A., & Hewitt, L. N. (2001). Volunteer work and well-being. *Journal of Health and Social Behavior, 42*, 115–131.

Thomas, P. A. (2012). Trajectories of social engagement and mortality in late life. *Journal of Aging and Health, 24*(4), 547–568.

Thomas, W., & Blanchard, J. (2009). Moving beyond place: Aging in community. *Generations, 33*(2), 12–17.

Thompson, S. (2013). *Reciprocity and dependency in old age: Indian and UK perspectives* (Vol. 8). New York: Springer Publishing Company, Inc.

Todorova, I. L., Guzzardo, M. T., Adams, W. E., & Falcon, L. M. (2015). Gratitude and longing: Meanings of health in aging for Puerto Rican adults in the mainland. *Journal of Health Psychology, 20*(12), 1602–1612.

Tornstam, L. (2005). *Gerotranscendence: A developmental theory of positive aging.* New York: Springer Publishing Company, Inc.

Townsend, M., Gibbs, L., Macfarlane, S., Block, K., Staiger, P., Gold, L., Johnson, B., & Long, C. (2014). Volunteering in a school kitchen garden program: Cooking up confidence, capabilities, and connections! *VOLUNTAS: International Journal of Voluntary and Nonprofit Organizations, 25*(1), 225–247.

Townsend, P. (1981). The structured dependency of the elderly: A creation of social policy in the twentieth century. *Ageing and Society, 1*(1), 5–28.

Townsend, P. (1986). Ageism and social policy. In C. Phillipson & A. Walker (Eds.), *Ageing and social policy* (pp. 15–44). London: Gower.

Tse, S.-C. (2014). *Harmonisation of the self: Narratives of older Chinese about ageing, health and wellbeing.* A thesis presented in partial fulfilment of the requirements for the degree of Doctor of Philosophy in Health Psychology at Massey University, Albany, New Zealand.

Tulle, E. (2008). *Ageing, the body and social change: Running in later life.* Basingstoke: Palgrave Macmillan.

Tuohy, R., & Stephens, C. (2011). Exploring older adults' personal and social vulnerability in a disaster. *International Journal of Emergency Management, 8*(1), 60–73.

Uehara, E. S. (1995). Reciprocity reconsidered: Gouldner's "moral norm of reciprocity" and social support. *Journal of Social and Personal Relationships, 12*(4), 483–502.

Unger, J. B., McAvay, G., Bruce, M. L., Berkman, L., & Seeman, T. (1999). Variation in the impact of social network characteristics on physical functioning in elderly persons: MacArthur Studies of Successful Aging. *Journals of Gerontology: Series B: Psychological Sciences and Social Sciences, 54B*(5), S245–S251.

Utz, R. L., Carr, D., Nesse, R., & Wortman, C. B. (2002). The effect of widowhood on older adults' social participation an evaluation of activity, disengagement, and continuity theories. *The Gerontologist, 42*(4), 522–533.

Van Campen, C., & Iedema, J. (2007). Are persons with physical disabilities who participate in society healthier and happier? Structural equation modelling of objective participation and subjective well-being. *Quality of Life Research, 16*(4), 635–645.

Van Cauwenberg, J., De Donder, L., Clarys, P., De Bourdeaudhuij, I., Owen, N., Dury, S., . . . Deforche, B. (2014). Relationships of individual, social, and physical environmental factors with older adults' television viewing time. *Journal of Aging and Physical Activity, 22*(4), 508–517.

van der Pas, S., Ramklass, S., O'Leary, B., Anderson, S., Keating, N., & Cassim, B. (2015). Features of home and neighbourhood and the liveability of older South Africans. *European Journal of Ageing, 12*(3), 215–227.

van Dijk, H. M., Cramm, J. M., & Nieboer, A. P. (2013). The experiences of neighbour, volunteer and professional support-givers in supporting community dwelling older people. *Health & Social Care in the Community, 21*(2), 150–158.

Van Ootegem, L., & Spillemaeckers, S. (2010). With a focus on well-being and capabilities. *Journal of Socio-Economics, 39*(3), 384–390.

Vassilev, I., Rogers, A., Sanders, C., Kennedy, A., Blickem, C., Protheroe, J., . . . Morris, R. (2011). Social networks, social capital and chronic illness self-management: A realist review. *Chronic Illness, 7*(1), 60–86.

Vaughan, M., LaValley, M. P., AlHeresh, R., & Keysor, J. J. (2016). Which features of the environment impact community participation of older adults? A systematic review and meta-analysis. *Journal of Aging and Health, 28*(6), 957–978.

Venkatapuram, S. (2011). *Health justice: An argument from the capabilities approach.* Cambridge: Polity Press.

Victor, C. (2010). *Ageing, health and care.* Bristol: The Policy Press.

Victor, C., Scambler, S., Bond, J., & Bowling, A. (2000). Being alone in later life: Loneliness, social isolation and living alone. *Reviews in Clinical Gerontology, 10*(4), 407–417.

Vineis, P., Kelly-Irving, M., Rappaport, S., & Stringhini, S. (2016). The biological embedding of social differences in ageing trajectories. *Journal of Epidemiology and Community Health, 70*(2), 111–113.

Viner, B. (2013, July 1). Glastonbury's night of the living dead as Rolling Stones rock the festival. *Daily Mail.*

Wahl, H.-W., Iwarsson, S., & Oswald, F. (2012). Aging well and the environment: Toward an integrative model and research agenda for the future. *The Gerontologist, 52*(3), 306–316.

Walker, A. (1981). Towards a political economy of old age. *Ageing and Society, 1*(1), 73–94.

Walker, A. (2002). A strategy for active ageing. *International Social Security Review, 55*(1), 121–139.

Walker, A. (2005). A European perspective on quality of life in old age. *European Journal of Ageing, 2*(1), 2–12.

Walker, A. (2008). Commentary: The emergence and application of active aging in Europe. *Journal of Aging & Social Policy, 21*(1), 75–93.

Walker, A. (2009). Why is ageing so unequal? In P. Cann & M. Dean (Eds.), *Unequal ageing.* Bristol, UK: The Policy Press.

Walker, A. (2013). *Active ageing: A policy for all ages?* Paper presented at the 20th IAGG World Congress of Gerontology and Geriatrics (IAGG June), Seoul, South Korea.

Walker, A., & Hennessey, C. H. (2004). *Growing older: Quality of life in old age.* Maidenhead, Berkshire, England: Open University Press.

Walker, A., & Maltby, T. (2012). Active ageing: A strategic policy solution to demographic ageing in the European Union. *International Journal of Social Welfare, 21*, S117–S130.

Walker, M., McLean, M., Dison, A., & Peppin-Vaughan, R. (2009). South African universities and human development: Towards a theorisation and operationalisation of professional capabilities for poverty reduction. *International Journal of Educational Development, 29*(6), 565–572.

Wallace, S., Nazroo, J., & Bécares, L. (2016). Cumulative effect of racial discrimination on the mental health of ethnic minorities in the United Kingdom. *American Journal of Public Health, 106*(7), 1294–1300.

Walsh, K., Scharf, T., & Shucksmith, M. (2014). Exploring the impact of informal practices on social exclusion and age-friendliness for older people in rural communities. *Journal of Community & Applied Social Psychology, 24*(1), 37–49.

Wang, A., Redington, L., Steinmetz, V., & Lindeman, D. (2011). The ADOPT model: Accelerating diffusion of proven technologies for older adults. *Ageing International, 36*(1), 29–45.

Wang, D., & MacMillan, T. (2013). The benefits of gardening for older adults: A systematic review of the literature. *Activities, Adaptation and Aging, 37*(2), 153–181.

Warburton, J. R., & Cordingly, S. (2004). The contemporary challenges of volunteering in an ageing Australia. *Australian Journal on Volunteering, 9*(2), 67–74.

Warburton, J. R., & Gooch, M. (2007). Stewardship volunteering by older Australians: The generative response. *Local Environment, 12*(1), 43–55.

Warburton, J. R., Oppenheimer, M., & Zappalà, G. (2004). Marginalizing Australia's volunteers: The need for socially inclusive practices in the non-profit sector. *Australian Journal on Volunteering, 9*(1), 33–40.

Wearing, B. (1995). Leisure and resistance in an ageing society. *Leisure Studies, 14*(4), 263–279.

Wells, T. (2016). Sens' Capability Approach. *The Internet Encyclopedia of Philosophy*. Retrieved from www.iep.utm.edu/sen-cap/

Wenger, G. C. (1997). Social networks and the prediction of elderly people at risk. *Aging & Mental Health, 1*(4), 311–320.

Wenger, G. C., & Tucker, I. (2002). Using network variation in practice: Identification of support network type. *Health & Social Care in the Community, 10*(1), 28–35.

Wheeler, J. A., Gorey, K. M., & Greenblatt, B. (1998). The beneficial effects of volunteering for older volunteers and the people they serve: A meta-analysis. *The International Journal of Aging and Human Development, 47*(1), 69–79.

Whitney, G., & Keith, S. (2006). Active aging through universal design. *Gerontechnology, 5*(3), 125–128.

Wiles, J. L. (2011). Reflections on being a recipient of care: Vexing the concept of vulnerability. *Social & Cultural Geography, 12*(6), 573–588.

Wiles, J. L., Allen, R.E.S., Palmer, A. J., Hayman, K. J., Keeling, S., & Kerse, N. (2009). Older people and their social spaces: A study of well-being and attachment to place in Aotearoa New Zealand. *Social Science & Medicine, 68*(4), 664–671.

Wiles, J. L., & Jayasinha, R. (2013). Care for place: The contributions older people make to their communities. *Journal of Aging Studies, 27*(2), 93–101.

Wiles, J. L., Leibing, A., Guberman, N., Reeve, J., & Allen, R. E. (2012). The meaning of "aging in place" to older people. *The Gerontologist, 52*(3), 357–366.

Wilson, K. B. (2007). Historical evolution of assisted living in the United States, 1979 to the present. *The Gerontologist, 47*(suppl 1), 8–22.

Wilson, N. J., & Cordier, R. (2013). A narrative review of Men's Sheds literature: Reducing social isolation and promoting men's health and well-being. *Health & Social Care in the Community, 21*(5), 451–463.

Wilson, N. J., Cordier, R., Doma, K., Misan, G., & Vaz, S. (2015). Men's Sheds function and philosophy: Towards a framework for future research and men's health promotion. *Health Promotion Journal of Australia, 26*(2), 133–141.

Winter, J., & Nowson, C. (2016). Promoting healthy and enjoyable eating in the elderly. *Medicine Today, 7*(6), 36–40.

Wolff, J., & de-Shalit, A. (2007). *Disadvantage.* Oxford: Oxford University Press.

World Health Organization. (1948). *Constitution of the World Health Organization.* Retrieved from www.who.int/about/mission/en/

World Health Organization. (1986). *Ottawa charter for health promotion.* Geneva: WHO.

World Health Organization. (2002). *Active ageing: A policy framework.* Retrieved from http://whqlibdoc.who.int/hq/2002/who_nmh_nph_02.8.pdf

World Health Organization. (2007). *Women, ageing and health: A framework for action: Focus on gender.* Retrieved from www.unfpa.org/upload/lib_pub_file/684_filename_ageing.pdf

World Health Organization. (2015). *World report on ageing and health.* Retrieved from www.who.int/ageing/events/world-report-2015-launch/en/: WHO.

World Health Organization. (2016). *Age-friendly cities and communities.* Retrieved from www.who.int/ageing/projects/age-friendly-cities-communities/en/

World Health Organization. (2007). *Checklist of essential features of age-friendly cities.* Geneva: WHO.

World Health Organization. (2012). *Aging and life course: Interesting facts about ageing.* www.who.int/ageing/about/facts/en/

Wylie, K., & Nebauer, M. (2011). "The food here is tasteless!" Food taste or tasteless food? Chemosensory loss and the politics of under-nutrition. *Collegian, 18*(1), 27–35.

Xavier, F. M., Ferraz, M., Marc, N., Escosteguy, N. U., & Moriguchi, E. H. (2003). Elderly peoples definition of quality of life. *Revista Brasileira De Psiquiatria, 25*(1), 31–39.

Xie, B. & Jaeger, P. T. (2008). Older adults and political participation on the internet: A cross-cultural comparison of the USA and China. *Journal of Cross-Cultural Gerontology, 23*(1), 1–15. https://doi.org/10.1007/s10823-007-9050-6

Zaninotto, P., Breeze, E., McMunn, A., & Nazroo, J. (2013). Socially productive activities, reciprocity and well-being in early old age: Gender-specific results from the English Longitudinal Study of Ageing (ELSA). *Journal of Population Ageing, 6*(1–2), 47–57.

Zaninotto, P., Wardle, J., & Steptoe, A. (2016). Sustained enjoyment of life and mortality at older ages: Analysis of the English Longitudinal Study of Ageing. *BMJ (Online), 355.* https://doi.org/10.1136/bmj.i6267

Zappalà, G., & Burrell, T. (2002). What makes a frequent volunteer? Predicting volunteer commitment in a community services organisation. *Australian Journal on Volunteering, 7*(2), 45–58.

Zumbro, T. (2014). The relationship between homeownership and life satisfaction in Germany. *Housing Studies, 29*(3), 319–338.

Zunzunegui, M. V., Rodriguez-Laso, A., Otero, A., Pluijm, S., Nikula, S., Blumstein, T., . . . CLESA working group. (2005). Disability and social ties: Comparative findings of the CLESA study. *European Journal of Ageing, 2*(1), 40–47.

INDEX

Italic page references indicate boxed text.